Executive's Guide to Pension and Retirement Benefits

Executive's Guide to Pension and Retirement Benefits

Mayer Siegel & Carol I. Buckmann

Law & Business, Inc.
Harcourt Brace Jovanovich, Publishers

Permissions, Law and Business, Inc.
757 Third Avenue, New York, N.Y. 10017

Printed in the United States of America

Library of Congress Cataloging in Publication Data

Siegel, Mayer.
Executive's Guide to Pension and Retirement Benefits.

Includes index.
1. Executives–Salaries, pensions, etc.–United States. 2. Old age pensions–United States.
I. Buckmann, Carol, joint author. II. Title.
HD7106.U5S53 331.25'29 80-27748
ISBN 0-15-003996-4

CONTENTS

PART TWO
PLANNING ALTERNATIVES

Introduction

HOW TO GET THE MOST OUT OF YOUR COMPANY'S RETIREMENT PLANS

Only a small number of retirement plans were in existence prior to World War II. However, within a period of about forty years, pension trusts maintained by private employers have become this country's greatest reservoir of capital, holding assets running into the hundreds of billions of dollars.

If you are in the work force, the chances are now better than even that you are covered by one or more retirement plans. In all probability, the benefits for which you are eligible under those plans, together with the benefits provided by Social Security, represent your largest single asset. If you are an executive, technical, or professional employee, the benefits provided under your company's plans are probably greater than those provided under Social Security.

The purpose of this book is to enable you to manage your most significant asset intelligently and to get the most out of your company's retirement plans. It will explain what types of benefits are provided by these plans, what requirements must be satisfied in order to share in those benefits, and most important, how to get the greatest individual financial benefit out of your plan participation by exercising your options wisely.

This book also describes the role of the Federal agencies responsible for regulating private pension plans and your rights as a plan participant under the Employee Retirement Income Security Act

(ERISA), the revolutionary federal pension reform legislation that was enacted in 1974.

The book is divided into two major parts.

Part One describes the types of retirement plans commonly offered by employers in this country, and shows how to qualify for benefits under them. Part One also includes a discussion of the significant changes in pension law introduced by all of the amendments to ERISA, including those contained in the Revenue Act of 1978, the Technical Corrections Act of 1979, and the Economic Recovery Tax Act of 1981 (ERTA).

Part Two explains, in great detail, the choices that are available to you at various stages in your working lifetime under your employer's retirement plans. This part of the book is divided into chapters which deal with the choices which are most important at different points in your own career.

A detailed table of contents and an extensive index have been provided in order to help you quickly find any specific information in which you are interested. Finally, since the subject of retirement planning has its own vocabulary which is unavoidably complex, a glossary of frequently used technical terms has been added.

This is the first book on the subject of retirement plans ever written for the educated layperson. In the course of our practice, we have often noticed the confusion of plan participants as they struggled to make sense of these complicated arrangements and adapt them to their individual needs. It is hoped that this book will dispel some of this confusion and enable executives to use more advantageously the best tax shelter available—their employer's retirement plans.

We would like to thank Christine Fryer, our former legal assistant, and her successor Roberta Mueller, for their invaluable help in the preparation of this book as well as Pat Richardson for her skill and patience in retyping many drafts of the manuscript.

Mayer Siegel
Carol I. Buckmann

Part One

BASIC CONCEPTS

Chapter 1

HARD FACTS ABOUT FINANCING YOUR RETIREMENT

If you retire sometime between ages 55 and 65 (as most people do), you can expect to live another 15 to 22 years if you are a man or 18 to 26 years if you are a woman. During this period, your earnings from employment will probably be minimal. If retirement means a sharp drop in your standard of living, the phrase "golden years" will have a hollow ring to it.

Since, ideally, your standard of living should remain the same after retirement (you hope, for example, not to be forced to move to a less expensive home) the ultimate goal of any preretirement financial planning is to bridge the gap between income and outgo after retirement by effectively replacing your salary. There are, essentially, four sources of funds available to you as a salary replacement after you retire. These are Social Security, your personal savings, your own Individual Retirement Account (IRA) and your employer's retirement plan. Unless your circumstances are quite unusual, the last of these, supplemented by your own IRA, should play the central role in your retirement planning.

Why is this? Why aren't Social Security and savings adequate? Why, by contrast, is a retirement plan able to do such an effective job in replacing preretirement income?

The blunt answer to why Social Security benefits are inadequate is that Social Security is not intended to provide managers and executives with an adequate retirement income, but rather was planned to satisfy the basic needs of lower-paid workers. Furthermore, the widely publicized financial plight of the Social Security system calls into question whether there will be sufficient funds to pay even these basic promised benefits.

Chapter 7 of Part One of this book is devoted to an overview of the Social Security system. There you will learn how the Social Security benefit formula is skewed against the individual with above-average earnings. If you have consistently earned more than the Social Security "taxable wage base" (the part of your income on which Social Security taxes are collected—the first $32,400 in 1982) your Social Security benefits will be a smaller percentage of your preretirement income, and will be smaller yet in relation to the Social Security taxes that you have paid, than if you had always earned less than the taxable wage base. This means that Social Security will provide you with only a small percentage of the income that you were earning before retirement—perhaps no more than 10 or 15 percent of that income, certainly less than a third (even taking into account the fact that Social Security benefits are tax-free).

Is it likely that you can accumulate enough savings to make up the lost two thirds (or more) of your income? A calculator with a compound interest function can produce what looks like an impressive accumulation of cash as the result of small systematic savings unrelated to any formal retirement plan. But don't let your calculator do your thinking. The United States tax system operates to hinder you from accumulating a retirement nest egg through systematic saving. Here is a typical example of naive retirement planning which failed to take this hard fact into consideration:

Bill Smith is thirty-five years old—thirty years from retirement, let us say—and he and his wife Jenny, who is also thirty-five, together earn $30,000 a year. What with mortgage payments, car payments, post-graduation payments on old student loans, the life insurance that was bought from Bill's old college buddy, the kids' tonsillectomies and the like, they have never had much left over for the proverbial rainy day. Today, however, Bill and Jenny have been inspired by financial columns about the funding problems of Social Security and a nagging sense of responsibility to think about a savings program.

Bill figures that a young couple on the way up can't lose if they save 15 percent of their income. Fifteen percent of $30,000 is a somewhat staggering $4,500 per year—close to a hundred dollars a week—but Bill, calculator in hand, virtuously plugs the number in. After all, as their salaries rise in the future, setting aside $4,500 a year should become easier.

For a long term interest rate, Jenny recalls that savings banks are offering long term certificates of deposit yielding 11 percent. Now Bill and Jenny have all the data they need for a calculation: deposits of $4,500 per year for 30 years, 11 percent interest compounded annually. The accumulation after 30 years is almost $900,000, a pretty fair sum by anyone's standards. Without touching the principal, it will (at 11 percent interest) provide an annual income of about $99,000 forever. If the principal is drawn down over 20 years (until Bill and Jenny reach 85), annual payments will be increased to about $113,000. Although Bill and Jenny may be satisfied that financing a secure retirement is a snap, they are actually right on course for retirement disaster. They have overlooked the following unpleasant facts:

Bill and Jenny Don't Yet Realize How Much It Costs to Save a Dollar

Bill and Jenny don't get to keep every dollar that they earn. They pay income taxes on their salaries and must, in order to have one dollar to save, earn roughly one dollar and fifty cents. To put aside $4,500 a year, when about one-third of their income is applied to taxes, they must commit $6,750 pretax dollars—almost a quarter of their income—as savings. Moreover, as their income rises, their marginal tax rate (the highest bracket in which their income is taxed) will rise, too. When their taxable income reaches the top bracket (about $86,000 in 1982, $109,000 in 1983, $162,400 in 1984, and increasing with inflation in later years) their tax rate will be 50 percent, the highest possible rate. At that point, saving $4,500 will cost $9,000 a year.

The implication of these numbers is that it will be a long time before Bill and Jenny can realistically expect to match their periodic savings goal.

Bill and Jenny Haven't Considered What Their Dollars Will Buy 30 Years From Now

You wouldn't think that people need to be reminded of inflation these days, yet the Smiths have entirely ignored its effects in making their calculations. Seeing the figure $900,000 they think of 1982 dollars. They should be thinking of the value of a dollar in the period beginning with the year 2012, when they both reach 65, and extending through the 15 to 25 years that they can expect to live thereafter.

If the average inflation rate between 1982 and 2012 is 5 percent per year (a rate that many people call "moderate"), the Smiths' $900,000 will have the purchasing power of only about $208,000 present day dollars. The income provided by this sum ($99,000) will have the purchasing power of only about $23,000 today (about $26,000 if the principal is drawn down over twenty years).

Inflation Plus Taxation Will Destroy Any Long-Term Savings Program

There is no need, however, simply to guess at the future rate of inflation in order to understand the error in the Smiths' projections. The Smiths assumed that their joint savings could earn a 11 percent per year rate of return. They did not consider the fact that this rate of return is taxed immediately or that current interest rates include a large allowance for inflation. By itself, the federal tax which is imposed on the income earned by the Smiths' investments makes the effective rate of return on their savings much less than the 11 percent which was projected in their calculations. If they are taxed at a marginal rate of 50 percent, they will really be earning 5½ percent interest (and even less if state and local income taxes are taken into consideration).

Bill and Jenny also ignored the fact that (after inflation) the rate of return on long-term investments is much less than 11 percent. Historically, the real rate of return has rarely been higher than 3 percent per year. Some economists would peg it at only a little above zero.

No matter what the rate of inflation is in the future, the Smiths cannot expect to earn more than the real rate of return—no more than 3 percent—on their money, unless they invest less conservatively and risk investment losses in the hope of greater gains.

What is more, the Internal Revenue Code does not distinguish between "real" and "nominal" rates of return. If a dollar saved earns eleven cents, the Smiths are taxed on eleven cents of income, despite the fact that seven or eight cents simply kept their income abreast of inflation. If their marginal tax rate is 50 percent, they retain after taxes, at the end of the year, only $1.055 out of their original $1.11 and each original dollar is worth about 96 cents in terms of beginning-of-the-year dollars.

Stated another way, the combined effect of inflation and the tax system is that when the rate of inflation exceeds 5½ percent (assuming a 50 percent tax rate), the real value of the Smiths' assets declines even if they are earning 11 percent interest, because there is, in effect, a negative interest rate after the rate of inflation reaches 5½ percent. In other words, if they are earning only 5½ percent per year but their assets decline in value due to inflation at the rate of 8 percent per year, they will end up with a net loss in asset values of 2½ percent for that year.

If inflation continues at the rate projected by economists, the outcome of a retirement savings program such as the one instituted by Bill and Jenny Smith will be to fall far short of the intended goal. Instead of accumulating an adequate retirement nest egg, the systematic saver will simply lose a race with inflation.

Individual Retirement Account (IRAs)

Beginning in 1982, the Economic Recovery Tax Act (ERTA) has made it possible to base a small portion of the kind of savings program instituted by the Smiths on pre-tax rather than after-tax dollars. As of January 1, 1982, all working individuals will be able to make an annual tax deductible contribution to an individual retirement account (commonly called an IRA, or Eye-Ar-Ay) not to exceed the lesser of earned income or $2,000. A married individual with a nonworking spouse may contribute and deduct up to $2,250 per year. (The new IRA rules and restrictions on IRA deposits are discussed in detail in Chapter 4.) An IRA program has an additional advantage over the Smiths' savings program because income earned by the contributions is not subject to tax while it remains in the account. In this way, income may compound on a tax deferred basis until it is withdrawn from the IRA at retirement age.

Despite the glowing and sometimes misleading advertisements now being sponsored by IRA sponsors which proclaim that young workers will easily accumulate a million dollars in their IRAs, the IRA remains only a supplementary retirement funding vehicle for two reasons. First, because contributions are limited to $2,000 per year rather than the $15,000 per year which you will find may be put annually into a Keogh plan or the much larger amounts which may be contributed by an employer under corporate profit sharing plans. Second, although it will be possible to accumulate a million dollars in an IRA if current interest rates hold over the long term, by the time the million dollars becomes payable it may cost $100 to buy a loaf of bread.

Although each eligible employee should contribute regularly to an IRA, since it is clearly better to have one than not to have one, it is unlikely that an IRA and a nondeductible forced savings program, even together with Social Security, will be able to provide executives with an adequate retirement income in these inflation-ridden times.

Qualified Retirement Plans

This brings us to retirement plans. If Social Security plus informal or formal personal savings programs, including IRAs, could provide most employees with an adequate old-age income, retirement plans would probably be an unusual fringe benefit existing in a handful of industries, as they were before World War II. In the current economic situation, a qualified retirement plan is not a luxury, it is a necessary part of almost every employee's financial planning, representing the difference between maintaining your accustomed standard of living after retirement and resigning yourself to a more limited and stringent existence.

Take note of the adjective "qualified" used to modify "retirement plan" because the advantages discussed in the succeeding paragraphs are available only to plans that satisfy (i.e., "qualify" under) a detailed set of standards laid down in the Internal Revenue Code.

For our purposes, only two Code requirements are important: an employer that establishes a qualified plan must place plan assets in an irrevocable trust fund, beyond the reach of creditors and of the employer itself. The employer cannot decide to reclaim the funds if, for example, there are business reverses which create a need for additional capital. With minor exceptions, the trust fund may be used only to pay retirement benefits and the plan's administrative expenses.

The second important requirement is that a pension plan cannot be qualified unless it does not discriminate in favor of officers, stockholders, or highly compensated employees (called the "prohibited group"). This means that a plan may not cover only members of the prohibited group or provide benefits to the prohibited group which are a higher percentage of compensation than the benefits provided to rank-and-file employees and still enjoy the tax benefits available under the Internal Revenue Code. ERISA strengthened this requirement that plans be nondiscriminatory by adding the rule that if two or more business are commonly owned, the entire affiliated group is to be considered a single entity for purposes of determining whether a plan discriminates in benefits or coverage.

There are two major reasons why a properly-designed tax qualified retirement program can accomplish what your own savings program can't:

1. When your employer makes contributions to a "qualified" retirement plan, it is allowed to deduct the contributions from its corporate income. In order to contribute one dollar, your employer has to earn only one dollar—not the $1.50 to $2.00 (depending on your tax bracket) that you have to earn in order to save an after-tax dollar. Although contributions to qualified plans are subject to certain limitations on maximum individual contributions or benefits, these limitations are so high as to affect very few individuals.

2. The income earned by a "qualified" retirement plan is not subject to any tax until it is actually distributed to employees. Therefore, the plan is not a victim of the "knockout" combination of inflation and taxation which destroyed the Smiths' informal personal savings program. In fact, plan distributions will probably be taxed at much lower rates when you actually receive them, since not only will you presumably be earning much less income (and will therefore be in a lower tax bracket) after you retire, but there are also a number of tax breaks available to the recipients of benefits from qualified plans. (Taxation of benefits is discussed fully in Chapter 11.) A small number of retirement plans even contain cost-of-living clauses which make limited adjustments to benefit levels to compensate for inflation. (These plans are discussed in Chapter 3.)

While an IRA savings program benefits from the same tax advantage of deductibility of contributions and deferral of tax on income, the annual limitation makes deductions too small to do the job of providing adequate retirement benefits alone, or even together with Social Security.

A retirement plan also has other economic advantages over an individual savings program or even an IRA. Because the trust fund accumulates money on behalf of many employees, it will have more funds to invest than the average individual saver. It can therefore invest more efficiently and effectively to yield higher rates of return than you could earn investing on your own. It also can afford professional investment management that would be beyond the means of all but the wealthiest individuals.

It should now be clear why a qualified retirement plan can effectively fill the gap between the postretirement income provided by your personal savings (including IRAs) and Social Security benefits and your preretirement salary.

The next two chapters will introduce you to the different methods which a qualified plan may use to calculate your benefits and will give you an idea of the relative advantages of various types of plans to participants in higher brackets.

Chapter 2

IDENTIFYING TYPES OF CORPORATE RETIREMENT PLANS

Under some qualified plans, annual contributions are discretionary on the part of the employer. Nevertheless, such plans sometimes provide large benefits. Under other plans, benefits may be much too low to supplement Social Security benefits and savings adequately, even though the plan sponsor is obligated to contribute each year. Before you can intelligently evaluate your employer's—or your prospective employer's—retirement plan, you need to know what type of benefits your employer's plan is designed to provide and whether your anticipated benefit will be sufficient to allow you to live well during retirement. You also need to have some familiarity with the latest features of modern plan design in order to judge whether your employer's plans are competitive with those of other corporations in its industry.

This chapter focuses on the families of corporate plans, as classified by employee benefit specialists. Since these precise classifications are not helpful until you have a general picture of the variety of ways in which benefits can be provided by qualified plans, Table I lists some key features of retirement plans alongside the types of plans which are required or permitted to incorporate those features. Some of these plans are quite straightforward in concept. Other types of plans, which may appear more complicated at first glance, are really variations of these simple plans or of the basic plan features which will be discussed in Chapter 3.

Table 1

Plan Feature	Plans Required or Permitted to Contain Feature
1. Benefits determined under a formula based on age and service, regardless of fund investment performance	All defined benefit plans
2. Benefits increase with good fund investment performance	Defined contribution and target benefit plans
3. Employer contributions	
–Mandatory	All plans
–Discretionary	Profit sharing
4. Employee contributions	
–Mandatory	Thrift plans Defined benefit plans
–Voluntary (not related to benefits provided by employer)	All
5. Benefit guaranteed by PBGC (plan insurance)	Defined benefit
6. Fixed contribution formula based on payroll	Fixed contribution profit-sharing plans Money purchase pension plans
7. Benefits integrated with social security (benefits skewed in favor of highly-paid employees)	All plans except ESOPs and TRASOPs
8. Substantial contributions of employer stock	ESOPs, TRASOPs, and other specially-designated defined contribution plans

MAJOR FAMILIES: DEFINED BENEFIT AND DEFINED CONTRIBUTION PLANS

Although there is great variation in the features of retirement plans, all retirement plans may be usefully grouped into two different families.

One group of plans provides periodic income in the form of an annuity usually beginning at age 65 and payable for life thereafter. The exact amount of each employee's benefit is determined in accordance with a formula which is related to the employee's length of service with the company and his or her earnings history. Such a retirement plan is technically called a "defined benefit plan" because benefits are expressed (or "defined") in accordance with a formula. Each year, regardless of the employer's profit picture, it must contribute whatever amount is necessary to fund the plan benefits which have been earned by participants through the end of that year. Annual funding is based upon predictions as to future salary levels, interest rates, mortality, and employee turnover. Since the employer is required to fund a determinable level of benefits, it will be required to make smaller contributions in periods in which the pension fund's investment performance is better than anticipated.

The second group of plans consists of plans under which a separate account is established for each participant. These are called "defined contribution plans" because the benefit which each participant receives is "defined" in terms of the portion of the employer's contribution which is allocated to his or her individual account.

All of these accounts, taken together, constitute the defined contribution plan's trust fund. At the end of each year, a share of the employer contribution made for that year is allocated to each participant's account, usually in proportion to compensation. Most such plans provide that a participant must be employed on the last day of the year to receive an allocation for that year. Each account also receives a proportionate allocation of trust fund investment gains and earnings, and is charged with its share of losses and expenses. In a defined contribution plan, the employee, rather than the employer, benefits from a good investment return on plan trust funds.

Under most defined contribution plans, employer contributions are made only out of current or retained earnings. Such plans are called "profit sharing" plans. In other defined contribution plans, annual employer contributions equal to a fixed percentage of compensation paid during the year are required, regardless of the employer's profitability. Such plans are called money purchase pension plans.

From the employee's point of view, there is one important distinction between these families of plans. A defined benefit plan promises a specified benefit *regardless* of the investment results obtained by the plan's trust fund. If an employer terminates its defined benefit plan, benefits are even guaranteed up to certain maximum dollar amounts by a government agency called the Pension Benefit Guaranty Corporation, or "PBGC." If your promised benefit is $1,000 a month, that is what you will receive, whether the trust fund invests successfully or not. In contrast, no specific benefit is promised under a defined contribution plan. If you are covered under a defined contribution plan, your benefit when you retire or leave the job for any other reason is simply the balance credited to your account as of that date.

A second point worth remembering is that no retirement plan is likely to provide adequate income to the employee hired at a relatively advanced age. In the case of a defined benefit plan the reason is that benefits are accrued in proportion to years of service with the employer, and in the case of a defined contribution plan it is because contributions are made over fewer years and have fewer years in which to earn income. However, if an employer maintains a defined benefit plan, there is somewhat more flexibility to provide higher benefits to older workers with relatively short periods of service. The benefit formula may provide for

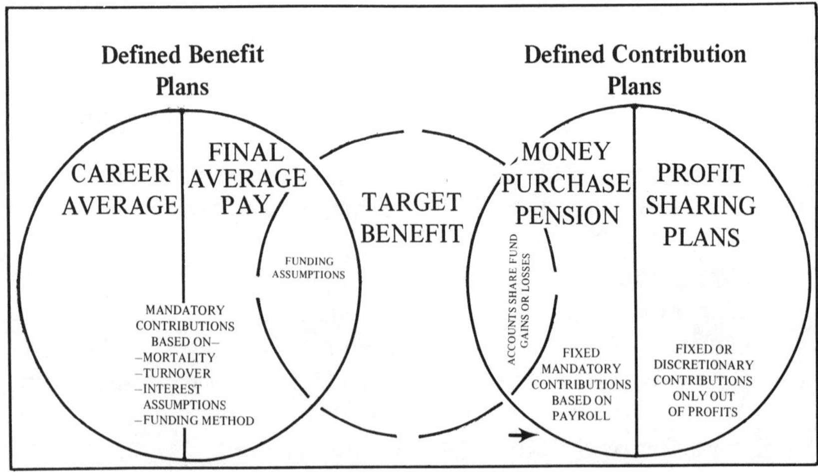

Figure 1. Families of Qualified Plans

greater accumulations of benefits in the initial years of service, although such provisions are unusual. More commonly, many defined benefit plans provide minimum benefits which will exceed the benefit which would otherwise be payable to an older worker under the plan's regular benefit formula (based on age and service).

Figure 1 illustrates the relationships among the various types of qualified plans which will be discussed in the remainder of this chapter.

DEFINED BENEFIT PLANS

Unit Benefit Plans and Flat Benefit Plans

These plans provide a benefit expressed as a fixed percentage of earnings (unit benefit) or a specified number of dollars (flat benefit) *for each* year of employment, and thus reward long-time employees with higher pensions per month than recently-hired employees at the same salary level. Most flat benefit plans cover hourly employees. Unit benefit plans are used to provide benefits to both hourly and salaried employees. A typical unit benefit percentage formula might be 1.5 percent of average compensation multiplied by the number of years of employment with the company. Sometimes, the pension is divided into what are called a "past service benefit" and a "future service benefit." The "past service benefit" typically represents benefits related to service before a pension plan is adopted or before benefits are increased and the future service benefit represents benefits attributable to employment after that event. Usually, the benefit per year of past service is less than the benefit per year of future service.

Unit benefit plans often contain a maximum limitation on the number of years which may be counted in the benefit formula and may provide, in addition, for a minimum monthly benefit.

> *Example 1.* The Interweave Textile Company pension plan is a unit benefit plan which provides an annual benefit equal to the sum of a past service benefit of 1½ percent of compensation during the period 1965–75, and a future service benefit of 2 percent of compensation during the years after 1975 (total service credit is not to exceed 30 years). The plan provides a minimum benefit of $2,400 per year for an employee who has completed at least 20 years of service.

Robert Morgan, who was hired by Interweave in 1965, remains an employee until he retires in 1995 at age 65. Morgan's compensation for the years 1965–75 is $100,000. His compensation for the period subsequent to 1975 is $800,000. Under the Interweave plan, Morgan will be entitled to an annual past service benefit of $1,500 (100,000 x .015) and a future service benefit of $16,000 (800,000 x .02), for a total benefit at age 65 of $17,500 per year (approximately $1,450 per month). This is greater than the minimum benefit.

The "Replacement Ratio"—A Measure of Plan Sufficiency

A defined benefit plan must be judged by comparing the dollar value of the pension it produces to the employee's salary immediately preceding retirement. This relationship is called the "replacement ratio" since it represents the portion of the employee's salary which is replaced after retirement by his or her pension benefit. Since the replacement ratio is directly related to the plan's benefit formula, the benefit formula is the key provision in a defined benefit plan. The following sections will explain how to calculate the replacement ratio in the most common unit benefit type of plan.

Career Compensation Plans

Under a "career compensation" benefit formula such as that illustrated in Example 1, an employee's pension benefit is based upon compensation during his or her entire career. A shortcoming of this approach is that the pension is based, in substantial part, upon relatively low compensation payable in the early working years. Because a career compensation approach averages in this relatively low compensation, it usually results in an inadequate replacement ratio.

Example 2. The Manuscript Publishing Company pension plan provides that upon retirement at age 65 an employee will receive an annual pension, payable in monthly installments, equal to 2 percent of compensation for each year of service.

David Williams began working for Manuscript as a management trainee on January 1, 1950 at a salary of $5,000. When he retired on December 31, 1979 at age 65, Williams was earning $50,000 a year. He had completed thirty years of covered employment under the Manuscript plan.

During his entire career at Manuscript, Williams earned a total of $750,000 (for an average salary of $25,000 per year). His annual pension is therefore $15,000 (2 percent of 750,000), or, stated another way, 60 percent of his average compensation while covered under the Manuscript Publishing Company pension plan.

In this case, Williams' pension of $15,000 per year constitutes only 30 percent of his compensation in the year immediately preceding retirement, a replacement ratio which is hardly sufficient. An impressive nominal pension benefit of 60 percent (2 percent times 30 years) produces a replacement ratio of only 30 percent because during the early part of his career, Williams' compensation was only a small fraction of his salary immediately preceding his retirement. Williams' compensation increased by a multiple of 10 (from $5,000 to $50,000 per year) during his 30-year career with Manuscript. Increases of such magnitude are obviously common during an executive's career, since they result from a combination of promotions to jobs of increasing responsibility, longevity raises and, perhaps most of all, from increases in compensation to offset the effect of inflation. However, the pension payable under a career compensation formula never reflects these increases adequately.

In order to overcome this shortcoming, employers sponsoring pension plans with career compensation formulas have been forced to update them at periodic intervals, generally every five years or so. In updating a pension plan of this type, an employer will usually revise its benefit formula so that benefits related to years of employment before the date of the revision are based only upon compensation during the year or years immediately preceding the revision.

Example 3. The Manuscript pension plan was amended in 1974 to provide that the portion of an employee's pension related to service prior to 1974 (the "past service benefit") would be equal to 2 percent of his or her 1973 compensation multiplied by the number of years of service prior to 1974. However, the portion of the pension related to service after 1973 would continue to be based on the employee's compensation after that date.

In Williams' case, his past service benefit would be equal to 2 percent of his 1973 compensation ($40,250), multiplied by 24 (since he has been employed for 24 years prior to 1974), or $19,320.

The future service (i.e., post plan revision) pension benefit for each year of employment after the date of the amendment (covering 1974–1979 in Williams' case), would be 2 percent of his compensation for those years. Since Williams earned an aggregate of $330,000 during those six years, he would receive an additional pension of $6,600 as a future service benefit. Williams' total annual pension benefit would therefore be $25,920 ($19,320 + $6,600).

Note that the 1974 update of pension benefits produced a dramatic increase in Williams' annual pension. It rose from *$15,000* in Example 2 to *$25,920* in Example 3. The replacement ratio has been increased from 30 percent to a more reasonable 52 percent ($25,920/50,000).

Employers retain career average benefit formulas in their pension plans despite their obvious shortcomings because they are unwilling to promise in advance to compensate for future inflation. In actual practice these employers intend to update their plans by increasing benefits at frequent intervals, so long as they are financially able to do so. Employees who are participants in career average plans nevertheless find it more difficult to plan for their retirement since they have no assurance that their plan benefit formulas will actually be updated in the manner illustrated in Example 3.

Final Average Pay Plans

Under a final average pay formula, the compensation base for determining pension benefits is usually the average of an employee's compensation during the five-year period (or other selected period, such as ten years) immediately preceding retirement. Some plans use a modified final average pay formula which recognizes compensation during the highest consecutive three or five years out of the ten years immediately preceding retirement. Final average pay formulas are chosen in order to avoid the continual updating required under career compensation plans to keep pension benefits current with inflated salaries. They also give employees greater security about the adequacy of their benefits, because they use a more realistic compensation base.

Since the typical employee's salary is constantly increasing as a result of both merit and inflation, use of the final average compensation base will result in a *substantially* higher pension than would an equivalent benefit formula based on career compensation.

> *Example 4.* The Manuscript pension plan is amended to provide a benefit of 2 percent of final average compensation multiplied by the number of years of service completed at retirement. David Williams' salary increased from $5,000 to $50,000 per year over a 30 year period. This represents annual increases in salary of about 8 percent during his career. As Example 2 indicates, Williams' average career compensation was *$25,000.* However, his average compensation during the five year period ending at age 65 was approximately *$47,000.* His annual pension under the amended formula is therefore about $28,200.
>
> Given an identical pension benefit formula (for example, 2 percent of compensation for each year of service) and the same 30 year earnings history, Williams' actual pension would be almost doubled if a final five year average compensation base were used rather than a career compensation base which was not updated.

Contributory Plans

Some defined benefit pension plans are contributory—that is, employees are required to contribute a designated percentage of compensation on a nondeductible basis in order to participate in the plan. Contributory defined benefit pension plans tend to be of the career average type, because under such a plan design it is easier to match up employee contributions made during a given year with the pension benefit accrued during that year. The trend for some time now has been not only to eliminate employee contributions, but to return to employees the contributions they have previously made to their employers' pension plan.

The two trends which have just been discussed—the conversion of pension plans from the career average compensation to the final average compensation type and the trend to eliminate employee contributions—have tended to reinforce one another.

When the employee contribution requirement is eliminated from a pension plan, participants are sometimes permitted to choose whether to withdraw their accumulated contributions with interest, leave them in the plan to purchase additional pension benefits, or transfer them to the employer's profit sharing or thrift plan (more about these in the following section on defined contribution plans), if such a plan is maintained by the employer.

DEFINED CONTRIBUTION PLANS

There is substantially more variation among defined contribution plans than among defined benefit plans. However, defined contribution plans have a common distinguishing feature—a separate account is maintained for each participant to which is allocated his or her share of contributions, gains and losses, and income and expenses.

The key provisions of a defined contribution plan describe the level of the employer's contribution and the method by which it is allocated among the participants.

Profit Sharing Plans

The most common type of defined contribution plan is the profit sharing plan. Some profit sharing plans contain a fixed formula for determining the amount of the employer's annual contribution. However, since a fixed contribution formula is not a legal requirement, most profit sharing plans provide that contributions are discretionary on the part of the employer. Such plans provide that an employer may contribute each year from current or retained earnings any amount up to 15 percent of the compensation of the participating employees. This limit is set because contributions in excess of 15 percent of participants' compensation would not be deductible on the plan sponsor's tax return.

Since no contributions are permitted if the employer has no current or retained earnings, profit sharing plan participation may be virtually meaningless if the employer is encountering serious financial difficulty. Furthermore, a discretionary contribution provision gives the employer the flexibility of skipping contributions in certain years, even if it has high profits. As you can see, profit sharing plans generally provide less retirement security than do pension plans.

In the simplest type of profit sharing plans, employer contributions are allocated to the participants in proportion to their relative compensation–*i.e.*, an employee who earns $20,000 per year will receive an allocation equal to twice that of an employee earning $10,000 per year. Some profit sharing plans are "integrated" with Social Security benefits (i.e., plan contributions are adjusted to reflect the value of Social Security benefits). These plans have more complex allocation formulas and are discussed in Chapter 3.

Thrift Plans

A thrift plan is a profit sharing plan with a mandatory employee savings feature. Thrift plans generally provide that an employee may contribute from 1 to 6 percent of his or her compensation through payroll deductions. Employee contributions are then matched by the employer at a predetermined ratio. Although the matching ratio may range from 10 to 50 percent of employee contributions, ratios of 25 to 33 percent are most common. No employer contributions are made on behalf of employees who do not contribute.

> *Example 5.* Joe Williams earned $30,000 in calendar 1982. The Trans-Global Communications Corporation maintains a thrift plan which provides that employees may contribute 1, 2, 3, 4, 5, or 6 percent of compensation. Williams' election to contribute the full 6 percent of compensation resulted in an aggregate contribution to his account of $1,800 in the calendar year 1982. The plan provides for matching employer contributions at the rate of fifty cents for each dollar contributed by the employee. The Trans-Global Communications Corporation therefore contributed an additional $900 to Williams' account for 1982.

Thrift plans typically contain restrictions upon withdrawal of *both* employer and employee contributions and related trust fund earnings as a condition of qualification and for administrative convenience.

Thrift plans have become very popular in recent years. Most employers sponsoring thrift plans maintain defined benefit pension plans as their basic retirement benefit vehicle. The thrift plan is added as a supplemental benefit plan for employees. It serves as a savings vehicle which enables the employee systematically to deposit money that earns an attractive rate of return and to receive matching employer contributions. An additional, and sometimes unrecognized, benefit is the deferral of tax on employer contributions and all investment earnings until they are actually withdrawn.

However, it is important to note that the return would be attractive even without the tax deferral feature. An employer is generally able to negotiate an arrangement with an insurance company under which the employee is guaranteed a substantially higher rate of interest on plan contributions than is available from a savings bank on a passbook account. These insurance contracts also guarantee the principal of the contributions in the same way that a savings bank guarantees the principal of a savings account. Many insurance contracts currently provide for interest guarantees of between 11 and 13 percent. Rates of return are sometimes even higher, depending on the prevailing level of long-term interest rates.

Moreover, most thrift plans offer the employee the choice of investing the balance of his or her account in a fixed income fund, under which the employee receives a guaranteed rate of interest, or in an equity fund, which is invested primarily in common stocks. Sometimes more than one equity fund is made available. Employees are often permitted to invest their contributions in more than one fund, or to transfer them from one fund to another on predetermined transfer dates. This additional investment flexibility allows a thrift plan to cater to participants with differing investment objectives. Since employee contributions to a thrift plan are not deductible while employee contributions under a cash and deferred compensation plan (discussed on page 32) on a salary reduction basis are excludable from gross income, many employers are considering converting thrift plans into cash and deferred plans. It is probable that both types of plans will continue to be popular.

Money Purchase Pension Plans

A less common type of defined contribution plan is one in which the employer makes annual contributions under a fixed formula without regard to its profit or loss picture. If the participants in a money purchase pension plan are not also covered under a profit sharing plan, there is no deduction limitation on the percentage of the compensation of participating employees which the employer may contribute to its money purchase plan. This should be contrasted with the 15 percent limitation applicable to profit sharing plans and the 25 percent limitation applicable where employees are covered by both a money purchase pension and a profit sharing plan.

> *Example 6.* The Gourmet Foods Corp. maintains a calendar year pension plan which provides that each year it will contribute an amount equal to 5 percent of the total salary of each employee who participates in the plan. In 1982, Wanda Black earned $10,000 and Bill Verde earned $20,000 at Gourmet Foods. Both Black and Verde were participants in the plan in 1982. Gourmet Food's plan is a money purchase pension plan, since contributions are made in accordance with a fixed formula which is independent of profits. Under the formula Ms. Black was allocated a $500 contribution and Mr. Verde was allocated a $1,000 contribution in 1982.

Money purchase pension plans are relatively rare because they lack the flexibility of profit sharing plans. Employers are tied to fixed contributions, even in loss years, and have no discretion to skip contributions in particular years, as they do under most profit sharing plans. Employers are also prevented from making greater contributions in very profitable years. Furthermore, large corporations want to be able to promise employees a fixed benefit which is not dependent on fund investment performance.

Money purchase plans do not usually provide large benefits to employees who begin to participate at a relatively advanced age.

> *Example 7.* Roberta Jones was 25 years old when she became a participant in the Gourmet Foods Corp. money purchase pension plan (see Example 6). During the 40 years she was covered under the plan, Gourmet Foods Corp. contributed $40,000 to her account, based upon her aggregate salary of $800,000. Jones' account balance at age 65 had risen to $200,000 because of the interest and dividends earned by those contributions. One hundred sixty thousand dollars, or 80 percent of her account balance, represented the earnings on her employer's contributions.
>
> Ralph Winters, in contrast, became a participant at age 50 and earned an aggregate of $500,000 during his 15 years of participation in the plan. Winters' account balance at age 65 totalled $42,000. Twenty-five thousand dollars of this amount represented his share of contributions actually made by the Gourmet Foods Corporation. Only $17,000, or 40 percent of his account balance represented the earnings on those contributions.

Note that earnings, rather than employer contributions, accounted for the major portion of Jones's account balance, while the opposite was true in Winter's case. This is because Jones was a participant (and thus her funds remained invested in the plan) for a much longer period of time.

One specialized use of money purchase plans should be noted. Some small employers whose work force consists largely of shareholder employees maintain money purchase pension plans despite their lack of flexibility in providing benefits because they function as a supplement to the companies' profit sharing plans. If both a profit sharing plan and a money purchase pension plan are adopted, aggregate annual deductible contributions to both plans may equal 25 percent of the compensation of participating employees. By adopting a profit sharing plan and a money purchase plan in tandem, rather than a single money purchase plan, the employer can exceed the maximum permissible annual profit sharing contribution of 15 percent of the compensation of participating employees without tying itself down to a greater fixed contribution, even in loss years. The combination of a 10 percent money purchase plan and a 15 percent profit sharing provides the most flexibility to an employer. In loss years, a contribution of only 10 percent of compensation need be made to the money purchase plan. In profitable years, the employer may contribute an additional amount equal to the lesser of 15 percent of compensation or the company's profits or retained earnings, or whatever lesser amount it desires, in its sole discretion, to contribute.

Use of the money purchase arrangement, either alone or in tandem with a profit sharing plan, also permits the small employer to avoid both the annual insurance premiums paid to the Pension Benefit Guaranty Corporation (PBGC) by all defined benefit plans and potential liability to the PBGC if the plan is terminated. It eliminates the necessity of filing complicated annual reports with the PBGC and of hiring an actuary (a mathematician with special training in probability) to determine plan contributions. Money purchase plans are thus much simpler and cheaper to administer than defined benefit plans. In addition, by maintaining a money purchase plan, an employer can avoid the inflationary increases in benefit costs associated with final average compensation defined benefit pension plans.

Target Benefit Pension Plans

Target benefit plans are a relatively recent innovation, and are also quite rare. They are an attempt to *combine* the best features of both defined benefit and defined contribution plans. For most purposes, target benefit plans are considered defined contribution plans. This means that, unlike defined benefit plans, they are not subject to PBGC insurance or PBGC regulations. Target benefit plans are a variant of the money purchase pension plan.

A target benefit plan, (sometimes called an *assumed* benefit plan) provides that funds are accumulated for each participant according to a benefit formula, as in a defined benefit pension plan. However, an employee's benefit as calculated under this formula is not guaranteed. This benefit is a goal or target which the employer will reach in the future only if the assumptions it has made about factors such as trust fund investment performance are realized. Unlike a defined benefit plan, a *separate account* is maintained for each participant in a target benefit plan. The participants, rather than the employer, get the benefit of investment gains or are charged with fund losses, since level annual contributions must be made to the account of each participant in a target benefit plan. The employer will *not* increase its contributions to compensate for fund losses or reduce them to offset gains.

> *Example 8.* The Zoom Camera Corp. target benefit plan provides for annual contributions for each employee equal to the amount required to accumulate a lump sum for him or her upon retirement at age 65 equal to the value of a pension of 1 percent of his or her salary in the year he or she first becomes eligible to participate multipled by the number of years of service which that employee will have completed when he or she reaches 65. In the year in which the plan was established, Kenneth Roberts, a new employee age 25, and Ray Green, age 45 with 20 years of service, each earned $20,000. Since Green also became an employee of Zoom at age 25, he and Roberts will be entitled to identical benefits at retirement of $8,000 per year. (1 percent x 40 years x $20,000) Assuming an interest rate of 6 percent, Zoom will deposit $2,174.76 per year in Green's account, but only $516.92 per year in Roberts's account. The reason larger annual deposits are made to Green's account is that only 20 years are available to accumulate a lump sum equal to the value of his pension (an $80,000 lump sum is equal in value to an annual pension of about $8,000–depending on the interest rate used–for a person aged 65) while in Roberts's case 40 years are available to accumulate the identical sum.

Note, however, that there is no assurance that Roberts or Green will each have $80,000 in his account at age 65. This will occur *only* if their salaries remain the same and the pension fund earns exactly 6 percent each year. If earnings average more than 6 percent, their account balances will be larger than this amount; if not, they will be smaller than $80,000.

Of course, this example assumes unrealistically that there have been no increases in either employee's compensation. Green and Roberts will obviously receive raises from time to time. In a target benefit plan the additional pension benefit associated with each increase in compensation is separately funded.

Example 9. Roberts and Green each receive a $1,000 raise in the following year. If mortality discounts are ignored, Zoom will contribute to Roberts' account an additional $26.89, which is sufficient to accumulate over 39 years, at 6 percent interest, an additional $3,900, the lump sum value of an additional $390 pension. The additional contribution for Green would be $115.52.

Plans Which Hold Substantial Amounts of Employer Stock

No more than 10 percent of a defined benefit plan's assets may be invested in shares of the employer. However, all defined contribution plans (other than money purchase plans which are not part of an employee stock ownership plan, a type of plan which is discussed in the next section,) may contain provisions which permit them to exceed this limitation. Defined contribution plans authorized to exceed the 10 percent limitation on investment in shares of the employer are called "eligible individual account plans." There are no special restrictions applicable to such plans except for the "pass through" of voting rights.

All eligible individual account plans other than profit sharing plans (including the leveraged and tax credit ESOPs discussed in the next section) which are maintained by employers and which acquire employer securities after December 31, 1979, whether or not those securities are traded publicly, must provide participants with the right to vote the shares allocated to their accounts. If the shares are not traded publicly, voting rights may be limited to corporate issues requiring more than a majority vote for decision.

Figure 2 illustrates visually the relationships among the various types of defined contribution plans which are authorized to invest more than 10 percent of their assets in employer stock.

Employee Stock Ownership Plans (Leveraged ESOPs)

A leveraged employee stock ownership plan uses a variant of the profit sharing plan called a stock bonus plan, or a combination of a stock bonus plan and a money purchase pension plan, all or most of whose assets are invested in shares of the employer. All leveraged ESOPs are eligible individual account plans. The leveraged ESOP is a technique of corporate finance which, as the name suggests,

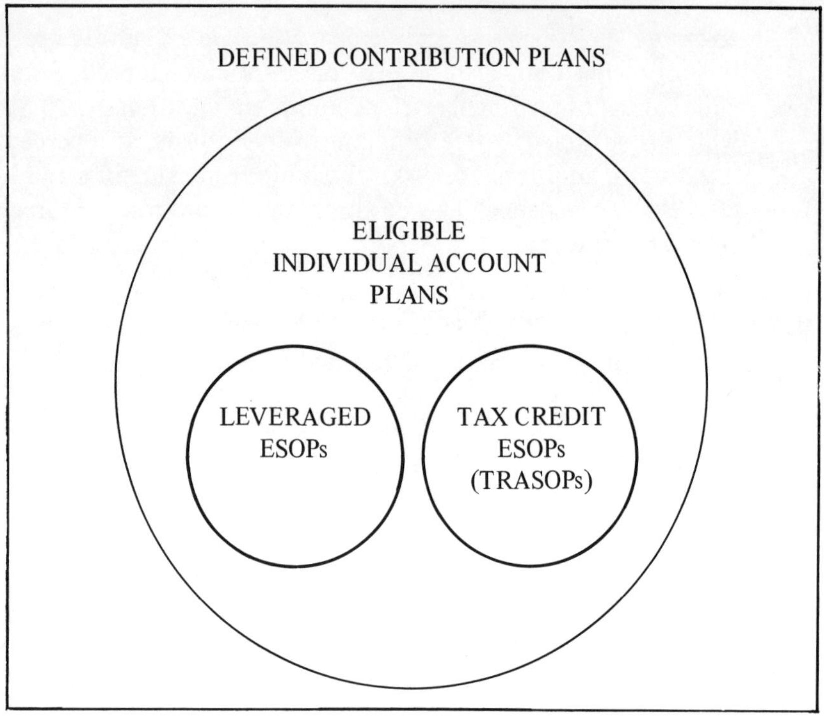

Figure 2. Plans Which Hold Substantial Employer Stock

involves the borrowing of funds in order to effectuate a purchase. Typically, such a plan is used where the employees of a subsidiary desire to purchase its shares from its parent corporation. It is also used to raise capital for new plant or equipment, and to buy out shareholders of closely held corporations.

The major advantage of using a leveraged ESOP as the mechanism for the purchase is that *the purchase price*—that is, the principal of the loan made to finance the purchase and not merely the interest—*becomes tax deductible.*

The mechanics of an ESOP transaction are quite intricate. The ESOP borrows money from a bank or government agency, and/or from the seller in the form of deferred payments. If the seller is the lender, the loan must be at least as favorable to the leveraged ESOP as an arm's length transaction. The loan which finances the leveraged ESOP must satisfy other stringent requirements, the most basic of which is that it may be used *only* to purchase or refinance employer stock. The loan must be without recourse against the leveraged ESOP and may be collateralized only with the securities purchased (or refinanced) by proceeds of the loan. It cannot have the net effect of "draining off" plan assets.

The leveraged ESOP then purchases employer stock with the proceeds of the loan. The plan sponsor makes annual contributions to the ESOP but unlike the case of any other profit sharing plan, up to 25% of the compensation of the participating employees may be contributed on a deductible basis to amortize the principal balance of the loan, and an additional amount (not subject to any percentage limitation) may be contributed on a deductible basis to pay the interest on the indebtedness. As the loan is amortized, a proportionate number of shares of stock is allocated among the participants. An ESOP may make distributions to a terminated participant or to his or her beneficiary in cash rather than employer securities, provided that the participants retain the right to insist upon a distribution consisting solely of employer securities.

> *Example 10.* Junior Corp. is a subsidiary of Universal American Corp. The parent corporation decided that Junior no longer fit into the mainstream of its business and offered to sell it to outside interests for $10,000,000. The executives of Junior Corp., learning of the impending sale, requested to be permitted to purchase it.
>
> To finance the purchase, the executives of Junior Corp. obtained $10,000,000: $3,000,000 in the form of a loan from the Economic Development Administration, $4,000,000 in the form of a loan from First National Bank, and the balance in the form of deferred payments from Universal American Corp.
>
> Under the terms of the loan agreements, Junior Corp. is obligated to contribute to the ESOP each year an amount sufficient to amortize the principal and interest on the indebtedness as it falls due. The loans are structured so as to amortize the entire indebtedness in equal monthly payments over a fifteen year period. As each year's contribution is made to the ESOP and a portion of the indebtedness is repaid, a similar portion of the Junior shares is allocated among the participants in the ESOP in proportion to their compensation. A participant who terminates employment will receive either the shares then in his or her account or cash equal to

> the value of those shares as determined by an appraiser that year. Each former employee who receives Junior shares from the ESOP is given an option to sell his shares to Junior Corp. at their appraised value. This creates a market which might not otherwise exist for the distributed shares.

A leveraged ESOP may also be used to raise capital. A corporation wishing to raise capital in this manner establishes a leveraged ESOP which then borrows money from an outside lender and purchases newly issued shares. The mechanics of the repayment of the loan and the allocation of the shares among the participants in the leveraged ESOP are substantially similar to those outlined in Example 10.

All leveraged ESOPs must satisfy very complex regulations which are not applicable to any other type of defined contribution plan (except for tax credit ESOPs, discussed below) and which restrict the circumstances under which ESOP securities may be bought and sold.

Participants in leveraged ESOPs that distribute securities that are not publicly traded *must* be given an option to sell (or "put") the shares to the employer. Although leveraged ESOPs, as a general rule, are not permitted to enter into buy-sell agreements or to issue put options, the ESOP may agree voluntarily to honor a participant's put option in place of the employer if the employer fails to do so.

A participant or recipient of ESOP stock who has exercised a put option may be paid in installments over five years. The installment period may be extended up to 10 years if the recipient consents and the purchaser puts up security for its obligation.

If a participant desires to sell his or her ESOP securities to a third party rather than to the employer or the leveraged ESOP, the plan sponsor or the leveraged ESOP may retain a right of first refusal if the security is not traded publicly. Any retained right of first refusal lapses no later than 14 days following written notice by the security holder that he has received a bona fide third party offer to purchase his ESOP securities. If the right of first refusal is exercised, the purchase price may not be less than the greater of the price per share arrived at under the plan's appraisal methods or the price offered by the third party.

Tax Credit ESOPs–(Tax Reduction Act Stock Ownership Plans)

A Tax Credit ESOP (formerly called a TRASOP) is a specialized form of ESOP whose original acronym was derived from the Tax Reduction Act of 1975, which first authorized this type of plan.

An employer otherwise entitled to a federal income tax credit equal to 10 percent of capital equipment purchased during the year (called the investment tax credit), is entitled to an additional 1 percent investment credit if contributions are made to a Tax Credit ESOP under certain conditions. In order to qualify for the extra 1 percent credit, the employer must contribute shares of its stock having a value equal to the additional 1 percent (or it must contribute cash equal to that amount which is then used to purchase shares of its stock) to a Tax Credit ESOP. The shares must then be allocated among all employees *in proportion* to their compensation.

A number of large corporations have adopted Tax Credit ESOPs. Tax Credit ESOPs are especially prevalent in capital intensive industries where the ratio of capital expenditures to payroll is high, resulting in significant allocations to participants in the plan.

Participants in Tax Credit ESOPs have the same rights to exercise put options and to insist upon distributions wholly in employer securities as do participants in leveraged ESOPs.

> *Example 11.* BZ Corp. established a Tax Credit ESOP in 1979. It purchased $3,000,000 of capital equipment in that year and would become entitled (in addition to the regular 10 percent investment credit of $300,000) to an additional 1 percent credit amounting to $30,000–when it contributes to the Tax Credit ESOP either shares of its common stock worth $30,000, or $30,000 in cash which is used to purchase its shares.
>
> The aggregate payroll for 1979 of the participants in the Tax Credit ESOP was $10,000,000. BZ Corp. elected to contribute 3,000 shares of its stock, worth $30,000. Edna Brown, who earned $10,000 therefore became entitled to 3 shares worth $30.

Payroll Tax Credit ESOPs

Because Tax Credit ESOPs have proven to be practical only in the case of a relatively few capital intensive companies, the law has been restructured effective in 1983 to provide employers with a tax credit based on the payroll of the participating employees. For 1983 and 1984 the credit is one-half of one percent of payroll; for 1985 through 1987 it is three-fourths of one percent of payroll. Although the provision permitting payroll tax credit ESOPs is now scheduled to expire in 1988, it is anticipated that it will be renewed at that time.

> *Example 12.* Ajax Supermarket establishes a Payroll Tax Credit ESOP in 1983. The payroll of its participating employees is $10,000,000 in 1983, and $10,000,000 in 1984. It contributes stock worth $50,000 in 1983 and $75,000 in 1984. It receives a tax credit of $50,000 and $75,000 on its 1983 and 1984 tax returns. Tom Smith who earned $10,000 in each of 1983 and 1984 will have stock worth $50 and $75 allocated to his account in 1983 and 1984 respectively.

Cash and Deferred Profit Sharing Plans

Lower-paid employees tend to prefer immediate cash bonuses while higher paid participants are more receptive to receiving deferred benefits under qualified plans because of the tax advantages of deferral. An attempt was made to design profit sharing plans which meet the needs of both groups (a provision limiting deferrals to the highly paid would violate the antidiscrimination rule) by permitting those employees who had an immediate need for funds (who were usually the lower paid) to withdraw a portion of the allocations made to their accounts, while the others could elect to leave their account balances untouched and thus to defer immediate taxation of their allocations. Such plans are called cash and deferred profit sharing plans.

> *Example 13.* Cash 'N Carry Retail Corp. established a 15 percent cash and deferred profit sharing plan in 1972 which provided that participants could elect to receive 50 percent of their yearly allocations (if any) in cash within 30 days of the date annual allocations were announced. Cash 'N Carry

authorized a contribution out of net profits of 10 percent of the compensation of participating employees in 1979. Paul Clark earned $20,000 at Cash 'N Carry in 1979, and was thus entitled to a $2,000 allocation. Under the Cash 'N Carry plan he had the right to elect to receive $1,000 in cash immediately, or to leave all $2,000 in the plan. If Clark declined to receive the $1,000 in cash, he would not be taxed currently on that amount. The remaining $1,000 would go into Clark's account regardless of whether he exercised his right to receive immediate cash payments.

The Internal Revenue Service at first approved these plans, provided that they met certain antidiscrimination tests. It then reversed itself and objected, (although plans in effect before it changed its position were permitted to continue in operation) so that the legal status of cash and deferred plans was unclear until the Revenue Act of 1978 gave them a new lease on life.

Effective January 1, 1980 a cash and deferred profit sharing plan may permit participants to withdraw a portion of the employer contribution allocated to his or her account, but such withdrawals are subject to a very complex set of rules. The rules apply to the participants as a group rather than to each participant individually and are designed to require lower paid employees to participate in the plan to a prescribed extent.

The basic rules are:

1. The participants are divided into two groups—the most highly compensated one-third of the participants and the lowest compensated two-thirds of the participants.

2. The highly compensated group may not defer a percentage of their compensation which is more than 50% greater than the percentage of compensation deferred by the lowest paid two-thirds of the participants.

All employer contributions which enter into these calculations must be *fully vested.*

Example 14. The Futuristic Products Profit Sharing Plan covers 30 participants. The employer contributes 15% of each participant's compensation to the plan and permits each participant to withdraw one-third of the contribution allocated to his or her account. The 10 highly paid participants make no withdrawals. All 20 lower paid participants withdraw one-third of the amounts allocated to their accounts.

The 10 highly-paid participants as a group earn $600,000 in salary and receive allocations of $90,000. The 20 lower paid participants as a group earn $500,000 in salary, receive allocations of $75,000 and elect to withdraw $25,000. The amount deferred by the higher paid participants is 15% of compensation ($90,000 divided by $600,-000) and the amount deferred by the lower paid participants is 10% ($50,000 divided by $500,000). The deferral percentage of the higher paid group is 150% of (i.e., 50% greater than) the deferral percentage of the lower paid group (15% divided by 10%). This meets the basic requirement for sufficient participation by the lower paid group.

3. More liberal provisions apply where employer contributions are equal to a lower level of salaries. For example, the deferral percentage of the higher paid group may be *250%* (rather than 150%) of the deferral percentage of the lower paid group if the deferral percentage of the higher paid group does not exceed that of the lower paid group by more than 3 percentage points.

Example 15. Assume the same facts as in Example 14 except that the employer contributes only 5% of compensation to the plan and the lower paid group elects to withdraw 60% of the contributions allocated to their accounts. The deferral percentage of the higher paid group is 250% of that of the lower paid group (5% divided by 2%) but since the differential is only 3 percentage points (5% – 2%) the alternative test is met.

4. Amounts which a participant may elect to withdraw from a cash and deferred plan, but which he or she chooses to leave in the plan, may not subsequently be withdrawn from the plan except in the event of retirement, death, disability, termination of employment, attainment of age 59½ or hard-

ship. Since hardship is the only permissible occasion for a distribution while an individual who is less than 59½ is an active employee, employers may be subjected to pressure to administer the hardship provision of a cash and deferred plan as liberally as is permitted by the Internal Revenue Service.

5. A cash and deferred profit sharing plan may provide that participants may elect to reduce their current compensation in return for which the employer will contribute an amount equal to the reductions into their respective accounts.

> *Example 16.* Tom Jones and Jennifer Williams are each active participants in the Free Enterprise Profit Sharing Plan and each earn $30,000 in basic compensation but Jones also receives a $5,000 bonus. The Plan provides that Free Enterprise will contribute 10% of basic compensation (excluding bonus) to each employee's account. It also allows each employee to elect to receive only 50% of his or her bonus currently with the balance to be contributed to the profit sharing account. Jones chooses to have an additional $2,500 (50% of his $5,000 bonus) deferred and allocated to his profit sharing plan account. Accordingly, an allocation of $5,500 is made to Jones' account and an allocation of $3,000 is made to Williams' account. This practice is permissible provided the 150% deferral percentage test and the other rules described in this section are adhered to.

It is likely that salary reduction cash and deferred profit sharing plans will become highly popular in future years.

Chapter 3

PLAN DESIGN – A GUIDE TO BASIC PLAN FEATURES

So far, we have described the most common types of plans maintained by corporations in this country—including plans such as ESOPs which are maintained for specialized purposes. Each of these types of corporate retirement plans must be tailored to the particular needs of employers by incorporating individually designed features. Differences in benefit and contribution formulas, which have already been discussed, account in part for variations among individual corporate retirement plans. Many of the remaining differences among individual plans may be accounted for by the basic plan features discussed in this chapter.

Four of the six basic plan features discussed here—integration of benefits with the Social Security System, the plan's compensation base, voluntary contribution programs, and segregated accounts—may be incorporated in *either* defined benefit *or* defined contribution plans. The remaining features are withdrawal penalties and cost-of-living adjustments. Withdrawal penalties are a feature of defined contribution plans. Cost-of-living adjustments may be incorporated in defined benefit plans.

Integration of Pension Benefits with the Social Security System

The Social Security System antedates most private pension plans, since it began in 1935 and the development of private plans began in a serious way only during World War II. This sequence of events allowed the designers of private pension plans to take into account the benefits provided by Social Security when setting the level of benefits under their plans. The technical name for this correlation of benefits is "integration." An elaborate body of rules and regulations—some highly technical—soon developed to govern the relationships between these two sets of benefits.

Although the principles underlying Social Security integration are quite complex, it is not necessary to understand the details in order to appreciate its effect. In a nonintegrated plan, all of a participant's compensation is given the same weight. Integration permits an employer to allocate *more* than a proportionate share of contributions or benefits to highly-paid employees. The Internal Revenue Service allows plans to integrate benefits with the Social Security system in order to compensate for the fact that the replacement ratio (that is, the percentage of preretirement salary represented by benefits) under the Social Security system is higher for low-income workers. Since the Social Security system is skewed in favor of workers with lower incomes, employers may, within prescribed limits, skew plan benefits in favor of highly compensated employees.

Integration of Defined Benefit Plans

THE "EXCESS" METHOD

There are basically two methods of integrating Social Security benefits with those provided by a private pension plan. The first method is called "excess" integration since compensation *in excess* of the Social Security taxable wage base—that is, compensation not recognized by the Social Security system—is given greater weight than compensation at or below the taxable wage base.

> *Example 1.* The taxable wage base in 1982 is $32,400. If Rebecca Cowan earned $40,000 in 1982, $7,600 of this amount is considered compensation in excess of the taxable wage base, or "excess compensation."

The integration rules for defined benefit plans permit a differential in the portions of the benefit attributable to compensation above and below the taxable wage base of up to 1.4 percent (depending on whether the plan provides death benefits) if a defined benefit plan has a career compensation base, and 1 percent if a 5 year final average compensation base is used. However, most integrated plans are not integrated to the maximum extent permitted by law. See the section on Integration Levels beginning at page 42.

Example 2. The Whiz Electronics Company pension plan provides a benefit which is 1 percent of compensation for each year of service. Since this is a career compensation plan, and it is desired to integrate it to the maximum permissible extent, the plan provides a benefit equal to 2.4 percent of "excess" compensation (the maximum permissible integration differential). Robert Wynn earned $52,400 in compensation recognized by the Whiz plan in the year 1982. He accrued a benefit of 1 percent of the first $32,400 ($324) and 2.4 percent of the remaining $20,000 ($480) for a total benefit of $804.

Example 3. The High Grain Cereal Company Pension Plan provides a benefit equal to 1 percent of average salary (not to exceed the taxable wage base) in the five years immediately preceding retirement multiplied by the number of years of employment. Since this is a final average pay plan, the maximum benefit which may be provided on compensation above the taxable wage base is 2 percent.

A final average pay formula adjusts an employee's actual compensation history to a certain extent, since it assumes that the employee has been earning that average wage during his or her entire career. If a plan containing a final average compensation benefit formula used as its breakpoint annual wages subject to Social Security tax in the year *preceding* retirement, benefits would be distorted because the breakpoint would be substantially higher than wages recognized by the Social Security system during the greater part of the employee's career. For example, in 1960 the breakpoint was *$4,800*. Therefore, when a plan which uses final average compensation is to be integrated with Social Security using the excess method, it is necessary to correct this imbalance by averaging the employee's taxable wage base during his or her entire career. This average taxable wage base is called an employee's "covered compensation." All employees born in the same calendar year have the same covered compensation since they are presumed to have started working at the same time and they will all reach age 65 in the same year. The Internal Revenue Service publishes a table of "covered compensation" which must be used by final average pay plans which employ the excess method of Social Security integration.

Many pension plans which were integrated with Social Security initially used the excess method since it produced a self-contained benefit formula which was relatively simple to administer. However, the excess method has come to produce somewhat unsatisfactory results (given the goal of skewing benefits in favor of the highly compensated) because Social Security benefits have become more and more weighted in favor of the lowest paid workers and also because the taxable wage base has been rising sharply. This means that the breakpoint above which skewed benefits are given is getting higher and higher. Benefits based on compensation up to the breakpoint continue to be proportional to compensation and service.

> *Example 4.* Consider the Whiz Electronics plan described in Example 2. Assume Robert Wynn also earns $52,400 in 1983 but that the taxable wage base in 1983 is $35,400 ($3,000 higher than in 1982). His accrued benefit in 1983 will be 1 percent of the first $35,400 ($354) and 2.4 per cent of the remaining $17,000 ($408), for a total benefit of $762. Thus Wynn's 1983 benefit was $42 less than his 1982 benefit solely because of the increase in the taxable wage base.

THE "OFFSET" METHOD OF INTEGRATION

Because the excess method has come to produce unsatisfactory results, most integrated defined benefit pension plans now use what is called the "offset" method. Under the offset method, an appropriate portion of primary Social Security benefits is subtracted from (or "offset" against) the benefits otherwise provided under the private pension plan. The primary Social Security benefit is the benefit payable to a participant exclusive of any related dependent or survivor's benefits which may be paid to members of his or her family. The maximum permissible offset at normal retirement date (depending on whether certain death benefits are payable) is generally 83-1/3 percent of the primary Social Security benefit.

> *Example 5.* The Mechanical Maid Appliance Co. pension plan provides a benefit equal to 2 percent of compensation in each year of service offset by 2 percent of the employee's primary Social Security benefit per year of service, with a thirty year cap on service for purposes of both the gross benefit and the offset. If an employee has completed fewer than 30 years of service at the time he or she retires at age 65, both the benefit and the offset are reduced proportionately.

In adopting this approach Mechanical Maid is saying that the combination of Social Security and private pension plan benefits should equal approximately 60 percent of an employee's pay at retirement plus the remaining 40 percent of the primary Social Security benefit (the 40 percent figure represents the amount not offset against the base benefit). It considers itself obligated to provide such a pension to an individual who has spent a full career (i.e., 30 years) with Mechanical Maid. If an employee worked for Mechanical Maid for only 15 years, Mechanical Maid would provide only half of a full pension to him or her. Since the pension which it was providing to the 15-year employee would be reduced, the Social Security offset would be similarly reduced.

Furthermore, since the participant's compensation and service credit are frozen as of his or her termination of service, the Social Security offset must also be frozen as of such date. Therefore, increases in Social Security benefits which occur *after* termination of employment may not be offset against plan benefits.

Integration of Defined Contribution Plans

Like defined benefit plans, defined contribution plans (except for ESOPs and TRASOPs, discussed in Chapter 2) may be integrated with Social Security. In a nonintegrated defined contribution plan, contributions are allocated in proportion to compensation; that is, a participant earning $20,000 a year gets twice the amount that is allocated to a participant earning $10,000 in that year. Although the specific integration rules are different for defined contribution plans and only the excess method of integration is used, the effect remains the same–it permits the employer to weight the plan in favor of the highly paid.

Since contributions rather than benefits are the focus of the defined contribution plan, it was necessary to develop a method of equating contributions to a private defined contribution plan with Social Security benefits. Actuaries have calculated that Social Security benefits derived from employer contributions are the equivalent of 7 percent of compensation up to the Social Security taxable wage base. Since an employer is deemed to have provided Social Security benefits worth 7 percent of compensation up to the taxable wage base it may provide an additional allocation related to compensation above the Social Security taxable wage equal to 7 percent of such excess. That is, a defined contribution plan may have an *integration differential* of up to 7 percent.

A profit sharing plan may therefore provide that contributions up to 7 percent of compensation above the Social Security taxable wage base will be allocated in proportion to such excess compensation, even if *no portion* of the contribution will be allocated to accounts of participants whose entire compensation is subject to Social Security tax.

> *Example 6.* Jean Jones and Ruth Smith are both participants in the Sparkle Jewelry Co. profit sharing plan. The plan provides that Sparkle Jewelry Co. will contribute each year, out of net profits or retained earnings, an amount up to 7 percent of compensation of participants in excess of the Social Security taxable wage base.
>
> Jean Jones' 1982 compensation was $62,400. Ruth Smith earned $20,000 in that same year. The taxable wage base in 1982 was $32,400. At the end of 1982 a contribution of $2,100 (7 percent of the difference between $62,400 and $32,400) was allocated to Jean Jones' account. Ruth Smith, who earned less than the taxable wage base in 1982 received no allocation at all under the plan for that year.

Some defined contribution plans combine features of integrated and nonintegrated plans.

Example 7. The Speculative Corp. money purchase pension plan provides that Speculative will contribute each year an amount equal to the sum of 5 percent of each participant's compensation up to the Social Security taxable wage base and 12 percent of that portion of his or her compensation which exceeds the Social Security taxable wage base. Jack Flynn's compensation for 1982 was $50,000. Of this amount, $17,600 represented compensation over the Social Security taxable wage base. At the end of 1982, 5 percent of $32,400 ($1,620) plus 12 percent of $17,600 ($2,112), or a total of $3,732, was allocated to Jack Flynn's account.

Profit sharing plans are sometimes also integrated on what is called a "spillover" basis. Contributions in an amount up to 7 percent of the compensation in excess of the taxable wage base are first allocated to compensation in excess of the taxable wage base. Any additional contributions are allocated in proportion to total compensation.

Example 8. The Advanced Development Corp. profit sharing plan provides for annual contributions of up to 15 percent of the compensation of the participants. An amount equal to 7 percent of compensation above the taxable wage base is first allocated in proportion to compensation in excess of the Social Security taxable wage base. The balance of the contribution (if any) is then allocated in proportion to total compensation.

Assume that Advanced Development contributes $100,000 to the profit sharing plan in 1982. The payroll of the participants in the plan is $1,000,000, $200,000 of which represents compensation in excess of the 1982 Social Security taxable wage base of $32,400. Advanced Development's 1982 contribution will be allocated as follows:

	Compen-sation	Allocations (1)	(2)	Total	Percentage Compensation
Excess Compensation	200,000	14,000	17,200	31,200	15.6
Comp. subject to Social Security Tax	800,000	-0-	68,800	68,800	8.6
Total	1,000,000	14,000	86,000	100,000	10

You should note that although Advanced Development contributes 10 percent of compensation to its profit sharing plan, the allocation based on participants' compensation in excess of the Social Security taxable wage base is equal to 15.6 percent of total compensation, while the allocation based on participants' compensation subject to Social Security tax is equal to 8.6 percent of total compensation. The difference between the two percentages, 7 percent (15.6 percent - 8.6 percent) represents the weight accorded to the Social Security benefits purchased by Advanced Development's contributions to the Social Security System.

INTEGRATION LEVELS

The rules governing Social Security integration are flexible enough to provide great variation in the weighting of benefits provided by both defined contribution and defined benefit plans. For example, excess plans need not provide *any* benefits based on compensation subject to Social Security tax if benefits on compensation above that level do not exceed the prescribed limits. Furthermore, in an "excess" plan the breakpoint at which the higher level of benefit accrual is applicable may be less than the Social Security tax base and the differential in benefits above and below the breakpoint may also be less than the maximum. For example, although a career compensation plan is permitted to provide an annual rate of benefit increment based on compensation in excess of Social Security covered compensation which is as much as 1.4 percentage points greater than the rate of benefit accrual on compensation at or below the breakpoint, most such plans in fact contain a differential in benefit accrual rates of only between .5 and 1 percentage point.

Similarly, while in a defined benefit "offset" plan the percentage of the primary Social Security benefit which is offset against the benefit can be any amount up to the maximum permissible percentage of 83–1/3 percent, plans which offset more than 50 percent of the primary Social Security benefits are uncommon.

PRESSURES FOR CHANGE IN THE INTEGRATION RULES

No attempt has been made to explain the technical principles and assumptions underlying the rules of plan integration here because few people believe them to be theoretically sound. Indeed, substantial changes in the principles governing Social Security integration have been proposed.

As previously stated, under current rules a private pension plan is not required to provide *any* benefits to employees all of whose earnings are subject to Social Security withholding.

It has been proposed that the rate of accrual of private pension benefits based upon compensation above the Social Security taxable wage base be limited so that it could not exceed twice the rate for benefit accrual in respect of compensation subject to Social Security. An employer would no longer be permitted to exclude entirely from its pension plan employees earning less than the Social Security taxable wage base. Because of this limitation on integration differentials, a plan sponsor that wished to provide adequate benefits to its executives would be required to provide reasonable benefits with regard to compensation below the Social Security breakpoint.

Such proposals, especially if combined with limitations on benefit increments, would drastically alter pension design; they have been vigorously opposed by employers and the pension community. Whether or not these particular proposals are ever enacted, it is safe to say that there will be substantial changes in Social Security integration within the next few years.

Much of the pressure for change in Social Security integration results from changes, implemented by 1977 Amendments to the Social Security Act, in the manner in which Social Security benefits are determined. These amendments, as well as the manner in which Social Security benefits are generally calculated, are discussed more fully in Chapter 7. In general, it can be said that although the Social Security taxable wage base will rise very substantially in the near future, Social Security benefits will not increase proportionately. In many cases, projected Social Security benefits will be *substantially* less than they would have been under the law in effect prior to the 1977 amendments, despite the fact that Social Security contributions will be much higher.

Employers that maintain offset pension plans (that is, the sponsors of *most* integrated defined benefit plans) have thus been subjected to increased costs from two directions as a result of Social Security reform. Their Social Security taxes have been substantially increased by the 1977 Social Security amendments, while at the same time projected Social Security offsets have decreased. The net result of lower offsets is that benefits under private pension plans—and therefore related costs—will increase. Employers who maintain excess pension plans have found that Social Security reform affects retirement plan costs in an opposite way. Both benefits and costs will decrease since the Social Security tax base will rise at a rapid rate under the 1977 Social Security amendments. Many employers with excess plans will be compelled to amend their plans to freeze the breakpoint or to increase benefit levels to compensate for these developments.

Excluded Compensation and the "Compensation Base"

When evaluating the adequacy of benefits under any plan, it is necessary to examine the elements which are included in the plan's compensation base. The compensation base, or compensation recognized by the plan, need not be equal to total W-2 compensation for the year. For example, some plans compute pension benefits or allocate contributions using only basic salary, and disregard overtime pay, shift differentials, bonuses or commissions. Other plans will credit one or more of these special forms of compensation, or will recognize them only up to a specified percentage of base compensation, such as 20 percent of base salary.

The only limitation on the employer's right to exclude compensation from the benefit base of a defined benefit plan or the contribution base of a defined contribution plan is that the effect of the exclusion may not be to discriminate in favor of highly compensated employees. This means that if only secretaries and clerical workers earn bonuses and overtime but executives who are more highly paid do not, bonus and overtime compensation may not be excluded from the compensation base.

Nondeductible Voluntary Participant Contributions

Any retirement plan other than a SEP or an IRA may permit participants to make nondeductible voluntary contributions to the trust fund. (Beginning in 1982, retirement plans may also permit participants to make deductible contributions subject to rules similar to those governing deductible contributions to IRAs. These are discussed in Chapter 4.) Nondeductible contributions are *in addition* to any contributions made to the plan on the participant's behalf by the employer and may be made in amounts which do not exceed 10 percent of compensation for each of the employee's years of participation in the plan. Where voluntary contributions are authorized to be made to a defined benefit plan, the voluntary contribution program is treated as a separate defined contribution plan.

Plans are permitted to incorporate a *carryover* feature which allows participants to make up unused contributions in subsequent plan years.

> *Example 9.* The Knotty Pine Furniture Company profit sharing plan permitted participants to make voluntary contributions in the maximum amount in both 1981 and 1982–that is, contributions of up to 10 percent of a participant's compensation could be made in each of those 2 years. Ann Foxe earned $50,000 in both 1981 and 1982 while a participant in the Knotty Pine Plan. Since she declined to make voluntary contributions in 1981, she will be permitted to make a *$10,000* contribution in 1982 (i.e., $5,000 attributable to compensation earned in 1981 and $5,000 attributable to her 1982 income).

If an employer institutes a voluntary contribution program at a time subsequent to an employee's commencement of participation in the plan, the participant may be permitted to use the carry over in order to make contributions attributable to years in which he or she participated in the plan *before it was amended* to authorize voluntary contributions.

Even though a participant is not permitted to take a personal tax deduction for these voluntary contributions, the right to make nondeductible voluntary plan contributions is far from meaningless. Voluntary contributions are an important and often ignored retirement planning device. From the time that contributions are placed into the trust fund until the time that the last dollar of contributions is withdrawn, any *income* which those voluntary contributions earn is sheltered from tax just as the earnings on the employer's contributions are sheltered. This means that these earnings will not be taxed until they are withdrawn, *even if* they remain in the fund for fifty years.

Voluntary contributions will not be taxed at all when they are returned to you or withdrawn, since they are made with after-tax dollars–that is, they were taxed when earned. The earnings attributable to these contributions may be taxed when withdrawn from the fund at rates which are lower than the rates which would have applied if the income were taxed when earned (when you are likely to have been in a higher tax bracket).

To make the voluntary contribution program even more attractive from the employee's point of view, employers may provide a choice of different funds with varying investment objectives, such as a "growth fund," a "balanced fund," a "money market fund," or a "bond fund," to which voluntary contributions may be allocated. Furthermore, even if participants are restricted to investing voluntary contributions in a guaranteed income fund—that is, a fund underwritten by an insurer which is similar to a savings account because both principal and a rate of interest are guaranteed—the employer will generally have negotiated a higher rate of return (which is even tax deferred) than a participant's savings would otherwise earn.

For all of these reasons, it usually makes sense to make the maximum permissible voluntary contributions under an employer's plan if you have cash available for investment. You should nevertheless be aware of restrictions which limit your right to withdraw your contributions and these earnings. These are discussed in the next section. You should also note that some plans prohibit any withdrawal of voluntary contributions prior to termination of employment, even where the participant may have an objectively determinable need for immediate cash which cannot be met from his or her other assets.

Withdrawal Penalties and Other Restrictions

Many profit sharing and thrift plans which permit inservice withdrawals (that is, withdrawals prior to termination of employment) for reasons other than hardship impose penalties or other restrictions on such withdrawals. Before 1982 the principle of taxation called "constructive receipt" applied to qualified plans. Under this doctrine (which is generally applicable under the Internal Revenue Code) property is constructively received when it is *made available* without restriction to a taxpayer regardless of whether possession is actually taken.

The simplest example of constructive receipt is the taxation of interest on an ordinary passbook savings bank account. The depositor is taxed on interest earned when the interest is credited, even if it remains in the account and is not withdrawn.

The application of the doctrine of constructive receipt defeats the purpose of qualified plans which is to *defer* the taxation of employer contributions and earnings. When ERISA introduced IRAs (discussed in Chapter 4) it excluded them from the doctrine of constructive receipt so that only *actual* distributions from IRAs are subject to tax. However, the doctrine of constructive receipt was applicable to qualified plans until the ERTA eliminated it effective January 1, 1982.

Many qualified plans contain penalty provisions or other restrictions designed to prevent the application of the rule of constructive receipt, although that is no longer the law. A common restriction in thrift plans is the suspension of a participant from participating in the plan for graduated periods of time depending on the nature of his or her withdrawals from the plan:

Money Withdrawn	Suspension Period
1. Unmatched employee contributions	None
2. Employee contributions matched by employer	6 months
3. Earnings on employee contributions (whether or not matched by the employer)	3 months
4. Employer contributions and earnings which have been in the plan at least 2 years (plans may not permit withdrawals of contributions made less than two years before date of withdrawal unless the employee was a participant for at least five years)	3 to 6 months

Example 10. Roberta Anderson is a participant in the Charter Airlines thrift plan. The Charter plan provides that participants may contribute up to 6 percent of yearly compensation. Charter will match employee contributions on a dollar for dollar basis to the extent that there are profits or retained earnings. The Charter plan contains penalties 1 through 3 from the chart above. Withdrawal of employer contributions and earnings thereon is not permitted prior to termination of employment.

On June 30, 1979, Anderson withdrew her own contributions to the plan, all of which had been matched by Charter. On November 30, 1979 she withdrew all of the earnings on her own contributions without a showing of hardship. As a penalty, her right to contribute was suspended until March 31,

1980 because the six month suspension period resulting from withdrawal of her own contributions must be followed by a three month suspension period based upon withdrawal of the earnings on her employee contributions, and the suspension periods may not overlap.

Anderson can never make contributions to the plan based upon her compensation earned during the period beginning on June 30, 1979 and ending on March 31, 1980.

Most plans have not yet been amended to remove penalty provisions or other restrictions no longer needed to avoid constructive receipt. Many plans will elect to retain some of these restrictions for administrative reasons—in order that plan administrators not be burdened by being required to process large numbers of small withdrawals. Notice also that cash and deferred profit sharing plans (discussed in Chapter 2) are subject to a separate set of rules and are not affected by the repeal of the doctrine of constructive receipt as applied to qualified plans.

Aside from considerations of administrative feasibility, there are a number of technical rules which limit the rights of employers to grant participants the right to make unrestricted withdrawals with respect to benefits derived from employer contributions:

1. In the case of defined benefit and money purchase pension plans (whether or not integrated with Social Security benefits) no inservice withdrawals are permitted until the participant attains his or her normal retirement date (generally age 65).

2. In the case of profit sharing plans which are integrated with Social Security, the integrated portion may not be distributed prior to termination of employment unless the participant attains his or her normal retirement date.

3. In the case of a profit sharing plan which is not integrated with Social Security benefits, an employee who has been a participant for fewer than five years may not withdraw contributions and related earnings attributable to the preceding two years.

Plan Adjustments for Inflation

Cost of Living Clauses

Inflation is the mortal enemy of retirees because it saps the purchasing power of their pension benefits. A limited number of defined benefit plan sponsors have therefore elected to adjust their benefits to compensate for the effect of inflation using so-called "cost-of-living" clauses. These clauses usually provide that benefits are to be increased in proportion to increases in the Consumer Price Index.

There are many examples of such adjustments in the public sector. Social Security benefits are now tied to increases in the cost of living, as are benefits under the federal Civil Service Retirement Plan.

Since it would be inordinately costly to provide benefits if there were no limitation on the adjustments to keep pace with inflation, private plans incorporating cost-of-living clauses usually place ceilings or caps on the cost-of-living adjustment. This limitation is most often expressed in terms of a percentage—typically 3 percent to 5 percent—by which the current year's benefit may not exceed the prior year's benefit.

If runaway inflation continues at its present rate, we can expect to see more and more defined benefit plans which contain such cost-of-living benefit adjustment clauses. Indeed, legislation has been proposed which would require pension plans to provide inflation-adjusted benefits.

Some alternative adjustments are being considered by employers to provide inflation adjustments which, unlike cost of living clauses, do not result in increased costs to them. Some employers which maintain both profit sharing or thrift plans, as well as pension plans are experimenting with methods of permitting participants to transfer a portion of their account balances under their defined contribution plans to fund cost-of-living increases under their defined benefit plans.

A second approach being developed is the addition of a payment option under the plan which has been actuarially adjusted so that it increases at a predetermined percentage, such as 5 percent each year. A participant's benefit would have to be substantially reduced initially to finance the yearly escalator. Sometimes the employer would partially subsidize the inflation adjustment to limit the reduction.

Other employers add voluntary contribution arrangements to their plans and encourage employees to set aside additional savings as a method of offsetting the loss in benefit purchasing power brought about by inflation.

You will undoubtedly be hearing more of these plan provisions in the next few years if the rate of inflation does not slacken.

Segregated Accounts

A small minority of defined contribution plans and defined benefit plans permit participants (generally, with the consent of the trustees or the retirement committee) to isolate their accounts from the rest of the trust fund and invest them independently. As you will recall, accounts are not ordinarily maintained for participants in defined benefit plans. However, an account can be established for a participant who has retired under such a plan, and elected an installment payment option. The value of the participant's accrued benefit is credited to such an account and is therefore paid to him or her along with the income earned in such an account.

If a defined contribution plan account is segregated, it will not share ratably in trust fund portfolio gains and losses, but will instead be charged with expenses and losses and credited with all gains resulting *from its separate investment experience*. Account segregation is a particularly desirable alternative for the participant whose plan does not offer a variety of investment funds or whose investment objectives are different from those of the plan trustees or the plan investment committee. Retired employees under defined benefit plans may request segregated accounts in order to obtain a guaranteed rate of return on their funds. However, if the fund has had a good investment return, the participant with a segregated account risks doing worse than the fund as a whole when left to his or her own devices.

Since an unrestricted right by employees to separately invest their accounts would result in overwhelming paperwork for plan administrators, virtually all plans which permit account segregation impose limitations on the right of participants to direct account investments. Often, participants will be limited to only particular alternative forms of investment, such as long term high yield savings accounts, if their accounts are segregated. Participants may also be limited as to the number of times per year at which they may change the investments in their segregated accounts.

Chapter 4

IRAs, SEPs AND KEOGH PLANS

The 1981 Tax Act greatly enhanced the attractiveness of Individual Retirement Accounts (usually called "IRAs"), Simplified Employee Pension Plans, and Keogh Plans. IRAs, in particular, will now become an important part of every employee's retirement planning as a vehicle for making deductible contributions during his or her working lifetime to supplement Social Security and employer-financed pensions at retirement. Although the new Tax Act did not change the rules for rollover IRAs, increased publicity about IRAs should also increase their popularity as a receptacle and tax deferral device for rollover distributions from qualified plans.

Although the rules governing eligibility to make IRA contributions have been greatly simplified effective January 1, 1982, there are substantial penalty taxes imposed upon improper distributions and withdrawals which could cancel out many of the tax benefits of IRA participation. Employees maintaining IRAs should familiarize themselves with these rules in order to avoid these pitfalls of individual retirement planning.

THE DEDUCTIBLE INDIVIDUAL RETIREMENT ACCOUNT

The IRA is a major innovation introduced by ERISA which was intended to enable employees not covered under qualified plans to save for their own retirement on a tax deductible basis. For years prior to 1982, the deductible IRA was therefore of comparatively limited interest to most persons covered by a qualified pension plan since active participants in qualified plans were not permitted to make deductible contributions to IRAs. Complicated regulations were issued by the Internal Revenue Service to determine under what circumstances an individual would be considered to be an "active participant" under a qualified plan so as to make him or her ineligible to contribute to an IRA. These rules were liberalized a number of times, but remained so complicated that employees often made contributions at times when they were ineligible despite their diligent efforts to abide by the rules. As a consequence, the Internal Revenue Service disallowed these contributions and imposed substantial penalties as well regardless of the depositor's intention to comply with the law.

Fortunately, the 1981 Tax Act has made most of these restrictive rules obsolete. We mention them here only to reassure you that you need no longer be concerned about them in respect of contributions made for years after 1981. (Note, however, that contributions made in 1982 in respect of 1981 are still subject to the old rules.)

The new rules for deductibility of contributions to IRAs are as follows:

1. You may contribute and deduct an amount equal to the lesser of $2,000 or 100% of your salary (the pre-1982 limitation was $1,500 or 15% of salary, whichever was less).

   Thus, as a practical matter, the elimination of the 15% of salary limitation means that just about every employed person is permitted to contribute $2,000 to an IRA each year and deduct that amount on his or her federal income tax return.

2. If you are married and your spouse is unemployed, and if you file a joint return with your spouse you may contribute to an IRA and deduct an additional $250. (This rule was also in effect prior to 1982.) You may divide your contributions between IRAs established for your benefit and for the benefit of your spouse in any proportion that you choose, provided that no more than $2,000 may be contributed for the benefit of either one of you. Therefore, if you wish to obtain the maximum $2,250 annual deduction you must contribute at least $250 to an IRA established for your spouse's benefit. Under prior law the spousal IRA deduction was available only if one-half of the contribution (i.e., one-half of $1,750, or $875) was made to the spouse's IRA. Effective 1982, an equal division of the contribution is no longer required.

Example 1. Donald Richards contributes $2,000 to his IRA in 1982 and also contributes $250 to the IRA of his non-working spouse, Ruth. In 1983, he reverses this procedure, contributing $250 to his own IRA and $2,000 to Ruth's IRA. Donald and Ruth can deduct $2,250 on their joint federal income tax return for 1982 and 1983.

Of course, where both spouses are employed each can establish his or her own IRA and make up to the maximum allowable joint contribution of $4,000 ($2,000 each).

Example 2. Ruth obtains part-time employment in 1984 and earns $1,500. She contributes that amount to her IRA. Donald contributes $2,000 to his IRA. They can deduct $3,500 in their 1984 federal income tax return.

3. Active participants in qualified retirement plans are permitted to make contributions to IRAs.

This is the most radical departure from prior law. Prior to 1982, some employees were permitted to elect not to be covered under their employers' qualified retirement plans in order to preserve their eligibility to make deductible contributions to an IRA. If you were offered the opportunity to opt out of participation in your employer's plan and if you availed yourself of it, that election should be terminated effective January 1, 1982.

Most employers that permitted such elections will no doubt eliminate them now that they are no longer necessary or in any employee's interest. If you are covered by such a provision you should inquire as to whether your employer intends to change its plan so as to eliminate the option not to be covered, or whether it will be necessary for your to affirmatively revoke your election in writing.

Deductible Voluntary Contributions to Qualified Plans

4. Employers may now amend their qualified retirement plans to provide that voluntary contributions made by employers are deductible to the same extent as if made to an IRA. These voluntary contributions would be in addition to the

nondeductible voluntary contributions up to 10% of compensation which could be made to qualified plans prior to 1982 (and which are still available). Thus, if your employer amends its qualified retirement plan in this manner, you could contribute to its plan and deduct up to $2,000 for each year beginning in 1982. However, if you have an unemployed spouse and wish to avail yourself of the additional $250 deduction, you must establish an IRA for the benefit of your spouse and contribute an additional $250 since spousal contributions may not be made to qualified plans.

Many employers will decide not to amend their plans to permit employees to make deductible contributions on a voluntary basis. Commercially available IRAs provide almost every conceivable type of investment strategy, from conservative investments in United States government securities and insured savings accounts to investments in aggressive growth stocks. Many employers therefore feel no need to amend their retirement plan to offer investment opportunities which are otherwise available. Some employers may choose as an alternative to facilitate employee IRA participation by making available payroll deduction plans for IRA contributions.

However, if your employer is among those that does make available the opportunity to make deductible voluntary contributions to a qualified retirement plan which it sponsors, you should compare it with commercially available IRAs and decide which is best for you. Bear in mind that you will not be able to avoid most of the IRA restrictions (except for the rules requiring withdrawals to commence at 70½ and limiting rollovers to once per year, which are inapplicable) or gain any favorable tax treatment by placing your contributions in your employer's plan as opposed to an IRA.

You may also split your deductible contribution between your employer's qualified retirement plan and one or more IRAs but the maximum limitation on the deduction remains the same.

Example 3. Jack Friedman is an active participant in the Republic Profit Sharing Plan which has been amended, effective January 1, 1982, to permit employees to make voluntary tax deductible contributions. Friedman, whose salary is $20,000, contributes $1,200 to his employer's plan by means of a payroll deduction program. He may establish an IRA and contribute $800.

The new law defines "voluntary" contributions in a highly technical way. Not only are contributions which are required to be made under the terms of a defined benefit retirement plan excluded from the definition of voluntary contributions, but all contributions which are in any way matched by an employer under thrift plans are similarly excluded from that definition.

Example 4. Jill Baker is covered under the Enterprise Thrift and Savings Plan. The plan permits employees to contribute 1, 2, 3, 4, 5, or 6 percent of compensation. The employer contributes fifty cents for each dollar contributed by an employee. Baker contributes $1,000 to the plan and the employer makes a matching contribution of $500. Baker cannot deduct her $1,000 contribution because it is matched by her employer, and is not considered to be a voluntary contribution.

Observe that in the above example, if Baker cannot afford to make both the maximum $2,000 deductible contribution to an individual retirement account and the maximum $1,200 contribution to her employer's savings plan, she will be forced to decide which alternative is more in her interest. Among the factors which she would have to consider are her income tax bracket (which would determine the value to her of the IRA tax deduction), the vesting schedule under her employer's plan and the likelihood that she will terminate employment, her employer's matching percentage under that plan, and the plan's investment performance.

Some employers are concerned that a sufficient number of relatively low salaried employees would elect to make deductible IRA contributions rather than non-deductible contributions which the employer matches thereby jeopardizing the plan's qualified status. It is too early to tell whether such fears are valid.

Beginning in 1982, an unemployed divorced spouse whose former spouse maintained an IRA for at least 5 years before the year in which the divorce decree was issued and made a deductible contribution for at least 3 of the last 5 years, may contribute and deduct an amount equal to the taxable alimony which the spouse receives during the year, up to a maximum of $1,125.

If the divorced spouse is employed but earns less than $1,125 during the year the combination of earnings and alimony may be taken into account up to the $1,125 maximum. If the divorced spouse's earnings alone exceed $1,125, the spouse would be subject to the regular limitations and the alimony would be disregarded.

> *Example 5.* Roberta Winston is divorced on December 1, 1982. She receives $900 in alimony in December, 1982. She obtains a Christmas job and earns an additional $300 in 1982. She may contribute and deduct $1,125 to an IRA for 1982.

There is a difference in the latest time by which a contribution must be made in order to be deductible for a particular taxable year, depending on whether the contribution is made to an IRA or to a qualified plan.

A contribution to an IRA for a taxable year may be made as late as the due date (including extension) for filing Form 1040 for that taxable year. Thus, if an individual obtains an extension until June 15, 1983 for filing his or her 1982 Federal income tax return, he or she has until that date to make his or her 1982 IRA contribution. However, deductible contributions to a qualified plan for a particular year must be made by April 15 of the following year, or such earlier cutoff date for making such contributions as the plan may provide.

An individual who has reached age 70½ before the end of a calendar year may not make a deductible contribution to an IRA or to a qualified retirement plan for that calendar year or for any subsequent calendar year. However, employer contributions may be made to SEP-IRAs for employees who are 70½ and older. (See the next section for SEP-IRA rules.)

SIMPLIFIED EMPLOYEE PENSION PLANS

The Revenue Act of 1978 authorized employers to contribute to their employees' IRAs under an arrangement called the Simplified Employee Pension Plan. Simplified Employee Pension Plans (also called SEPs) may be used by employers during tax years beginning in or after 1979 even if they maintain other qualified plans.

The innovation in the Simplified Employee Pension scheme is that it authorizes an employer to make contributions to an employee's IRA in excess of the $2,000 limitation which would ordinarily be applicable to the employee's contributions. Employer contributions to SEPs must be included in gross income, and are fully deductible by the employee, so the net effect is a deferral of tax on the employer contribution, even if the employee is also covered by a qualified plan.

A Simplified Employee Pension arrangement is possible only if an employer makes a nonforfeitable contribution to the IRA for each employee who has attained age 25 and performed service for the employer for at least three of the five preceding calendar years in accordance with the terms of a written plan. The plan may not discriminate in favor of officers, shareholders, the self-employed, or the highly compensated. Employer contributions to Simplified Employee Pensions will be considered discriminatory unless contributions to employee IRAs are proportional to compensation (up to the first $200,000). However, SEPs may be integrated with Social Security by offsetting the Social Security contribution made on behalf of an employee against the employer's contribution. Compensation in excess of $200,000 is not recognized. The employer may not limit or prohibit employee withdrawals from Simplified Pension Plans.

If these conditions are satisfied, the employer may contribute annually to each IRA an amount up to the lesser of $15,000 or 15 percent of the employee's compensation, and the employee may take a deduction for the employer's contribution on his or her tax return. However, if compensation in excess of $100,000 is taken into account, the employer must contribute at least 7½% of the first $100,000 of compensation, subject to its right to offset Social Security contributions as discussed in the preceding paragraph.

An employee's right to make deductible IRA contributions is not affected by his or her participation in a SEP. Deductible IRA contributions may even be made directly to the same SEP-IRA.

> *Example 6.* The Constructive Manufacturing Co. adopted a Simplified Employee Pension Plan, effective January 1, 1982, the terms of which provide that it shall contribute to each eligible employee's IRA an amount equal to the lesser of 10 percent of each employee's compensation or $15,000. Rae Beth Wilson and Andrew Mills were employed by Constructive in 1982 and each maintained an IRA. In calendar 1982, Mills earned $10,000 and Wilson earned $30,000 attributable to services for Constructive and Constructive contributed $1,000 and $3,000 to their respective IRAs. Mills and Wilson may each contribute $2,000 to their respective IRAs since, as in the case of employees covered under other qualified retirement plans, IRA contributions which an employee may make are now entirely independent of those made by the employer.

There are advantages to both the small employer and the employee under the SEP arrangement. The employee receives contributions which may exceed his or her maximum permissible "ordinary" IRA contribution, and the employer is spared much of the burdensome paperwork (to be discussed in Chapter 10) and expense associated with maintaining a qualified pension plan.

IRA PENALTIES

The IRA rules impose penalties of Byzantine complexity upon improper contributions (called "excess contributions") and "early and late withdrawals," regardless of whether or not the IRA is maintained as part of a SEP.

Excess Contributions

The IRA depositor is subject to an annual nondeductible penalty of 6 percent of the entire balance in his or her IRA account resulting from contributions in excess of the allowable limitations.

Example 7. Jane Doe contributes $3,000 to an IRA in 1982. On December 31 of that year, the balance in her IRA account was $3,100. Jane Doe will be subject to a penalty of $66 ($1,100 x 6%) unless the excess contribution is withdrawn in the manner discussed in the section headed "Relief Provisions."

Since all withdrawals from IRA accounts are subject to tax, and as excess contributions to an IRA are not deductible, an excess contribution is really subject to a double tax unless it is withdrawn in the manner discussed in the "Relief Provisions" section.

Early Withdrawals

The IRA depositor is subject to a 10 percent penalty tax if he or she withdraws any part of the balance in the IRA before reaching age 59½ unless he or she has become disabled. Distributions from qualified corporate plans (other than those consisting of deductible voluntary contributions and their earnings) are neither subject to the age 59½ rule nor to the other IRA penalties. If an IRA depositor borrows from the IRA, pledges it as security for a loan or invests the IRA in a collectible such as precious metals or artwork prior to age 59½, a taxable distribution also subject to early withdrawal penalties will be deemed to have been made from the IRA.

Example 8. Fred Mason had contributed $7,500 to an IRA over the last 5 years. In 1982, when he is 40 years old, Mason is faced with the need for immediate cash to meet his mortgage payments. Since he is not yet age 59½, Mason will be subject to a penalty tax of 10 percent of the amount withdrawn if he withdraws money from his IRA to pay off his mortgage. If Mason withdraws $1,000 from his IRA for this purpose in 1982 his 1982 federal taxable income will be increased by $1,000 and, in addition, his 1982 federal tax liability will be increased by a penalty equal to 10 percent of $1,000, or $100. The same penalty would apply if part of the amount withdrawn had been contributed under a Simplified Employee Pension arrangement.

The 10 percent penalty on early withdrawals is imposed without regard to whether the original contribution was a proper deductible or rollover contribution, or whether it was an excess contribution.

Relief Provisions

In order to mitigate the Draconian penalties imposed on excess contributions, the following exceptions have been provided:

Exception A. Any excess contribution made in a calender year may be withdrawn without the payment of any income tax or penalty if withdrawn prior to the due date (including extensions) of the federal income tax return for that year.

Example 9. Richard Rowe made a 1982 contribution of $4,250 to an individual retirement account on February 23, 1983. In fact, he was not eligible to make any deductible contribution in excess of $2,250 to an IRA for 1982. He withdrew the excess contribution in the IRA account on April 10, 1983. Rowe is not subject to tax on the $2,000 upon withdrawal, nor is he subject to the 10 percent penalty on early withdrawals and to the 6 percent penalty on excess contributions.

Note, however, that if the excess contribution earned any net income, that net income must be distributed along with the excess contribution in order for Exception A to be applicable. The net income is subject to tax in the year of distribution.

Example 10. Assume the same facts as in Example 9 except that the withdrawal was made on April 20, 1983 and Rowe did not receive an extension of time within which to file his 1982 federal income tax return. Rowe is subject to the 6 percent penalty tax in 1983. Rowe must include the $2,000 withdrawal in income in 1983 and is subject to a $200 penalty ($2000 x 10%) in 1983.

Exception B. An excess contribution of less than $2,250 for which no deduction has been allowed may be withdrawn at any time without being subject to the 10 percent penalty on early withdrawals and without being subject to income tax in the year of withdrawal. However, the 6 percent penalty on excess contributions would be imposed for each year in which on December 31st the excess contribution had not been withdrawn.

> *Example 11.* Assume the facts were the same as in Example 10 except that the contribution for which no deduction was allowed was only $1,000. Rowe is subject to a penalty of $60 ($1,000 x 6%) in 1982 but is not subject to tax on the withdrawal of $1,000 in 1983 or to the 10 percent early withdrawal penalty in 1983.

Exception C. An excess rollover contribution (see discussion of rollovers later in this chapter) attributable to erroneous information may be withdrawn at any time without being subject to the 10 percent penalty on early withdrawals and without being subject to income tax in the year of withdrawal. However the 6 percent penalty on excess contributions would be imposed for each year in which on December 31st the excess contribution had not been withdrawn.

> *Example 12.* Linda Robinson received a distribution of $10,000 from her employer's profit sharing plan in 1982. Her employer erroneously informed her that this distribution could properly be rolled over into an IRA. In fact, the distribution could not properly be rolled over. Robinson rolled the $10,000 into an IRA in 1982 and withdrew it in 1984 when she discovered that the rollover was improper. Robinson is not subject to tax on the early withdrawal in 1984, nor is she subject to the 10 percent early withdrawal penalty in that year. However she is subject to the 6 percent penalty on excess contributions during 1982 and again during 1983.

Exception D. An undercontribution in a later taxable year may be applied to reduce an excess contribution in a prior taxable year.

> *Example 13.* William Jones improperly contributed $1,000 to an IRA in 1981. This constituted an excess contribution since he was covered under a qualified plan in that year. In

1982 Jones contributed $1,000 to an IRA. Since Jones could have contributed $2,000 in 1982 he could apply the $1,000 1982 undercontribution to eliminate the $1,000 1981 excess contribution. This has the same effect as if he withdrew the $1,000 excess contribution in 1982 and then recontributed it in that year.

Jones is therefore subject to the 6 percent penalty on excess contributions in 1981. He is entitled to a $2,000 deduction in 1982.

Withdrawals Between Ages 59½ and 70½

An IRA depositor may withdraw any amount—or no amount—which he or she wishes between ages 59½ and 70½ without penalty. The doctrine of constructive receipt does not apply to IRAs, therefore only amounts actually withdrawn are subject to tax.

Minimum Mandatory Withdrawals after IRA Depositor Attains Age 70½

Beginning with the taxable year in which he or she attains age 70½, an IRA depositor must begin making at least minimum withdrawals in order to avoid the penalty on excess accumulations. The minimum mandatory withdrawal during each year is the balance in the IRA account on the last day of the preceding year divided by the unexpired number of years of life expectancy of the depositor or (if he or she is married) the combined joint life and last survivor life expectancy of the depositor and his or her spouse when the depositor was 70½. Life expectancy is based upon tables issued by the Internal Revenue Service.

One of the few differences between IRA contributions and deductible voluntary contributions to qualified plans is that this rule does *not* apply to deductible voluntary contributions, which may remain in the plan until retirement.

Example 14. Frances and Larry Warren had been married on August 18, 1981 when Larry, an IRA depositor attained age 70½. Under the appropriate table, their joint and last survivor life expectancy was then 20 years. The balance in Larry's IRA account on December 31, 1980 was $100,000. Larry must withdraw at least $5,000 (1/20th of $100,000) in 1981 in order to avoid a penalty. In 1982 Larry must withdraw 1/19 of the balance in the IRA account on December 31, 1981. If the account balance was $96,000 on that date, Larry must withdraw $5,053. However any withdrawal in excess of the minimum amount required in an earlier year is credited against the minimum required withdrawal in a later year.

A penalty equal to 50 percent of the difference between the minimum required withdrawal and the actual withdrawal will be imposed unless the depositor can establish that the shortfall was due to reasonable error and reasonable steps are being taken to withdraw the required amount.

Example 15. Assume that the facts are the same as in the previous example except that Larry withdrew only $4,000 in 1981. A penalty of $500 (50 percent of the difference between the required withdrawal of $5,000 and the actual withdrawal of $4,000) will be imposed.

Example 16. Assume the facts were the same as in the previous example except that Larry was erroneously informed by his accountant that Frances and Larry's joint life and last survivor life expectancy was 25 years. The error was discovered in 1982 and Larry thereafter immediately withdrew an additional $1,000. No penalty would be imposed since a $4,000 withdrawal in 1981 would have been appropriate if their joint life expectancy were in fact 25 years, Larry reasonably relied on the advice of his accountant, and he corrected the withdrawal immediately upon discovery of the error.

Where the IRA depositor dies without having begun to receive payments under a period certain option, any remaining balance in his or her IRA account must, within five years after his or her death, be applied to provide annuity payments to his or her designated beneficiaries. Similarly if a married IRA depositor and spouse both die before the expiration of the period of their joint life expectancy, the balance must be applied within five years after the death of the survivor to provide annuity payments to the designated beneficiaries.

ROLLOVER IRAS

An employee may want to establish a *nondeductible* rollover IRA after receiving a lump sum (i.e., all money has been paid in one tax year) plan distribution. Nondeductible employee contributions may not be rolled over. However, the portion of the distribution attributable to employer contributions, deductible employee contributions and any earnings on those contributions will remain tax sheltered to the extent that the property received or the proceeds from the sale is rolled over to an IRA within 60 days of the last payment. A rollover can be used to avoid immediate income taxation on the distribution received, since taxation is postponed until the year of distribution from the IRA.

In order for an employee's lump sum payment to become eligible for a tax deferral by reason of this "rollover" procedure, the following requirements must be met:

1. The distribution must be received on account of a plan termination, separation from service, *or* after attaining 59½.

2. The cash or other property received from the qualified plan must represent the *entire* account of the participant, if it is a defined contribution plan, or the participant's entire benefit, if it is a defined benefit plan.

3. Provided that a total plan distribution is made, all or any part of the cash or other property attributable to employer contributions or the proceeds from its sale may be transferred to the IRA. (You will recall that property attributable to nondeductible employee contributions and the proceeds thereof may not be rolled over.)

4. The cash or other property being transferred to the individual retirement account must have been received from a qualified plan within one calendar year.

5. The rollover must be made within 60 days of receiving the last payment of the lump sum distribution.

It is also possible for the spouse of an individual who dies while a participant in a qualified plan to make a tax free rollover of any lump sum death benefit received on account of such participant's death.

There is no limit on how many individual retirement accounts can be established so long as all the transfers are made within sixty days after receipt of the lump sum distribution. Since brokerage houses provide the most flexible IRA arrangements, large rollovers are usually made to IRAs maintained by brokerage houses. However, a rollover distribution may be made to any existing deductible or rollover IRA. The amount rolled over is never offset against an individual's maximum allowable IRA deduction for the year, since it is not counted against the $2,000 or $2,250 limitation. However, a separate rollover IRA should be maintained (and deductible contributions should not be made to the rollover IRA) if an employee contemplates that he or she might later want to make a tax free transfer of the rollover funds and their earnings to the plan of a new employer.

The examples which follow illustrate the operation of the rollover rules.

> *Example 17.* Richard Brown left his job with Creative Consultants Corp. and received two distributions from its profit sharing plan: one on February 11, 1978, and the other on December 1, 1978. He transferred the total of the amounts received into an individual retirement account on January 29, 1979. The two distributions from the profit sharing plan qualified as a lump sum distribution since they were received within one taxable year. The transfer qualified as a rollover since the deposit was made within sixty days after the last distribution and distribution was made as a result of termination of employment.

> *Example 18.* Bill Carver, who is 65 years old, received a distribution of the entire balance in his account under his employer's profit sharing plan. Carver may, if he so chooses, deposit the entire amount or any portion of the amount received in an individual retirement account since he has passed the age of 59½ years, regardless of whether he remains on the job. The amount not rolled over is taxed as ordinary income.

> *Example 19.* Bob Chandler became a participant in a profit sharing plan on January 1, 1975. On January 1, 1979 his

employer completely discontinued contributions to the plan. On June 30, 1982 Chandler received a lump sum distribution of $7,000.00, which represents employer contributions allocated to his account plus their earnings. Chandler is entitled to roll over the amount received or any portion of that amount by transferring it to an individual retirement account even if he is under 59½ years of age, since the distribution was made on account of a plan termination.

More specific advice about deductible and rollover IRAs will be given in Part II of this book, which discusses the retirement planning decisions you are likely to be called upon to make at various stages in your career.

KEOGH PLANS

A qualified plan maintained by a self-employed individual or a partnership as opposed to a corporate employer is called a "Keogh" plan. Although Keogh plans may be of either the defined contribution or the defined benefit type, defined benefit Keogh plans are relatively uncommon.

The maximum annual contribution which may be made to a defined contribution Keogh plan on behalf of a self-employed individual is the lesser of $15,000 or 15 percent of earned income (up to the first $200,000). There is a minimum Keogh contribution of 100 percent of earned income up to a maximum of $750 which may be made by self-employed individuals who have small amounts of earned income during the year. Keogh plans are inferior to corporate pension plans for two of the same reasons as IRAs. The maximum contribution which may be made on behalf of individual participants is lower, and, like IRA depositors, self-employed individuals who are sole proprietors or partners with a more than 10% interest in a partnership maintaining Keogh plans are subject to early withdrawal penalties if distributions (including loans) are received prior to age 59½. However, there is one instance in which the Keogh rules are more lenient. Unlike an IRA depositor, a self-employed individual who is a sole proprietor or a partner with more than 10 percent interest in a partnership is not prohibited from making contributions after the age of 70½ if he or she is still employed at the time the contributions are made although such individual will be required to receive distributions from the plan during the same years that additional contributions are being made.

A detailed discussion of Keogh plans is beyond the scope of this book. However, there is one very common situation in which a self-employed person is able to maintain a Keogh plan *even though* he or she is covered simultaneously by a corporation's qualified plan. If he or she has self-employment income which is not reflected in the W-2 which the employer provides, and which results from the independent rendition of services for compensation (if, for example, the employee does some free-lance accounting or tax work), an employee can deposit up to $15,000 or 15 percent of his or her annual free-lance income into a Keogh plan, and also take advantage of the $750 minimum contribution.

> *Example 20.* Roberta Blue resigned from ZAB Corporation on January 31, 1983 after being covered under its calendar year pension plan for the month of January, 1983. Blue earned $20,000 over the remaining eleven months of 1980 doing free-lance accounting work. Blue may contribute $2,000 to an IRA for 1983. Blue may also make a deductible contribution to a Keogh plan based on her $20,000 in income from self-employment. Her maximum 1980 Keogh contribution is $3,000 (15 percent of $20,000). Blue may not make Keogh contributions based upon income earned in 1983 as an employee of ZAB, since salary checks from ZAB are *not* income from self-employment.

The right to maintain a Keogh plan is a retirement planning device which should not be overlooked by corporate executives who provide free-lance consulting services or maintain an independent accounting or tax practice on a part time basis.

Now that you are familiar with all of the types of plans which can be maintained by employers or individuals, including Keoghs and SEPs, you are ready to grapple with the rules for qualifying for benefits under those plans. These rules are explained in the next chapter.

Chapter 5

QUALIFYING FOR BENEFITS

Qualifying for full benefits under a pension plan can be compared to running an obstacle course. Most employers are eager to provide adequate retirement benefits and will make surmounting these obstacles relatively effortless for full-time employees, who will qualify merely by accumulating seniority. Nevertheless, there are three specific obstacles—discrete sets of plan rules covering participation, vesting, and benefit accrual—which you will need to satisfy before becoming entitled to receive benefits under your plan. For the most part, these rules are applied in the same manner in both defined benefit and defined contribution plans. For introductory purposes, it will suffice to say that a *participant* must be *vested* in an *accrued benefit* before he or she can receive payments from a qualified plan. (For a definition of terms, see Glossary.) Under most defined benefit plans, pension payments must begin no earlier than the participant's normal retirement date (usually the participant's 65th birthday) if he or she is to receive an unreduced benefit.

ELIGIBILITY TO PARTICIPATE

It is important to note at the outset that the term "participant" is somewhat of a misnomer. Only participants, former participants, and their beneficiaries can ever receive benefits under a plan. However, you can be a participant and still not be entitled to receive any benefits after you resign or are discharged. When you become a "participant," you simply become eligible to receive benefits at a later date, provided that you satisfy the additional requirements of vesting and that benefits have accrued on your behalf. Generally, all employees who have completed a "year of service" and have reached age 25 must be permitted to participate in a qualified plan.

A Year of Service–the Eligibility Threshold

ERISA has highly technical rules defining the term "year of service" which determines when and whether you become a plan participant. If you are a steady full-time employee, you need not be concerned with these rules, since you will satisfy them in the ordinary course of performing your job. If you are a part-time employee or have a record of frequent leaves of absence these rules could be of some importance to you.

Basically, ERISA authorizes two optional methods for determining whether an employee has completed a year of service. These are commonly known as the "hours of service" and "elapsed time" methods of calculating service. The operation of each method is described briefly below.

Hours of Service

If an employee completes at least 1,000 hours during a twelve-month period, he or she is considered to have completed a year of service. Since an employee who worked a full 40 hour week would complete 2,080 hours of service in a year, an employee who works only half of the normal work week–that is, on a half-time basis–must be included in an employer's pension plan. Depending on the terms of the plan, the employer may actually count hours, or it may assume that an employee who was on the books during any payroll period will be deemed to have completed a certain number of hours prescribed by regulation (one permissible method of crediting service without counting hours is automatically to credit employees with 45 hours of service for every week during which they work even one hour). Vacation time and other time for which pay is received even though no services are performed, as well as certain unpaid leaves of absence will be credited toward the required 1,000 hours.

Elapsed Time

An employee will be deemed to have completed a year of service on each anniversary of his or her date of hire, without the necessity of counting hours. Even part-time employees who do not complete 1,000 hours of service within a year are included automatically.

Both methods of computing years of service are quite common. In fact, they are sometimes combined in one plan. You will have to read your plan or summary plan description to determine which method or methods are utilized by the plan under which you are covered.

Where a combination of the two methods is used, it is most common to count "hours of service" for eligibility only (which may have the effect of excluding some part-time employees), but to use the elapsed time method of calculating service for purposes of vesting and benefit accrual.

There is one exception to the rule that a plan may not impose a service requirement for participation which is longer than one year. A plan which provides for immediate full vesting (this means it provides that no part of your benefit will ever be forfeited) may have an eligibility rule requiring continuous service for a period of three years, without an intervening interruption in service.

Minimum and Maximum Age Limitations

With two exceptions, a plan may not exclude by reason of age an employee who has completed a year of service. Defined benefit plans are permitted to exclude employees first hired within five years of the normal retirement date. Your normal retirement date is generally your 65th birthday. In practice, most plans with maximum age limitations exclude employees first hired after their 60th birthday. However, under ERISA, it is permissible for an employer to delay the normal retirement date until an employee reaches the tenth anniversary of plan participation, if this is later. Plans which use this definition of normal retirement date may not exclude employees hired after age 60 since such employees can never be within five years of their normal retirement dates when first hired. Both defined benefit plans and defined contribution plans may establish a minimum age for plan participation which is not more than age 25.

You must be permitted to become a participant no later than six months following your completion of your plan's eligibility requirements. Plans satisfy this latter rule either by providing for semiannual entry dates on which employees become participants, or by admitting participants retroactively after they have completed the age and service requirements.

Many plans which require the completion of 1,000 hours of service provide that if you do not complete a year of service in your first twelve months of employment, your eligibility computation period shifts to the plan year (that is, to the plan's accounting period, which usually coincides with the employer's fiscal year). If you did not complete a year of service in your first twelve months of employment, you must be permitted to become a participant no later than six months following the end of the first plan year during which you complete a year of service.

However, if you have not satisfied the plan's minimum age requirement when you complete a year of service—if, for example, you are 23 but the minimum age for participation set by the plan is 25—you must become a participant no later than six months following your 25th birthday, assuming that you are still employed on your 25th birthday. Here are some examples which illustrate the way in which ERISA's eligibility rules operate:

> *Example 1.* Robert Bennett began work at Speedy Airlines, Inc. on June 15, 1979. The Speedy Airlines elapsed time pension plan has a plan year which begins on June 1 and ends on the succeeding May 31. It provides that each employee who completes twelve months of continuous service shall become a participant on the first day of the plan year coinciding with or next following the employee's date of hire. Between June 15, 1979 and June 14, 1980, Bennett completes a year of service. Bennett becomes a participant in the Speedy Airlines Plan as of June 1, 1980.

You should note that ERISA would have permitted Speedy Airlines to defer Bennett's participation until no later than December 15, 1980, which is six months following Bennett's completion of ERISA's minimum eligibility requirements.

Example 2. Rose Reardon began work at the Excelsior Corporation on January 8, 1979. Excelsior sponsors a profit sharing plan which provides that employees become participants on the first entry date (January 1 or June 1) following the anniversary of their first day on the job if they complete at least 1,000 hours of service in their first 12 months on the job. Any employee who does not complete at least 1,000 hours of service by the anniversary of his or her first day on the job will become a participant on the first entry date coinciding with or following the end of the first plan year during which he or she completes at least 1,000 hours of service. Reardon completes 2,000 hours of service between January 8, 1979 and January 7, 1980. She will become a participant in the Excelsior plan on June 1, 1980, the first entry date following her completion of a year of service.

Example 3. Marie Omega began work at the High Speed Business Machines Company on October 15, 1979, which was also her 22nd birthday. The High Speed pension plan provides that all employees become participants on the first entry date (April 1 or October 1) coinciding with or following the first "eligibility computation period" during which the participant has both completed 1,000 hours of service and attained age 25. The plan defines "eligibility computation period" as the first twelve months following an employee's first day on the job and all plan years (April 1 to March 31) beginning on or after the starting date.

Omega completes 1,000 hours of service in the twelve month period ending on October 14, 1980. However, she cannot become a participant on April 1, 1981, which is the first entry date following the end of the first "eligibility computation period" during which she completes 1,000 hours of service, because she will not yet have attained age 25. Omega will become a participant on April 1, 1983, if she is still employed on that date. This will be the first entry date following her completion of *both* the age and service eligibility requirements.

Omega will become a participant on that date *even if* she does not complete at least 1,000 hours of service in the plan year ending on March 31, 1983, since she fulfilled the service requirement for eligibility prior to the first anniversary of her employment starting date. It will not be necessary for her to fulfill the service requirement for eligibility more than once so long as she remains employed by High Speed.

VESTING

A synonym for vested is "nonforfeitable." Benefits which are vested cannot be lost even if you subsequently resign or are discharged. However, under certain circumstances they can be lost if you die prior to the plan's earliest retirement age. A participant who has no vested rights in an accrued benefit of $100 a month will not be entitled to *any* benefit if he or she quits or is discharged. However, a plan vesting provision is not necessarily an "all or nothing" rule. A participant who is 60 percent vested in his or her accrued benefit will become entitled to receive 60 percent of that benefit (perhaps only upon reaching age 65 or another specified age) even if he or she quits or is fired. The remaining 40 percent will be forfeited under those circumstances.

Prior to ERISA the Internal Revenue Code did not require that a plan contain provisions for vesting prior to the time an employee reached his or her normal retirement date. Thus, for many years, it was possible for a retirement plan to provide that an employee who terminated service at any time prior to attaining age sixty-five would receive *no benefits whatsoever*.

Over the years many employers voluntarily liberalized the vesting provisions of their plans in recognition of the unfairness of denying pension benefits to employees who had worked for them for substantial lengths of time. The Internal Revenue Service encouraged this trend by refusing to qualify many retirement plans, especially small ones, unless they "voluntarily" adopted liberal vesting provisions.

ERISA imposed stringent minimum vesting standards as a matter of law rather than informal Internal Revenue Service policy. These rules apply to all qualified plans other than Tax Credit ESOPs, which must provide for immediate full vesting.

In essence, most employers are now offered three choices of minimum vesting provisions to be placed in their plans in addition to full vesting at normal retirement date. Generally speaking, the definition of a year of service for the purpose of these vesting rules is the same as that discussed in the section on eligibility.

However, an employer is permitted to exclude the following years of service when calculating service for vesting purposes.

- –Years of service prior to adoption of the plan.
- –Years of service before ERISA became effective (generally on the first day of the plan year beginning in 1976), if that service would have been disregarded under the rules of the plan in effect prior to ERISA.
- –In the case of a plan *requiring* employee contributions, such as a thrift plan, years in which the employee declined to contribute.
- –Years of service prior to age 22 (if the plan does not have "Rule of 45" or "4–40" vesting). This means, for example, that if your plan requires ten years of service for vesting (the "cliff vesting" rule discussed below) and incorporates this additional provision, *no* employee can have any vesting rights in his or her accrued benefit prior to reaching age 32.

Cliff Vesting

Cliff vesting is an "all or nothing" rule under which an employee is completely vested only after having completed ten years of service but is not vested to any extent prior to that time. An employee who resigns or is discharged prior to completing ten years of service receives no benefits at all. Almost all major retirement plans have chosen the ten year cliff vesting rule, because of two key advantages which it provides. First, it is easy to understand and explain to employees. Second, it eliminates plan accounting problems of having to deal with employees who leave the job with partially vested interests and thus forfeit a portion of their accrued benefits. However, the Internal Revenue Service will not permit new plans sponsored by relatively small employers to use ten year cliff provisions if the employer has a high turnover rate of rank and file employees. (In pension parlance, the term "rank and file" means employees who are not officers or shareholders and who are not highly compensated.)

Fifteen Year Graduated Vesting

Under this graduated vesting schedule an employee is 25 percent vested after having completed five years of service and then vests at the rate of 5 percent per year during each of the next five years of service (so that he or she is 50 percent vested after having completed ten years of service) and continues to vest at the rate of 10 percent a year for the next five years. An employee is fully vested only at the end of fifteen years.

Rule of 45 Vesting

The Rule of 45 provides that an employee becomes 50 percent vested after the sum of the employee's age and the number of his or her years of service equals 45, provided that he or she has completed at least five years of service. The employee must wait until completion of five years of service before acquiring vested rights to an accrued benefit if he or she is 35 or older on the date of hire. Thereafter the employee continues to vest at the rate of 10 percent for each year of service. However, all employees must be at least 50 percent vested upon completion of 10 years of service. This vesting schedule is used less frequently than the two other statutory minimum vesting schedules because it is so complicated. A young participant can be forced to wait the longest period of time before having any vested rights under the Rule of 45, even though years of service completed prior to age 22 may not be excluded if Rule of 45 vesting is used.

> *Example 4.* Johanna Blake begins work at the Nifty Widget Company at age 25. The Nifty Widget pension plan has Rule of 45 vesting. Assuming that she is continuously employed after her date of hire, Blake will not have any vested rights in her accrued benefit until she has reached age 35, when the sum of her age (35) and her years of service (10) equals 45 and she has completed 10 years of service. Note that Blake would have been 100 percent rather than 50 percent vested at age 35 if her plan had 10 year cliff provisions. Under the Rule of 45, she will not become 100 percent vested until she is 40, assuming that she has by then completed 5 additional years of service.

4-40 Vesting

ERISA also empowers the Internal Revenue Service to impose more rapid vesting schedules than the three which have been discussed. The Internal Revenue Service often attempts to require new plans of small employers to adopt so-called "4–40" vesting schedules under which a participant is 40 percent vested upon completion of four years of service, and vests at the rate of an additional 5 percent for each of the following two years of service, and then 10 percent for each of the next five years of service. Under 4–40 vesting a participant is therefore fully vested after completing eleven years of service. The Internal Revenue Service usually insists upon 4–40 vesting in new plans unless the employer can demonstrate turnover rate for rank and file employees not more than twice as high as that of the highly compensated employees.

Unless an employer follows the practice of discharging employees immediately before their interests under a retirement plan would become vested to prevent them from ever receiving benefits (which is also a criminal offense under ERISA), it is generally believed that the Internal Revenue Service may not require vesting schedules more rapid than this "4–40" schedule.

Table 2 on the following page illustrates the comparative rates of vesting under the statutory minimum vesting schedules.

The statutory minimum vesting provisions apply only to benefits derived from employer contributions. If a defined contribution plan requires or permits employee contributions, any benefits related to those contributions (which means the contributions themselves *plus* all earnings derived from those contributions) must always be fully vested. Participants in contributory defined benefit plans are also fully vested in the benefits derived from their own contributions. Special conversion factors contained in regulations issued by the Internal Revenue Service are used to make these calculations.

The vesting provisions required by ERISA are only minimum standards. Plans may and do provide vesting provisions which are more liberal than those required by ERISA, even to the extent of providing full and immediate vesting in all employer contributions. Defined contribution plans such as thrift plans and profit sharing plans tend to provide faster vesting than do defined benefit pension plans.

Accelerated Vesting Under Special Circumstances

Most defined contribution plans (and a few defined benefit plans) provide for immediate full vesting in the event of death

Table 2

Comparison of Statutory Vesting Schedules

Years of Service Completed	5-15 Year	10 year Cliff	Rule of 45 (age 26 or younger when hired)*	Rule of 45 (age 35 or older when hired)*	4-40
0-1	0 %	0 %	0 %	0 %	0 %
1-2	0	0	0	0	0
2-3	0	0	0	0	0
3-4	0	0	0	0	0
4-5	0	0	0	0	40
5-6	25	0	0	50	45
6-7	30	0	0	60	50
7-8	35	0	0	70	60
8-9	40	0	0	80	70
9-10	45	0	0	90	80
10-11	50	100	50	100	90
11-12	60	100	60	100	100
12-13	70	100	70	100	100
13-14	80	100	80	100	100
14-15	90	100	90	100	100
15+	100	100	100	100	100

*Employees hired between ages 27 and 34 who are covered by a plan which provides vesting in accordance with the rule of 45 will be 50 percent vested within 6–9 years as follows:

Age when hired	Number of Years Required for 50% Vesting
27–28	9
29–30	8
31–32	7
33–34	6

(in which case the death benefit is payable to a designated beneficiary or to the participant's estate) or disability regardless of the plan's vesting schedule which is otherwise applicable to employees who resign or are discharged. Others add a minimum age or service requirement for full death vesting which may provide more liberal vesting than the plan's ordinary vesting schedule.

Finally, all plans must provide that the benefits of affected participants must be fully vested in the event that the plan is fully or partially terminated. (See discussion in Chapter 16.) In the case of a defined contribution plan, a complete discontinuance of contributions is considered the equivalent of a plan termination.

Breaks in Service

Plan participation stops when an employee incurs a break in service. This means that an employee ceases to earn benefit credits when the break in service occurs and the plan's vesting schedule determines whether he or she is entitled to the benefit earned up to the break in service. Prior to ERISA, it was not uncommon for plans to provide that even a short layoff experienced by a long-term employee constituted a break in service. However, ERISA requires plans to contain complex rules which prevent forfeitures of benefits and benefit credit due to brief absences from work.

In a plan which counts *hours of service*, a break in service occurs as of the first day of any plan year (or other computation period) in which the participant fails to complete at least 501 hours of service. A participant in an *elapsed time* plan does not incur a break in service unless he or she fails to perform an hour of service for twelve consecutive months. Although many plans incorporate more liberal rules for crediting service during leaves of absence, the law requires certain minimum credit for leaves of absence. If a participant in an *elapsed time* plan goes on a leave of absence and later resigns, the participant is deemed to have terminated employment as of the earlier of the date on which he or she resigns or the first anniversary of the day the leave of absence began.

An employee who returns to work after incurring a break in service must reenter the plan as of his or her date of reemployment, provided that he or she subsequently completes a year of service.

Example 5. Philip Quinn was employed by the Work Flow Consulting Co. during 1977. Work Flow sponsors a calendar year defined benefit plan which uses the hours of service method of crediting service. Quinn became a participant in the plan on January 1, 1978, the first entry date following the anniversary of his first day on the job, because he completed at least 1,000 hours of service during his first 12 months on the job. Quinn completed more than 1,000 hours of service in the plan year ended on December 31, 1979. In 1980, Quinn worked only 420 hours before resigning. Quinn is rehired by Work Flow on February 2, 1981.

Quinn remained a participant in the Work Flow plan in 1979. He did not incur a break in service in 1979 because he completed more than 500 hours of service in that year. However, Quinn incurs a break in service, and he ceases to be a plan participant, in 1980, because he completes fewer than 501 hours of service in 1980.

Quinn will become a participant again as of *February 1, 1981*, the date of his reemployment, if he completes 1,000 hours of service in either the first 12 months following his reemployment or the plan year of his reemployment (January 1 to December 31, 1981).

Example 6. Joan Lincoln has been a participant in the Cloudburst Umbrella Corporation's calendar year elapsed time pension plan since January 1, 1978. On February 20, 1980, Lincoln begins an unpaid leave of absence of indeterminate length. On November 1, 1980, Lincoln returns to work for Cloudburst. Lincoln is a participant in the Cloudburst plan during the entire period beginning on February 20, 1980 and ending on November 1, 1980 because she has not incurred a break in service.

If Lincoln had instead informed Cloudburst on November 1, 1980 that she did not intend to return, November 1 would be considered her termination date. She would have incurred a break in service on February 20, 1981.

ERISA usually requires that all service prior to a break in service be counted if the participant returns to the employ of the plan sponsor, although plans may require that a participant complete a year of service as a condition of recognizing service completed prior to the break. There is one exception to the rule that service prior to a break in service must be counted. This rule involves the unusual situation in which an employee who has not become vested in any portion of his or her benefit terminates employment and has a break in service which is longer than the period worked for his or her employer prior to the break. If such an employee is rehired, the "rule of parity" provides that the prior period of service need not be counted for *any* purposes under the plan–including vesting and benefit credit. Such an employee must fulfill the service requirement for participation a second time if he or she is subsequently rehired.

> *Example 7.* Karen Breck began employment with the Rainbow Paint Company on January 2, 1977. Rainbow Paint Company sponsors a calendar year pension plan which requires ten years of service before any rights to benefits are vested, and one year of service for eligibility. The plan incorporates the rule of parity. Breck left the job voluntarily on December 31, 1979, after completing three full years of service.
>
> On January 2, 1984, Breck is rehired by the Rainbow Paint Company.
>
> Breck loses credit for her prior service for all purposes under this plan, since she had no vested rights to benefits and the length of her break in service (4 years) exceeded the length of her prior period of service (3 years). She must complete a year of service in the plan year ending on December 31, 1984 (or a subsequent plan year) or in the twelve months following her date of reemployment before she can participate in the Rainbow Paint Company plan again.

BENEFIT ACCRUAL–HOW MUCH WILL YOU RECEIVE?

A participant who terminates employment becomes eligible to receive his or her vested accrued benefit (if any) under the plan, perhaps only upon reaching a specified age. Under a defined contribution plan, a participant's accrued benefit is the balance in his or her account. As you will recall from Chapter 2, participants in defined contribution plans receive an allocation of a portion of the employer's contribution and forfeitures (if any) for each year during which they are a participant. However, the account balance will also reflect the fund's investment performance, since accounts will share ratably in fund earnings or losses.

The term "accrued benefit" has quite a different meaning in a defined benefit plan. In this case a participant's accrued benefit at any time is the amount to which he or she would be entitled under the plan's benefit formula at normal retirement date if he or she stopped working at the time the calculation is made.

For purposes of calculating an accrued benefit, if a plan uses the offset method of integration, the Social Security offset will usually be computed on the assumption that the participant will continue to earn the same salary until retirement as the salary earned when the calculation was made and that the Social Security benefit levels will remain unchanged.

ERISA contains complicated rules to insure that benefits accrue no more slowly than at an approximately even rate throughout the period of your plan participation.

It is perfectly permissible for plans to provide that participants will accrue benefits faster during the first years of employment. This accelerated benefit accrual is called "frontloading." The only benefit accrual limitation which is of importance to you is the prevention of "backloading." This means that a defined benefit plan cannot make you wait until the years immediately prior to retirement before accruing the bulk of your benefits. If backloading were permitted it would be a method of evading the vesting provisions, since during the initial years of participation, participants would have vested interests in small or even negligible benefits.

ERISA does not require a plan to provide that participants continue to accrue benefits after their normal retirement date.

ERISA provides you with a right to receive an annual statement of the accrued benefit to which you would be entitled at your normal retirement date upon written request to your plan administrator. Most employers furnish this statement automatically.

LOSS OR DENIAL OF VESTED ACCRUED BENEFITS

There are three major exceptions to the rule that an employee may never lose benefits once they have been earned and become vested.

Death Prior to Retirement

A defined *contribution* plan may provide that a participant forfeits benefits if he or she dies prior to having become fully vested. However, most defined contribution plans contain provisions for immediate full death vesting. A defined *benefit* plan may provide that a married employee's benefits are lost if while employed he or she dies prior to the plan's earliest retirement age or age 55, if it is later. The benefit of a single employee may be forfeited if he or she dies while employed prior to normal retirement date, even if the plan provides for early retirement and he or she would have qualified on the date of death to retire early. Provisions incorporating these rules are used in many defined benefit plans, since they result in significant cost savings to the employer.

However, a pension plan must provide that a married employee who is within ten years of his or her normal retirement date (generally, an employee who reaches age 55) and whose plan provides for early retirement be given the opportunity to "purchase" a death benefit for the surviving spouse (if the participant dies while employed) equal to 50 percent of the benefit that would have been payable to the employee had he or she elected to retire early immediately prior to death.

> *Example 8.* When Ronald Green reached age 55 he elected to have a benefit payable to his wife, Ruth, under his pension plan in the event of his death while employed prior to age 65. Green died at age 60. If he had retired at that age having elected a joint and 50 percent survivor annuity he would have become entitled to a pension of $100 a month, beginning immediately. His widow is entitled to a pension of $50 per month beginning immediately after his death.

ERISA does not require that this death benefit be subsidized by the employer. The employee who elects a survivorship option can be made to pay for this benefit himself or herself. This "payment" is made by means of a reduction in the benefit which otherwise would have been payable to the employee when he or she retires.

The death benefit reduction is generally based on the period for which the option has been in effect. The reduction made to an employee's pension is usually in the range of between ½ percent to ¾ percent for each year that the option is in effect. However, the majority of employers choose to subsidize the preretirement death benefit of married employees and not make reductions in the pensions otherwise payable to participants who live through the death benefit period.

> *Example 9.* Assume that Green's plan requires that employee to bear the cost of a preretirement death benefit. Green elected the death benefit, then lived through the payment period and, instead, retired at age 65. At age 65 his accrued pension under the plan's benefit formula is $300 per month. However, since the optional early survivor election was in effect for ten years, Green's pension will be adjusted by making a cumulative reduction of $15, from $300 per month to $285 per month.

Under the majority of defined benefit plans, however, Green would have remained entitled to receive $300 per month on his normal retirement date.

ERISA contains complicated notice provisions to cover situations in which the preretirement death benefit is elective rather than automatic. Employees must not only be notified of the existence of the election, but must also be given a sufficient opportunity to elect such coverage prior to the plan's earliest retirement date (or age 55, if later).

An employer that improperly fails to notify an employee eligible to elect preretirement death protection risks legal penalties. If it can be shown that an employee did not avail himself or herself of the right to make the election because the employer did not notify the employee of its existence, the employer could be held liable to pay a survivorship annuity to the employee's surviving spouse.

Death after Retirement

Most retirement plans contain a number of optional methods of payment of retirement benefits. These options will be discussed in detail in Chapters 6 and 13.

There are two important ways in which these optional payment rules affect the availability of death benefits. First, ERISA requires that if a plan provides life annuities, a married participant must receive his or her pension in the form of a qualified joint and survivor annuity, unless he or she formally declines to receive the pension in this form. A qualified joint and survivor annuity will be payable for the joint lives of the participant and spouse, with anywhere from 50 percent to 100 percent (depending upon the plan) of the benefit payable during the participant's life continuing to the surviving spouse upon the participant's death. The participant's lifetime payments are reduced to compensate for the fact that payments will be made over a period of two lives instead of one. The younger the spouse and the larger the spouse's monthly benefit, the greater will be the reduction in the participant's monthly benefit.

However, if a participant has formally declined the qualified joint and survivor annuity in order to elect a form of payment with no death benefit feature (i.e., monthly payments for the participant's lifetime only), no additional benefits will be provided by the plan by reason of the participant's death. Death benefits may be lost in this manner *even if* the employee dies before having received a single benefit payment.

> *Example 10.* Judith King, a participant in the XYZ Corporation pension plan, retires on her normal retirement date. Since her husband is eligible for a generous pension under his own pension plan, and thus does not need to be assured of an income in the event Judith dies, she declines the qualified joint and survivor annuity and elects to receive deferred retirement benefits in the form of equal monthly payments for her lifetime commencing on the first day of the calendar year following her normal retirement date. King dies prior to the date pension payments were to commence. Her husband does not become entitled to receive any benefits upon her death,

even though King did not receive even one pension payment from the XYZ plan.

Withdrawals Under Contributory Plans

A second major exception to the nonforfeitability rule applies to defined benefit plans requiring employee contributions as a condition of participation. Any benefits attributable to employer contributions may be forfeited upon withdrawal of employee contributions if the employee is less than 50 percent vested in the benefit derived from employer contributions.

Underfunding

You should also be aware that even if you are a fully vested participant in a defined benefit plan, there is no assurance that your full accrued benefit will actually be paid to you if the plan terminates. Often plans are not fully funded—that is, they do not contain sufficient assets to pay all accrued benefits. If you participate in a terminated defined benefit plan which has insufficient assets in the trust fund to pay all accrued benefits, you will receive only *the greater* of your funded accrued benefit or the maximum benefit insured by the Pension Benefit Guaranty Corporation. The PBGC insurance guarantees vested benefits, *up to certain maximum dollar amounts*, to the extent that plan assets are insufficient to provide them. (PBGC insurance will be discussed in Chapter 16.) The effect of this limited PBGC guarantee is to make a minimum level of benefits available to participants in underfunded plans which are terminated.

Final Note

You should have acquired by now sufficient familiarity with both the requirements of ERISA and the arcane terminology used by pension technicians to be able to evaluate not only how you become entitled to benefits under any retirement plan, but also the likelihood of your obtaining benefits under your employer's plan.

Chapter 6

HOW AND WHEN PLAN BENEFITS ARE PAID

Defined benefit plans often authorize benefit payments at different times than those authorized by defined contribution plans. In addition, defined benefit and defined contribution plans virtually always provide different standard forms of payment to the employee who has not elected a plan payment option. However, there is one overriding rule imposed by ERISA which you should keep in mind while reading this introduction to how and when your plan dollars will become available. All qualified plans must provide that payment of benefits is to commence (unless the participant consents in writing to a postponement) no later than 60 days after the end of the plan year in which the participant reaches normal retirement date, unless the participant continues to work after normal retirement date. In that case, unless the participant consents to a deferral, payments must begin not later than 60 days after the end of the plan year in which he or she retires.

DEFINED BENEFIT PLANS

Standard Forms of Payment

All defined benefit pension plans are built around the anticipated retirement of the participants at their normal retirement date, which is usually age 65. The normal form of benefit (that is, the benefit provided to all single participants who have not elected otherwise) provided under such a plan is a life annuity beginning at the normal retirement date. A life annuity contains no death benefit element. The last payment made is the payment in the month in which the participant dies. Of course, any eligible married participant who did not decline the qualified joint and survivor annuity during the statutory election period will instead be paid in that form. Plans may require that employees be married to the spouse for at least one year prior to retirement or death (or both) as a condition of receiving the qualified joint and survivor annuity.

Under a qualified joint and survivor annuity, if the participant dies the surviving spouse must be entitled to receive a pension, after the participant's death, equal to at least 50 percent of the pension which the participant was receiving (or would have been entitled to receive) prior to death. However, the qualified joint and survivor annuity will be calculated by adjusting the monthly benefit which would otherwise be payable to the participant as a single life annuity to an actuarially equivalent smaller monthly benefit payable over the lives of the participant and the spouse. Even though it is provided in situations in which the employee has made no affirmative election, the qualified joint and survivor annuity is really a form of payment option.

Payment Options

It is recognized that a limited choice between a life annuity and a qualified joint and survivor annuity does not best suit the needs of some participants. Therefore, most pension plans provide for alternative payment options.

Nonsubsidized optional forms of pensions (including the qualified joint and survivor annuity) have two basic characteristics:

(i) they may provide a form of death benefit, which, in the case of benefits other than the qualified joint and survivor annuity, is often payable to anyone the participant chooses, including the participant's estate, and

(ii) they are actuarially equivalent—that is, they have the same economic value.

> *Example 1.* Under the ABD pension plan, Frank Smith is entitled to a pension of $500 per month for life. This pension has a *lump sum value* of $58,000, i.e., a $500 per month annuity can be purchased or funded for a man Frank Smith's age at a cost of $58,000. Under the terms of the pension plan, Smith can elect to receive the lump sum in lieu of a life annuity.

> *Example 2.* Angela Woods is entitled to receive a lifetime pension under the Smooth Sailing Watercraft Corporation pension plan of $600 per month beginning at age 65. Woods is married and does not decline the plan's 50 percent qualified joint and survivor annuity during the statutory election period. Since the pension earned by Woods will now be paid out over the joint lifetimes of Woods and her husband (i.e., until the survivor dies), Woods' monthly pension will be reduced to approximately $480 per month and her husband (provided that he survives Woods) will be entitled to receive 50 percent of the $480, or $240 per month for the remainder of the period during which he survives Woods.
>
> The exact reduction made in the lifetime pension is based upon the exact ages of Woods and her spouse. If Woods's spouse had been younger the reduction made in the employee's pension to "finance" the survivor option would have been greater.

There is, however, an exception to the general rule that all options are actuarially equivalent. In some pension plans, the qualified joint and survivor option is either fully or partially subsidized in the same way that the preretirement death benefits of married active employees (discussed in Chapter 5) are subsidized.

> *Example 3.* Tom Jones is entitled to receive a pension under the ABE pension plan of $600 per month for the balance of his life beginning at age 65. However, since he is married, the plan provides that if Jones does not decline the qualified joint and survivor annuity and if his wife, Mary, survives him

she will be eligible at his death to receive $300 per month for the balance of her life.

This is a subsidized joint and survivor option. If this option were not subsidized, the pension payable during Jones' lifetime would have been reduced in the manner illustrated in Example 2.

Full subsidization of the joint and survivor annuity is rare because it adds substantially to the cost of a pension plan. However, a substantial number of employers provide for partially subsidized joint and survivor annuities. Under many of these arrangements the employer pays about 50 percent of the additional cost of providing the survivorship annuity. It will generally be to your advantage to select even a partially subsidized qualified joint and survivor option if your employer has made one available.

Commonly Available Payment Options

The most common elective forms of payment under defined benefit pension plans and the death benefits or other guaranteed benefits provided under them are summarized in Table 3 and described in more detail in the pages which follow. One rule imposed by the Internal Revenue Service which is worth keeping in mind while reading the rest of this chapter is that regardless of the alternative payment method elected, at least 50 percent of the value of an accrued benefit payable to a retired participant must be payable over his or her life expectancy. The purpose of this rule is to insure that no more than 50 percent of a retired participant's benefits may be converted into a death benefit to his or her beneficiary, thereby escaping estate tax. A 100 percent survivor feature, under an annuity option or a period certain, equal to the retired participant's life expectancy is the largest permissible survivorship benefit. This latter rule means that benefits may be paid out over a period certain equal to *twice* the retired participant's life expectancy.

1. OTHER JOINT AND SURVIVOR ANNUITIES

In addition to the statutory or "qualified" joint and survivor annuity, most defined benefit plans contain a similar option, sometimes called a "contingent annuitant option," which is identi-

Table 3

Payment Options

Option	Death Benefit	Guaranteed Payment Period
Lump Sum (cost of a lifetime annuity in amount of your accrued benefit)	Payable to beneficiary in full if you die prior to payment date. No death benefit if participant dies after receiving payment.	None.
Period Certain (Annual Install-ments)	Unpaid installments payable in full to beneficiary	Full period certain elected
Life Annuity	None.	Life of the participant.
Life Annuity–Period Certain	Only if participant dies before the expiration of the period certain.	Longer of full period, certain elected or life of the participant
Joint and Sur-vivor Annuity	Usually, choice of 50 percent, 66-2/3 percent, or 100 percent of death benefit.	Joint lifetimes of participant and joint annuitant.
Cash Refund Annuity	Only if the participant dies before receiving lump sum value of pension.	Until lump sum value is paid.

cal to the qualified joint and survivor annuity except that the person who receives the pension after the death of the employee need not be a spouse and that the survivorship benefit can be a percentage of the participant's benefit other than the percentage under the qualified joint and survivorship annuity (i.e., a participant may elect a survivorship benefit of 66 2/3 percent to the surviving spouse if the plan otherwise limits the qualified joint and survivor annuity to a 50 percent survivor benefit).

This option can be selected if a participant wishes to protect a relative such as a brother or sister. It can also be used to protect a person with whom the participant is living if they are not married.

The higher the percentage of the participant's pension under any joint and survivor annuity that is elected as the continuation pension to the spouse or other annuitant, the larger will be reduction in the participant's pension. That is, a participant electing a 75 percent survivorship benefit receives a higher lifetime benefit than would be paid if he or she had elected a 100 percent survivorship benefit. Since any joint and survivor annuity is payable over two estimated lifetimes, the reductions made are related to the ages of the participant and joint annuitant. As with the qualified joint and survivor annuity, the younger the joint annuitant, the greater will be the reduction in the lifetime pension payable to the employee.

In order to prevent last minute switching of beneficiaries, many plans require that all joint and survivor elections be made at least one year prior to the commencement of benefit payments.

The qualified joint and survivor annuity and, in some cases, the contingent annuitant option protect an employee who works past his or her normal retirement date. This means that the surviving spouse of an employee who did not elect not to receive a qualified joint and survivor annuity within the statutory election period and who elects not to retire at age 65 and then dies while actively employed will receive a survivor annuity. A survivor annuity would also be paid to the beneficiary of a participant who elected a nonstatutory joint or survivor annuity if the plan made election of that option effective on the normal retirement date.

An employee who retires prior to his or her normal retirement date but who elects to defer the commencement of his or her pension until that date is also covered by the qualified joint and survivor annuity if he or she has not declined the qualified joint and survivor annuity in order to elect another form of payment.

> *Example 4.* Jack Brown retired under the Acme pension plan at age 55 and elected to defer the commencement of his pension until age 65. The Acme pension plan provides for a 100 percent qualified joint and survivor annuity. At the time Brown retired, he was married and had not declined the qualified joint and survivor annuity. Brown died at age 60 survived by his widow, Alice Green. Alice will be entitled to a survivorship annuity even though Brown died before his pension payments started.

If an employee has elected an ordinary contingent annuitant option, however, a plan may provide that no benefits will be paid (i.e., the election may be considered null and void) if the employee dies prior to age 65.

2. LIFE ANNUITY

A life annuity provides the highest monthly pension of any of the options since it contains no death benefit element. However, this option should be selected only by the employee who has no dependents whom he or she wishes to protect.

3. LIFE ANNUITY–PERIOD CERTAIN OPTION

Under this optional form of payment, benefits are *guaranteed* for a prescribed number of years. If a retired employee dies before the end of the specified period, benefits continue to his or her designated beneficiary for the balance of the guaranteed benefit period. A ten year guaranteed payment period is the most common, although many pension plans provide for periods certain of 5, 15 or 20 years, and in some cases as long as thirty years.

> *Example 5.* Beverly Brown is entitled to a life annuity of $1,000 per month beginning at age 65 under her company's pension plan. Instead, she has selected a 10 year certain and life option and designated her husband Ray, as her beneficiary. She will therefore receive a pension of $900 per month. If she dies within 10 years, that is, before she reaches age 75, Ray will receive $900 per month for the balance of the 10 year period. If Beverly lives longer than 10 years after retirement, benefits will continue until her death, with no benefit payable to Ray.

Under some pension plans the period certain option may also be combined with the joint and survivor option.

> *Example 6.* Frank Shea has selected a joint and survivor 20 year certain option under the ZAB pension plan, naming his wife as the contingent annuitant and their son as the contingent beneficiary. Under this option, if both Frank and his

> wife die before having received 240 monthly pension checks (12 months x 20 years), the remaining payments will be made to their son.

The life annuity-period certain option is generally chosen by individuals who can afford to receive a reduced pension (usually because they have other sources of income) and who are unwilling to take a "death gamble," i.e., such individuals are unwilling to assume the risk that they will live long enough to receive substantial life annuity payments from their plan.

The combination of a joint and survivor and period certain option may be an especially attractive one. The employee is able to protect his or her children against the untimely deaths of both spouses by using this option in the manner illustrated in Example 6.

4. CASH REFUND OPTION

Under a cash refund option, a retired participant who dies before having received aggregate monthly installments equal to the lump sum value of his or her pension will have payments continued to the designated beneficiary until that lump sum dollar amount is recovered.

> *Example 7.* Alan Barnes is entitled to a pension under the Excelsior Corp. pension plan of $1,000 per month for life. Instead, he chooses to receive his pension in the form of a cash refund annuity and therefore will receive a reduced benefit of $820 per month. Barnes' pension has a lump sum value of $120,000. If he dies before the total of his monthly pension payments equals $120,000 the remaining payments will be made to his designated beneficiary.

The cash refund option performs much the same function as a period certain option. Since the period certain option is more flexible—that is, a participant may usually choose from among a number of different periods certain—the cash refund option has been dropped from many pension plans.

5. LUMP SUM OPTION

Under this option a participant is entitled to receive the value of the normal form of his or her pension in a single lump sum, i.e., a sum equal to the aggregate monthly benefits which would be paid out over his or her life expectancy, discounted at a rate of interest which could be earned by the funds during the period they are available to the participant.

Lump sum options have not been popular in defined benefit plans, since they seem inconsistent with their goal of providing regular periodic income. However, since ERISA created the option to postpone taxation of lump sum distributions by rolling them over into IRAs, additional pressure has been brought upon employers to provide the lump sum option.

In times of high interest rates, if a life annuity is discounted using the conservative long-term interest rate assumed by the actuary for purposes of calculating costs under the pension plan (see Chapter 9), the amount of the lump sum will be large. Therefore, some plans provide that the lump sum will be equal to the cost charged by a representative life insurance company for the purchase of an immediate annuity (since insurance companies make less conservative interest assumptions), or even an amount geared to a long term bond index rate. A lump sum calculated in this manner will be smaller than the lump sum equivalent of the identical benefit which has been discounted using the interest assumption adopted in funding the plan.

> *Example 8.* Carol Robinson is entitled to a pension of \$10,000 per year under the DFL Pension Plan. The plan's actuary uses an interest assumption of 6 percent in calculating the annual pension contribution which the employer must make under the pension plan as explained in Chapter 9. This interest rate is appropriate for funding purposes, since it represents the average return expected over a long period of time on the existing trust assets and on all contributions to be made during future years. It is possible, however, to purchase an immediate annuity from a life insurance company which will guarantee an interest rate of 11 percent.

> The *discounted* value of a lump sum at 11 percent is much less than at 6 percent. Because the plan could go out and purchase an annuity of $10,000 a year for Ms. Robinson from an insurance company at a price equal to the value calculated using an 11 percent interest assumption, she will be entitled only to this smaller sum.

Although the large dollar amount is superficially attractive, unless a rollover to an IRA is contemplated, the lump sum election is probably not wise. The lump sum option does not provide adequate protection for dependents and often leads to substantial tax liability. Remember that a lump sum attracts income tax immediately. The after-tax balance will then be invested without a tax shelter and may be subject to estate taxes when the employee dies.

Generally speaking, lump sums are selected under two circumstances.

1. When the participant is entitled to a relatively small pension, the advantageous 10 year income averaging discussed in Chapter 11 will result in a relatively moderate tax on the lump sum. The balance after payment of the tax can be used by the participant without any further restriction.
2. A participant may prefer to receive the lump sum and roll it over into an individual retirement account, thereby postponing the tax on the lump sum until the amount is actually withdrawn. This alternative is explored fully in Chapters 4 and 11.

Time of Payment

A participant in a defined benefit plan may not begin drawing benefits while employed prior to the normal retirement date. However, pension plans generally provide that participants who retire prior to their normal retirement date may begin to receive immediate benefit payments.

Early Retirement Reductions

A defined benefit plan's early retirement date is the first date at which an employee can retire and be entitled to receive immediate benefit payments. The most common age at which early retirement is permitted is age 55, although many plans do not permit early retirement prior to age 60, or even 62. Many plans which permit early retirement also require that, in addition to reaching the prescribed age, a participant must also have completed a certain number of years of service. The early retirement service requirement is generally ten or fifteen years, but sometimes even more. It can delay initial eligibility for early retirement. For example, if a plan has a "55 and 10" rule, that is, if it requires participants to be at least 55 with 10 years of service in order to retire, and a participant has only 5 years of service at age 55, the earliest age at which that participant may retire is *60*.

Although ERISA does not require that a plan permit participants to retire earlier than age sixty-five, such early retirement provisions have become increasingly common. However, unless a plan provides fully subsidized early retirement benefits, the plan's normal retirement date is the earliest date at which a participant can get full benefits in either the normal form or under one of the options *without* reductions for early payment.

When a participant elects to have his or her pension payments begin upon early retirement, the monthly benefit is smaller than it would have been had it begun on normal retirement date for two reasons. One is that the employee has completed fewer years of service and therefore has accrued a smaller benefit than he or she would have earned if actively employed until age sixty-five. In addition, if immediate payments are elected by an early retiree, the amount payable is further reduced to compensate for the fact that benefits will be payable over a longer period of time than if payments had begun when the employee reached age 65. This adjustment produces what is called an "actuarially equivalent" benefit. The term "actuarially equivalent" has the same meaning here as it does in the case of options. Actuarially equivalent benefits are benefits which have the same economic value.

Generally, the actuarial reduction made in the benefit of a participant retiring at age 62 is approximately 20 percent and at age 55 it is approximately 50 percent.

Example 9. Claude Brown is covered under a career average pension plan which provides a unit benefit of 1 percent of compensation for each year of service. Brown was hired at age 35. The plan permits early retirement at age 55 if the employee has completed ten years of service. Assuming that he remains on the job, Brown will become eligible to retire at age 55 because he will have completed more than 10 years of service at that time. Note, however, that if Brown retires at age 55 he will have completed only twenty years of service whereas if he remained an employee until age 65 he would have completed thirty years of service and therefore would have accrued a benefit which is at least 50 percent higher.

Example 10. If Brown were entitled to a projected pension of $150.00 a month at age 65 (assuming that he had remained an employee until that date and been compensated at the same yearly rate) his pension would be reduced to 2/3 of $150.00 or $100.00 a month, if he retired at age 55 having elected that commencement of payments be postponed until age 65. It would make sense to postpone payments in this manner if Brown left his employer and obtained a job elsewhere to provide income during the period of deferral.

If Brown wanted his pension to begin immediately at age fifty-five, or at some other time prior to his sixty-fifth birthday, a further actuarial reduction would be made. Generally speaking, a pension beginning at age fifty-five is about 50 percent of an equivalent pension beginning at age sixty-five.

Thus, Brown's pension of $100 beginning at age 65 would be only $50 if he elected to have payments begin at 55. If he elected that payments were to commence at some date between age 55 and age 65 the reduction would be proportionately adjusted.

As you can see, actuarial reductions are quite large. However, the reductions are directly related to projected life expectancy. An employee at age sixty-five is generally predicted to have a life expectancy of between twelve and fifteen years, depending on the mortality table used. If his or her pension began at age fifty-five rather than sixty-five, it would have to be paid over a period almost twice as long as the payment period for a payee who deferred payments until age sixty-five.

Subsidized Early Retirement Benefits

Because actuarial reductions take such a large bite out of pension payments, many plans provide for subsidized early retirement benefits. Subsidization occurs when plans which permit employees to retire early provide for actuarial reductions which are less than those which would be made to compensate the plan for the making of immediate payments. In some cases, plans subsidize benefits to the extent of making no actuarial reductions at all.

Subsidized early retirement benefits are becoming increasingly common because employers favor liberal early retirement policies. Furthermore, employers use subsidized retirement as an opportunity to allow younger people to assume positions of leadership by making it more attractive for older executives to retire early.

Vested Former Participants

A vested former participant who terminated employment when too young to retire will become entitled to begin receiving benefits upon reaching the earliest retirement age under the plan.

> *Example 11.* George Fields participated in the New Horizons Development Corporation pension plan from 1965 to 1975, when he left New Horizons to accept an executive position with another firm. Fields was thirty-five years old and fully vested in his accrued benefit when he terminated employment with New Horizons, since the plan has a ten-year cliff vesting schedule and he had completed ten years of service.
>
> The New Horizons pension plan provides for early retirement at age 55 with 10 years of service and defines normal retirement date as a participant's 65th birthday. Fields will begin receiving payments *only* when he attains age 55, and he will, therefore be required to wait a full 20 years after he leaves New Horizons before benefits commence.
>
> If the New Horizons plan did not permit early retirement, Fields' initial benefit payment could be postponed until his normal retirement date.

Deferred Retirement

No employer within the scope of federal age discrimination law and certain state laws may force employees (other than certain executives who are entitled to receive large pensions) to retire at age 65. If employees take advantage of their legal rights to work beyond age 65 (these are discussed in Chapter 15), pensions need not begin to be paid until 60 days following the end of the plan year in which employment terminates. Although a plan could authorize participants to receive payments while working after their normal retirement date, very few plans permit this practice.

ERISA does not require that a pension be increased because pension payments have been delayed. Some employers will increase the amount of a deferred retiree's pension which would otherwise be payable by voluntarily adding interest or increasing the monthly benefit to compensate for the shorter projected payout period if the employee retires after his or her normal retirement date. However, it is possible for a deferred retiree's monthly benefit to be *reduced* if an option is chosen and a plan does not freeze the monthly benefit at the level which would have been payable at the normal retirement date. If a participant on deferred retirement elects a single life annuity, the monthly benefit is not reduced, but the total value of the pension is always reduced.

DEFINED CONTRIBUTION PLANS

When Payments May be Made

Most defined contribution plans (even money purchase pension plans) will permit participants to begin receiving benefits as soon as they leave the job, or at least no later than a reasonable time after the end of the plan year in which they incur a break in service, without any requirement that participants reach their normal retirement date. Profit sharing plans are even permitted to provide for withdrawals by active employees of nonintegrated employer contributions (i.e., contributions not integrated with Social Security benefits) and their earnings which have been in the plan at least two years. Integrated contributions and their earnings are forbidden to be withdrawn prior to termination of employment or attainment of normal retirement date.

No actuarial adjustments are made under a defined contribution plan if participants receive benefits prior to or after the plan's normal retirement date. Instead, they are always entitled to receive either the balance in their accounts at that time or a benefit which can be purchased with that amount.

If participants who are only partially vested in their account balances receive lump sum payments under a defined contribution plan prior to the time they incur a break in service, they have a period not exceeding the earliest of two years from their date of reemployment, or the end of the plan year in which they first incur a break in service or five years from the date of the withdrawal to repay these amounts to the plan. If a participant takes advantage of this so-called "buyback rule," any forfeitures from his or her account which resulted from the termination of employment will be *fully restored*, unadjusted for any gains or losses incurred by the trust fund subsequent to the date of payment.

Even though the rules for defined contribution plans are generally much more flexible than the rules for payment of benefits from defined benefit plans, you should note one strict rule: A participant may not receive a distribution of employer contributions or related earnings from a money purchase pension plan prior to normal retirement date except upon termination of employment.

Payment Options

Although defined contribution plans such as profit sharing plans, thrift and savings plans, and money purchase pension plans are permitted to provide the same wide range of options as defined benefit plans, in virtually all cases the number of options provided by such plans is much more limited. Typically, defined contribution plans provide only a lump sum option (which may be the automatic form of payment if no option is elected) and an installment option for a period certain, most commonly for ten years. In each case the basis for the payment will be the vested account balance of the participant at the time he or she leaves the job. If a participant elects an installment option, he or she will also be entitled to earnings on the unpaid balance which remains in the trust fund.

The majority of defined contribution plans do not provide any options payable in annuity form, since the Internal Revenue Service has interpreted ERISA to require that if benefits are payable in the form of any type of life annuity, the joint and survivor annuity must be the normal form of benefit for married participants failing to decline it. After having lost a case on this point, the Internal Revenue Service announced early in 1982 that it intends to change its regulations dealing with joint and survivor annuities in profit sharing plans to provide that such annuities must be declined only where a participant *actually chooses* to have his benefit payable in the form of a life annuity, not where a life annuity is merely *available* under the terms of the profit sharing plan.

Since the joint and survivor annuity is difficult to administer, with complicated statutory election periods, and since the typical profit sharing plan is not designed to provide periodic lifetime income to retirees, most profit sharing plans have dispensed with all life annuity forms of options. The holdouts may all dispense with such options because of the problems resulting from compliance with new rules on sex discrimination in the payment of benefits.

The considerations involved in the selection of an option either under a defined contribution plan or a defined benefit plan will be discussed in greater detail in Chapter 14.

Chapter 7

SOCIAL SECURITY BENEFITS

Regardless of whether your company's retirement plan is integrated, it will provide you with benefits which serve only to supplement your basic Social Security benefits. Some knowledge of the Social Security benefit structure is therefore necessary for effective preretirement financial planning. This benefit structure was revamped extensively in 1977 in an attempt to balance the Social Security budget until 2026 and to compensate for the fact that as a result of the recent decline in birthrates, there will be only about two active workers supporting each Social Security beneficiary in the future, in contrast to the three workers now actively supporting each Social Security beneficiary.

EFFECT OF THE NEW AMENDMENTS

The reasons your benefits will never replace your preretirement salary were briefly discussed in Chapter 1. The Social Security System is skewed against the executive, since it will provide you with a benefit which is both a smaller percentage of your preretirement income and smaller in relation to the Social Security taxes which you have paid than the benefit which a lower-paid worker receives. In January 1979, when the first of the changes in the Social Security law implemented by the 1977 amendments became effective, the system became even more skewed in favor of lower-paid workers. Indeed, if you are an executive with an annual salary equal to the Social Security taxable wage base, it has been estimated that under new wage-indexed formulas which became effective beginning January 1, 1979, your "replacement ratio" (i.e., the ratio of your initial annual primary Social Security benefit to your earnings recognized by the Social Security System in the year immediately preceding retirement) will stabilize (after a sharp decrease until 1981, when a slow rise towards stable ratios is projected to begin) at approximately 30 percent as compared to a ratio of approximately 55 percent for a low-income worker. When total earnings are considered, this ratio will be much lower for executives with salaries above the wage base. The maximum monthly benefit for an employee retiring at age 65, in 1981, for example, is approximately $750.00 (although you should note that these benefits are tax free).

You should also be aware that the "revamped" Social Security system will demand sharply increased contributions both out of your paycheck and from your employer in future years. You will not recoup these contributions in proportionate benefit increases, since the new benefit formula was designed by Congress to stabilize replacement ratios for workers retiring at age 62 at a level of about 5 percent below that which would have been provided under the old benefit formula. However, the increased contributions required of employers may be a spur to adoption of more integrated plans which *do* provide executives with proportionately higher benefits than workers earning less than the taxable wage base.

With the specific planning goal of projecting retirement income in mind, this chapter will attempt to explain how "basic" Social Security benefits and benefits derived from the basic benefit (i.e., spouse's and survivors benefits and disability benefits) are calculated, particularly after all of the radical changes in the system which were enacted by Congress in 1977 become effective. It will skirt past those other benefits provided by the Social Security system (such as Medicare benefits) which were not designed as regular income replacements.

SOCIAL SECURITY SIMPLIFIED

System Input-Contributions

Employers and employees pay equal amounts of tax which are expressed as a percentage of the taxable wage base for the calendar

Table 4

Calendar Year or Period	Wage Base	Contribution Percentage (the employee and the employer *each* contribute this percentage)	Maximum Tax Paid
1937-1949	$ 3,000	1.0 %	$ 30.00
1950	3,000	1.5	45.00
1951-1953	3,600	1.5	54.00
1954	3,600	2.0	72.00
1955-1956	4,200	2.0	84.00
1957-1958	4,200	2.25	94.50
1959	4,800	2.5	120.00
1960-1961	4,800	3.0	144.00
1962	4,800	3.125	150.00
1963-1965	4,800	3.625	174.00
1966	6,600	3.85	254.10
1967	6,600	3.9	257.40
1968	7,800	3.8	296.40
1969-1970	7,800	4.2	327.60
1971	7,800	4.6	358.80
1972	9,000	4.6	414.00
1973	10,800	4.85	523.80
1974	13,200	4.95	653.40
1975	14,100	4.95	697.95
1976	15,300	4.95	757.35
1977	16,500	4.95	816.75
1978	17,700	5.05	893.85
1979	22,900	5.08	1,163.32
1980	25,900	5.08	1,315.72
1981	29,700	5.35	1,588.95
1982	32,400	5.40	1,733.40

1983 and after—wage base and maximum tax determined under automatic wage escalation clause—

1983-1984		5.40	
1985-1989		5.70	
1990		6.20	

year. The wage base is the maximum amount of earnings recognized by the Social Security System. Although tax is never paid on compensation in excess of the taxable wage base in any year, the "flip side" of this exemption from tax is that compensation over the taxable wage base goes unrecognized for *all purposes* under the system, including the calculations of base compensation which is used in fixing your benefit level. This is a principal reason that the system's "replacement ratio" is so low at higher income levels. The maximum tax and base amounts which have been used to determine maximum contributions are listed in Table 4, together with the contribution percentage rates for future years.

The wage base escalator clause did not become significant until 1982, since Congress specified the new wage bases for the years 1978–1981 when passing the Social Security Act Amendments of 1977. Under the new escalator clause, rises in the wage base are tied indirectly to increases in the Consumer Price Index because they are based on an existing benefit escalator clause keyed to the Consumer Price Index.

The wage base escalator clause operates so as to increase the wage base after each escalator increase in benefit levels. Benefit levels increase when the cost of living rises 3 percent or more each year.

However, the law provides that there can be no automatic escalator adjustments in a year following a year in which a general benefit increase was either enacted by Congress or became effective.

This cost-of-living escalator raised benefits approximately 11 percent in June, 1980 and is expected to raise them in future years. It is therefore anticipated that the taxable wage base will continue to rise sharply after it is tied into the benefit escalator, beginning in 1982.

Coverage Status

An individual who has at least 40 calendar quarters of coverage is said to be "fully insured" by the Social Security system.

Generally, you were credited with a quarter of coverage during each calendar quarter in which you earned $50 in covered employment for years prior to 1978. You were also credited with four calendar quarters for each year in which you earned at least the taxable wage base (even if you didn't work in all four calendar quarters), if this would give you additional coverage. (Note that under no circumstances will a quarter be counted more than once.)

Beginning in 1978, you will be credited with four quarters of coverage if you have earnings of at least $1,000 during the year (and do not die during that year), and one quarter for each $250 earned up to the maximum of four calendar quarters, whether you are an employee or self-employed. This minimum is to be adjusted annually to reflect increases in average wages.

For purposes of the discussion which follows, it will be assumed that you will have become "fully insured" under Social Security (i.e., you will have at least forty calendar quarters of coverage) prior to your 62nd birthday. The 62nd birthday is, of course, the earliest date at which a covered employee who is not disabled may begin to collect benefits as a wage earner.

You can request a report from the Social Security Administration which indicates your quarters of coverage and total contributions to the system by writing directly to the central office in Maryland. Simply request Form OAR-7004 and file it with the Social Security Administration, P.O. Box 57, Baltimore, MD 21203. It is advisable to obtain this information from time to time, especially if you have worked for a number of employers, or for employers which have gone out of business. If you have any questions about the extent of your coverage at the present time, you can obtain detailed information from your local Social Security office.

System Output–Benefit Payments

COMPUTATION OF SOCIAL SECURITY BENEFITS

Although the new benefit formulas have no effect on retirees currently receiving benefits, the 1977 amendments *reduce* benefits for employees born in 1917 or later. There will be three basic methods of calculating benefits, and you will be entitled to the highest possible benefit produced by the methods which you are eligible to use. Your eligibility to use these methods is keyed to your initial eligibility for Social Security benefits (that is, to your 62nd birthday) even if you don't retire or apply for benefits upon reaching age 62.

There are also "special minimum benefits" provided by the Social Security System, but these are useful only for workers with long periods of relatively low earnings and will therefore be ignored in the discussion which follows.

THE PRIMARY INSURANCE AMOUNT (PIA)

The Primary Insurance Amount is the monthly benefit to which you will become entitled if you retire or become disabled, and which will go to your eligible survivor (if any) when you die.

The Actual Earnings Method

The method used to calculate this PIA benefit prior to 1979 was based upon an Average Monthly Wage (AMW), which is equal to the compensation (recognized for Social Security purposes) earned during benefit computation years divided by the number of months worked during those years. Generally, an individual's benefit computation years equal the number of years after 1950 but before the year in which he or she reaches 62–disregarding the 5 years during that period on which his or her earnings were lowest. A retiree reaching 65 in 1980, for example, will have 21 benefit computation years. When computing disability or survivor's benefits, these years are calculated as if the individual had turned 62 in the year in which he or she became disabled or died.

A simple PIA table then lists the benefits available at each wage level. Using this method, a retiree at age 65 in 1981 who has earned at least the taxable wage base in all years received a benefit of $752.90. As benefits are increased in proportion to increases in the Consumer Price Index, new tables are published.

The PIA method was abandoned because it resulted in a doubling up of benefits. Each time an increase in the Consumer Price Index occurred, it caused both an increase in the taxable wage base and an increase in benefits per dollar of average monthly wage. People who had not yet retired got a double benefit from inflation–i.e., an increase in average monthly benefit plus a larger benefit per dollar of average monthly wage.

The Indexed Earnings Method

This method or the Transitional Guarantee Method described in the next section must be used for those who become 62 in 1979 or thereafter. The benefit computation years are determined in the same manner as under the actual earnings method but instead of basing benefits upon actual wages earned, it uses a formula based upon *indexed* earnings. Indexing inflates earnings in earlier years by incorporating a factor equal to the ratio of average wages in the previous year to average wages in the year being indexed. Wages are indexed beginning with the second year prior to the year in which a person is eligible to receive benefits, becomes disabled, or dies. If you retire at 65 in 1982, for example, (that is, you became 62 in 1979) 1977 will be the indexing year. 1976 wages and wages in years prior to 1976 will be indexed by multiplying earnings up to the taxable wage base by the ratio of average earnings in that year to average earnings in the subsequent year. Earnings in 1977 and later years are not indexed.

A three-part formula is then used to calculate the PIA based upon graduated percentages of the average indexed monthly wage. For those eligible in 1980, the PIA was 90 percent of the first $194, plus 32 percent of the next $977 plus 15 percent of the excess over $1,171. The brackets ($194 and $1,171) are inflated in later years, based on the ratio of earnings in the indexing year to earnings in 1977. The brackets for 1981 are $211 and $1,274. New brackets will be published each time they are changed.

The Transitional Guarantee Method

This method is available to workers whose initial eligibility years are in 1979–83 (that is, those born between 1917 and 1921) and is intended to insure that they receive at least as much as would have been payable under the 1978 tables. Under the Transitional Guarantee Method, the December 1978 PIA table is used, and no earnings on or after the year on which you attain age 62 may be used to calculate your benefit. You will, however, be credited with benefit increases granted after your 62nd birthday.

Under this method, a retiree at age 65 in 1982 who has had earnings of at least the taxable wage base in all years will receive a benefit of $679.30.

OTHER BENEFITS BASED ON THE PIA

Certain members of a covered worker's family also become entitled to receive monthly payments upon the worker's attainment of retirement age or earlier disability. These benefits are a fraction of the PIA. The following benefits are available to family members (bear in mind that there are specific limits on the aggregate benefits which one family can receive, and that some of these benefits will be reduced actuarially if payments begin early).

–Spousal (or divorced spouse) benefit equal to 50 percent of PIA available while the wage earner is alive.

–Surviving Spouse (or surviving divorced spouse) benefit equal to 100 percent of PIA if surviving spouse has reached retirement age (65) or 75 percent of PIA if the surviving spouse has not reached age 65 but is caring for your dependent child. Since 1978, widows and widowers who remarry after age 60 will not lose benefits because of their remarriage.

–Divorced Spouse's benefit to those former spouses who have been married for the specified number of years needed to qualify as a "divorced spouse" and receive benefits based upon the other spouse's earnings record. The minimum period of marriage has been reduced by the 1977 Amendments from 20 to 10 years.

–Dependent Children's benefit equal to 50 percent of PIA while the wage earner is alive, or 75 percent of PIA after his or her death. (Stops at age 18 or, if child is an unmarried secondary school full-time student, age 19. Those students who were entitled to child's benefits as of August, 1981 and who were enrolled in college prior to May, 1982 may continue to receive benefits until the earlier of their attainment of age 22 or their graduation from college.)

You should note that the spousal benefits listed are based upon the earnings record of the *other* spouse. If both spouses work and one (for example, the wife) would be entitled to equal or higher benefit based upon *her own* earnings record, she will be entitled to collect on her own record.

This rule also applies to other types of dependent benefits. If a woman becomes entitled to a PIA on her own record which is at least 50 percent of the PIA of her former husband, she will not receive benefits as a divorced wife.

Lump Sum Death Payment

The Social Security system provides a lump sum death benefit of $255 for each worker with at least six quarters of coverage during the 13 quarter period ending with the quarter in which he or she dies.

ADJUSTMENT TO BENEFITS

Actuarial Reductions for Early Payments

The reason behind early retirement reductions and methods of making those reductions is the same under Social Security as under private pension plans.

If you elect to begin receiving payments exactly at age 62, your PIA will be reduced by 20 percent to compensate for the longer payout period. If you elect to begin receiving payments at any time between your 62nd and 65th birthdays, your benefit will be reduced proportionately. The reduction is 5/9 of 1 percent for each month that your pension is paid before the month in which you reach 65.

> *Example.* The reduction made in a benefit of 489.70 if payments begin precisely at age *63* is computed as follows:
>
> a) 5/9 x 1/100 x 489.70 x 24
>
> b) .0055 x 11752.80
>
> c) The reduction made is therefore 64.64 (rounded off to 64.70)
>
> d) actual benefit payable at age 63 is:
>
> 489.70
> -64.70
> \$425.00

Spousal benefits will also be reduced–however, the formula is different. If a spouse or divorced spouse begins receiving benefits exactly at age 62, the benefit reduction will be 25 percent. Thereafter, the benefit is reduced by 25/36 of 1 percent for each month that the pension is paid before the recipient reached age 65.

An eligible widow or widower may apply for a reduced benefit commencing as early as age 60. The pension will be reduced by 19/40 of 1 percent for each month that the pension is paid before the recipient reaches age 65.

If the wage earner was receiving a reduced benefit, the survivor's benefit cannot exceed the larger of what the wage earner would have received if he or she were alive or 82.5 percent of the wage earner's unreduced benefit.

The Retirement Earnings Test

Retirees aged 72 and older (70 and over after 1982) may earn unlimited income without concomitant reductions in their Social Security benefits. However, if you work even part time after you begin collecting Social Security benefits but prior to the calendar year in which you reach age 72 (age 70 in 1983 and thereafter), one dollar will be deducted from all benefits being paid based upon your account for each $2 that you earn in excess of specified limits. This reduction is made in addition to the usual Social Security and Medicare deductions which will be taken from your post-retirement salary.

When applying the earnings test, you must count all earnings for the year even though you may have become entitled or ceased to be entitled to benefits during that year and *even* earnings which exceed the taxable wage base. "Earnings," is limited to compensation for services. It excludes dividends, interest, rents, royalties, capital gains, and any income in the form of pension benefits or insurance. Therefore, your monthly pension benefit check will have *no* effect upon your Social Security benefit. There is an offsetting small benefit which may come to you in conjunction with the retirement earnings reduction–post-retirement earnings will be used in computing your benefit, if they would increase it. An automatic recomputation is made by the Social Security Administration whenever earnings in the period during which benefits are being received would result in an increase in the PIA.

In 1981, workers between 65 and 72 who continued to work after benefit payments began could earn $5,500 before reductions were made. Workers who retired earlier and did not become 65 during the year could earn only $4,080 before reductions were made. There is an additional monthly test which applies only in the year a worker begins to receive benefits and eases the restrictions slightly–a worker who reached age 65 in 1981 was paid a full benefit for any month in which he or she earned no more than $458.33 (i.e., $5,500/12) and was not self-employed during the year; and no more than $340 (i.e., $4,080/12) if the worker is between 62 and 64 and did not engage in self-employment. Beginning with the month in which you reach age 72 (age 70 beginning in 1983) full Social Security benefits are paid monthly *regardless* of the amount which you earn. Although you may be familiar with a general and additional monthly limit on earnings, that monthly benefit test for all years after the initial benefit year was phased out by the 1977 amendments.

The annual amount which may be earned without resulting in a reduction in a worker's Social Security benefit changes each year during the period between the time benefits commence and the month in which he or she reaches age 72 (age 70 after 1982) in accordance with the following table:

Year	Annual Limit	Monthly Limit (for Initial Year Test)
1978	$4,000	$333.33
1979	4,500	375.00
1980	5,000	416.67
1981	5,500	458.33
1982	6,000	500.00

However, for those workers who will not attain age 65 until after 1982, the annual earnings test limit will be determined using escalator provisions which are keyed to rises in national average taxable wages. The escalator provisions of the law will also determine limitations for workers who have reached 65 but have not yet attained their 70th birthday, beginning in 1983. (You will recall that beginning in 1983, you are not subject to the retirement earnings test from your 70th birthday on.)

If you become subject to the retirement earnings test, excess earnings will be charged first against the first month in the year in which you had excess earnings.

If there is an unused excess, it will be carried over to succeeding months in that taxable year, except for months in which you:

- were not entitled to benefits, or
- were at least 72 (70 after 1982) years of age for at least one day of the month
- received a disability benefit, or
- (initial year *only*) did not receive wages higher than the monthly limit or render "substantial services" in a self-employed capacity.

However, your unused excess will *not* be carried over to subsequent taxable years.

The following simple example should help you understand how the "retirement earnings test" is applied.

> *Example 2.* Walter Dexter retired in late December, 1977 and began receiving benefits in January 1, 1978 at age 65. In 1978, Walter became entitled to receive a benefit of $118.80 per month, which was raised to $126.60 in June, 1978. His wife, Ann, was entitled to receive 50 percent of this amount as a spouse's benefit. In March, 1978, Walter began work at a temporary job which paid him $1,500 in March, $300 in the month of April and $1,400 in each of the months of May and June, for total earnings of $4,600. He earned no other income in 1978. Since Walter turned 65 and began receiving benefits in 1978, he became entitled to earn $4,000, without benefit reductions in 1978. (Note that the earnings limit has been increased since 1978 in accordance with the table on page 117.)
>
> Since 1978 was Walter's initial benefit year, a *monthly* benefit test was also applied. Since Walter earned less than $333.33 (the monthly limit) in January, February, April and July through December, these are "free months," whose benefits cannot be reduced by the chargeoff of excess earnings. Thus, Walter and Ann both received full benefits in January and February.

Here is how reductions in benefits would be made and allocated:

Step 1–Determine ½ Annual Excess Earnings

$$
\begin{array}{r}
\$4600 \\
\underline{-4000} \\
\$600/2 = \$300
\end{array}
$$

The excess is divided in half to determine the amount deductible from benefits, since this is the equivalent of a $1 deduction for every $2 of excess earned income.

Step 2–(a) Begin allocation in first month with excess earnings. (March, 1978)

$$
\begin{array}{rl}
\text{Total Benefit} = \$118.80 & \text{(Walter)} \\
\underline{59.40} & \text{(Ann)} \\
\$178.20 &
\end{array}
$$

since the excess amount ($300) exceeds the monthly benefits payable, no benefit is received by Walter *or* Ann for March.

(b) Determine the unallocated excess to carry forward:

$300.00
-178.20
$121.80

Step 3—Allocate excess carryover to May. (Walter and Ann were both entitled to full benefits in April, since Walter earned less than $333.33.)

$178.20
-121.80
$ 56.40 (actual benefit)

The remaining benefit is allocated (or, conversely, reductions are made) in the same 2:1 ratio as original benefits, (you will recall that Ann's benefit is exactly half of Walter's) so that Ann receives $18.80 and Walter receives $37.60. Remaining monthly benefits are unaffected.

If Walter had earned $8,600 rather than $4,600 during those same months in his initial benefit year (so that ½ of total excess earnings was equal to $2,300) the additional excess could be allocated only insofar as possible to the month of June, since July through December would be nonchargeable free months.

> *Example 3.* If Walter earned the same $1,500 in March, $300 in April, and $1,400 in each of the months of May and June 1979, no monthly benefit test would be applied, since 1979 is not Walter's initial benefit year. Excess earnings (earnings over $4,500, the 1979 earnings limit) would be charged off beginning in the month of March (the first year in which there were excess earnings), with the excess simply carried over to succeeding months of 1979. Any benefit remaining due to partial setoff by the carryover would be allocated in the same 2:1 ratio as original benefits.

Although the earnings limit has been increased, the process of reducing benefits by 50% of excess earnings continues to operate as explained in the above examples.

Required Reports

If you are subject to the retirement earnings test and expect your total earnings in any year to exceed your annual exempt amount, you must report this fact to the Social Security Administration. A formal annual report must be filed within 3½ months (with a 3 month available extension) of the close of your tax year.

Additional benefit reductions may be made as a penalty for failing to comply with these requirements.

Deferred Retirement Credit

A worker who elects to work up to or past his 72nd birthday whether or not he or she is collecting benefits and thus subject to the retirement earning test, will be entitled to a 7 percent increase in basic and surviving spouse benefits only. Such a worker's benefit can also be increased if his or her earnings were high during those employment years, since it will be recalculated automatically.

The actual formulas used to provide the deferred retirement credit is 1 percent of the PIA for each year (1/12 of 1 percent per month *after 1970*) that retirement is delayed past age 65, with a 7 percent cap. This credit is not available to workers who have elected early Social Security retirement benefits (that is, who began collecting actuarially-reduced benefits prior to age 65).

> *Example 4.* Andrew Cook would have been entitled to a primary benefit of $300 a month if he had retired at age 65 on January 1, 1978. Instead, Andrew works until his 70th birthday. Apart from cost of living increases, Andrew's monthly benefit will be increased by 5 percent or $15, since his retirement was delayed for 60 full months *after 1970.*

For workers reaching age 65 after 1981, the maximum credit will be increased 3 percent per year (¼ of 1 percent per month). The 1977 amendments provide that the credit is to become available to these workers even if actuarially reduced early retirement benefits were elected prior to age 65.

You should note that the deferred retirement credit does *not* compensate you fully for the delay in payment. The government still keeps your unpaid benefits plus interest at far more than 3 percent per year, if you retire at 72 as opposed to 65. Your monthly benefits aren't sufficiently increased to account for the fact that you will be receiving benefits for a period up to seven years less than the period over which you would otherwise have collected benefits.

Your resulting financial dilemma will be discussed more fully in Chapter 15 on "Deferred Retirement." However, you should be aware that the limited deferred retirement credit is only one of several reasons why you will usually not benefit financially from deferred retirement–in fact, there will be a distinct financial disadvantage which may or may not be offset in your eyes by nonfinancial factors such as the interest level of your work.

Further Information

This chapter on the extremely complex subject of Social Security benefits is necessarily sketchy. If you desire more detailed information about the Social Security system, you should contact your local Social Security office.

Chapter 8

ADMINISTERING ERISA: WHO PROTECTS PLAN PARTICIPANTS' RIGHTS?

ERISA is administered by three separate agencies of the federal government–the Internal Revenue Service, the Department of Labor, and the Pension Benefit Guaranty Corporation (often called the "PBGC" for short). Between them, the Department of Labor and the IRS protect both your entitlement to benefits under ERISA and your right to know about the operation of the plans under which you are covered. This protection continues throughout the time that you participate in a plan and even thereafter–since ERISA also creates rights for deferred vested participants and for retirees and beneficiaries receiving benefits. The PBGC provides invaluable additional protection, including plan termination insurance which guarantees accrued benefits up to certain maximum dollar amounts, to participants and beneficiaries in qualified defined benefit plans.

THE REGULATORY SYSTEM

Each of these three agencies has both a unique sphere of regulation and an area of responsibility which it shares with other agencies. The current spheres of jurisdiction of the primary agencies administering ERISA are illustrated graphically in Figure 3 below. There are other federal agencies with less important regulatory roles relating to other aspects of pension plan operation. For example, the Equal Employment Opportunity Commission has authority under the Civil Rights Act of 1964 and the Equal Pay Act to prohibit employers from engaging in sex discrimination in compensation and benefits and under the Age Discrimination in Employment Act, to prevent age discrimination in retirement plans. Securities and Exchange Commission rules must be obeyed by plans which permit employee contributions to be invested in employer stock. For simplicity, these additional agencies are not included in Figure 3.

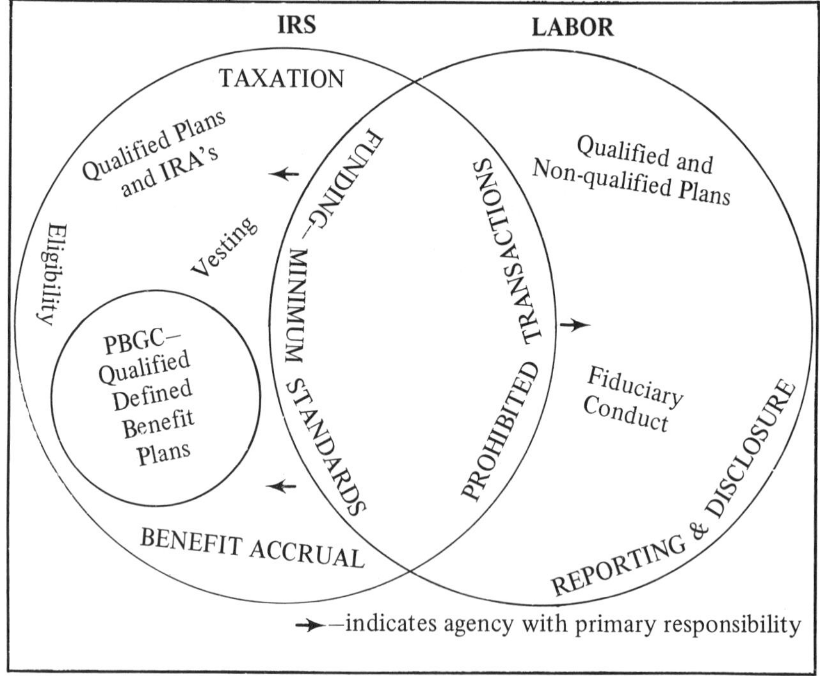

Figure 3. Administrative Oversight of ERISA

THE IRS

The Internal Revenue Service is concerned only with the regulation of pension plans which are qualified for tax-exempt status—that is, which meet requirements set forth in certain sections of the Internal Revenue Code, including the rules governing eligibility, vesting, benefit accrual, and funding. The Internal

Revenue Service does not regulate the provisions of nonqualified pension or deferred compensation arrangements.

It is not difficult to understand why more intense regulation of qualified plans than of nonqualified plans was desired by Congress. The impact of qualified retirement plans on tax revenues is a substantial deferral of revenue over a very long period of time (since employer contributions to plans are deductible when made, pension funds pay no taxes on their earnings, and benefits are not taxed until distributed from the plan), and in some cases complete elimination of tax (for example, if an individual receives annual benefits less than his or her exemptions and deductions). Taxation of benefits will be discussed in Chapter 11.

Although contributions to other types of nonqualified pension and deferred compensation arrangements are also deductible for federal income tax purposes, those types of plans generally give rise to taxable income in the hands of the participants during the same year as the deduction is claimed by the employer. As a result, the potential for revenue loss is much smaller when dealing with nonqualified plans.

The Internal Revenue Service maintains control over qualified retirement plans in two ways—through the advance determination letter process, including the imposition of requirements for qualification and, to a lesser extent, through audits.

Determination Letters

The determination letter process, which provides for advance Internal Revenue Service determination that plans satisfy the requirements for qualification, arose to fill a very clear need. Because of the huge amount of money involved in annual contributions to retirement plans, the immense sums held by their associated trust funds and insurance arrangements, and the fact that tax consequences to participants are dependent on the qualified status of the plans, employers found it impractical to have the qualified status of funds dependent upon the results of audits taking place many years after the plans were established. Under the determination letter process, an employer, by filing an application at the local Internal Revenue district office prior to or soon after the establishment of a retirement plan, is able to secure a letter stating that its plan is tax qualified. The Service, as a condition to issuing a favorable determination letter, can require a plan to adopt amendments containing provisions satisfactory to it. The importance of this amendment process cannot be overemphasized. If the IRS determines, for example, that the eligibility rules in a plan which was submitted for an advance determination do not satisfy ERISA, the plan will not be disqualified. Instead, the employer will generally be permitted by the service to adopt a retroactive amendment correcting the defect.

The Service has enormous discretion in determining whether or not to issue a favorable determination letter. This is true not only because the technical rules governing qualified plans are incredibly complex, but also because it is empowered to issue an unfavorable determination letter if in its judgment the plan is "discriminatory" in its coverage, contributions or benefits—that is, if the plan would *operate* in a discriminatory manner.

A plan is "discriminatory" if, by its terms or in operation, it does not cover lower-paid employees in sufficient number, or if benefits or contributions are skewed impermissibly in favor of higher-paid employees.

Although the Service has issued a number of rulings on the subject of discrimination, and much litigation has arisen over impermissible discrimination, the determination of whether a plan discriminates improperly is largely a subjective one. An employer which does not secure an advance determination as to a plan's qualified status is assuming the risk that its plan provisions do not satisfy the nondiscrimination rules of the Code.

Plan Changes

The Internal Revenue Service will rule on the qualified status of a plan not only when it is established, but also at the time amendments are adopted, or when a plan is terminated or merged with another retirement plan.

Intervention in the Qualification Procedure

You as a participant are permitted to intervene in the determination process. Before requesting a favorable determination letter, an employer is required to post in a prominent place or to distribute to its employees a notice which states, in standard obscure federal prose, that you may petition the Internal Revenue Service directly, or through the Department of Labor, to require changes in the terms of the plan as a condition to its being granted qualified status.

Although this was conceived by Congress as a meaningful change in the qualification process, it has not worked in this manner, because individual participants in qualified plans have not been reading the notices or intervening in the qualification proceedings. However, there have been a few situations in which labor unions have intervened on behalf of their members. Although the Department of Labor is also authorized to intervene on its own initiative, it has rarely taken any part in plan qualification proceedings.

Minimum Standards

As a corollary to its role of ruling upon whether plans are qualified, the IRS determines by regulation and rulings the minimum standards for participation, vesting, and funding which will satisfy the Code and ERISA.

The Audit Process

Although the qualification process is the most important way in which the Internal Revenue Service regulates qualified retirement plans, it could not be the exclusive method of regulation because it deals primarily with sufficiency of the written terms of the plan—that is, in provisions appearing in the plan documents—and is based upon the facts as submitted by an employer at the time of its application for determination. The qualification process is thus essentially a snapshot, dealing with the condition of the plan at one moment in time; it cannot deal with the ongoing cycle of plan operation.

When an Internal Revenue agent examines an employer's tax return, he or she also reviews the status of its retirement plan. If this review indicates the probability of a violation of the Internal Revenue Code, a full scale audit of the plan may follow. In such an audit the actual operation of the qualified plan—i.e., admission of employees to membership, when employees vest, how benefits are paid—is carefully examined. In addition, the IRS audits retirement plans under a separate audit program which is independent of audits of the corporate tax returns.

If the agent concludes that a plan was not operated in accordance with its terms or was operated in a discriminatory manner, and if the problem cannot be solved by remedial amendments to the plan, the Internal Revenue Service is empowered to disqualify it.

Tax Court Declaratory Judgments

ERISA permits an employer whose plan the Internal Revenue Service has determined not to be qualified, or with respect to which the Service has not issued a determination within 270 days after the application was filed, to bring an action in the Tax Court for a declaratory judgment. This is a court order stating whether the plan meets the standards for qualification.

Only a handful of cases have been brought to the Tax Court since this procedure became available under ERISA. An employer will want to avoid using the declaratory judgment process whenever possible. The Internal Revenue Service is very serious about its obligations under the qualification process and manages to work out an accommodation with plan sponsors which, in almost all instances, spares employers the cost and time expenditure of a lawsuit.

Other IRS Functions

The Internal Revenue Service has sole jurisdiction over Individual Retirement Accounts, including the imposition of IRA penalty taxes and excise taxes on prohibited transactions. (See the section on Department of Labor functions which follows, for discussion of these issues.) The IRS jurisdiction is the result of a quirk in ERISA which gives the Department of Labor control only over plans adopted by employers or self-employed individuals, and not over employee IRAs. The IRS will sometimes rule, upon request, on IRA problems, such as eligibility for rollovers and permissible distributions from IRAs.

THE DEPARTMENT OF LABOR

The Department of Labor was made a part of the retirement plan regulatory scheme by ERISA. It recently became the primary overseer of fiduciary conduct standards and prohibited transactions. These two sets of rules require that fiduciaries, who are the persons responsible for operating plans (for example, trustees and members of plan administrative committees), act solely in the interests of plan participants and beneficiaries, and forego personal gain and conflicts of interest in the investment and handling of plan assets.

The Department of Labor also oversees compliance with the reporting and disclosure provisions of ERISA. These provisions require that plan participants be given information regarding how they may qualify for benefits under the plan, as well as the financial condition of the plan's trust fund. They will be discussed in Chapter 10.

Ombudsman Functions

It was intended by the draftsmen of ERISA that the Department of Labor would represent the individual plan participant to make certain that he or she was treated fairly under the employer's retirement plan. The Department may perform this function in two specific ways:

1. It may intervene (as previously discussed) when an employer submits a request for a favorable determination letter to the Internal Revenue Service, either on its own initiative, or at the request of plan participants.
2. It is also authorized to bring lawsuits on its own initiative, or to intervene in lawsuits brought by plan participants, to take whatever actions may be required to prevent violations of ERISA.

In contrast to its reluctance to intervene in the qualification process, the Department of Labor has taken advantage of its power to intervene in or initiate lawsuits, primarily in the area of fiduciary responsibility, and has also participated in the reorganization and "cleaning up" of some scandal-ridden plans.

Regulation of Nonqualified Plans and Payments Made Outside Qualified Plans

The Department of Labor has sole jurisdiction over retirement plans which are not qualified under the Internal Revenue Code. Labor's jurisdiction in this area has created problems. ERISA requires that all retirement plans, *whether or not qualified* under the Internal Revenue Code, be funded and contain eligibility and vesting provisions identical to those contained in qualified plans. However, it is impractical to fund nonqualified plan arrangements, such as severance pay plans or out-of-pocket pension supplements for employees, in advance, since contributions to such plans would not usually be deductible until taxed to the recipients.

The effect of these restrictions is that it is impractical for an employer to make out-of-pocket payments to encourage early retirements (as an alternative to layoffs), except under a qualified pension plan.

However, under recently enacted legislation, severance pay arrangements and certain supplemental pension payments designed to take into account increases in the cost of living (up to a maximum of the highest of 3% per year or one third of the increase in the cost of living for the year) are not considered pension benefits and therefore may be paid directly by the employer.

THE PENSION BENEFIT GUARANTY CORPORATION

The PBGC is the federal agency charged with the responsibility of insuring benefits provided under defined benefit pension plans. This agency, which was created by ERISA, can be compared to the Federal Deposit Insurance Corporation (FDIC). Like FDIC savings account insurance, PBGC insurance has maximum dollar coverage limitations. Both federal corporations were created to solve specific problems: the FDIC to end the loss of savings accounts because of bank insolvencies, and the PBGC to prevent "broken promises"—that is, to insure that plan participants are not denied their promised vested and accrued benefits when insolvent or under funded benefit plans are terminated.

Under ERISA, if a defined benefit plan is terminated and assets are insufficient to provide all vested benefits other than benefits which become vested solely by reason of the termination (subject to certain maximum dollar limitations), the PBGC will make up the shortfall and hold the employer liable for an amount up to a ceiling of 30 percent of its net worth. Liability will be determined on a controlled group basis, which means that a parent, subsidiary, or affiliate may be compelled to assume the liabilities of a related plan sponsor which goes bankrupt.

An employer that wishes to terminate a defined benefit plan must file a notice of intent to terminate with the PBGC and must also notify its employees at least ten days prior to the proposed date of termination of the plan. The notice of termination which is required to be filed with the PBGC must contain detailed information about the plan's financial condition. This required information includes:

—the number of active participants (both vested and nonvested), separated participants with deferred vested rights, and former participants and beneficiaries receiving payments;

—the aggregate amount of monthly benefit payments;

—the proposed method of distributing assets;

—a statement indicating whether plan assets are believed to be sufficient to pay vested benefits, other than benefits which became vested solely because of the termination.

If the PBGC determines that plan assets are sufficient to pay its liabilities, it will issue a Notice of Sufficiency to the plan administrator and it will establish a deadline before which final plan distributions must be made.

PBGC Reports and Insurance

For plan years beginning on or after January 1, 1978, the Pension Benefit Guaranty Corporation assesses each defined benefit pension plan a premium equal to $2.60 per plan participant. The original premium of $1.00 per participant was raised because the costs of operating the Pension Benefit Guaranty Corporation and its insurance program have risen substantially. The PBGC has recently proposed to increase the annual premiums to $6.00 per participant.

The Pension Benefit Guaranty Corporation requires pension plans under its jurisdiction to file annual reports (this requirement is now satisfied by filing Form 5500—see Chapter 10) and an annual premium payment form. In addition, the occurrence of specified events, which are indicative of a weakening in the financial status of the defined benefit plan and which may, therefore, signal difficulty in paying vested and accrued benefits, must be reported to the Pension Benefit Guaranty Corporation.

A "reportable event" occurs if, for example, the number of participants in the plan is reduced by more than 20 percent, or if an employer files a petition under the bankruptcy law. Other reportable events include amendments which decrease benefits payable (for example, an increase in service requirements for entitlement to benefits); inability of a plan to pay benefits when due, even if plan assets exceed liabilities; plan terminations, plan mergers, and corporate dissolutions; and violations of ERISA's funding requirements (these are discussed in Chapter 9).

Plan Divisions and Mergers

The Pension Benefit Guaranty Corporation has joint jurisdiction with the Internal Revenue Service over the merger and division of pension plans, which generally occur as a result of acquisitions or divestitures.

Each agency has an interest in these events because of its individual objectives. The IRS sees that no participant's benefits are decreased as a result of the merger or spinoff. The Pension Benefit Guaranty Corporation is interested because it must ascertain that its liability is not increased (for example, because of a plan's falling into the hands of a weak plan sponsor after a business has been sold) by reason of an acquisition or divestiture.

Effect of PBGC Coverage

The establishment of employer liability for insufficiently funded defined benefit pension plans and the attendant required insurance premiums and reports have caused many small employers to terminate their plans. However, a number of these plans have been replaced by defined contribution pension plans which, in most cases, are a more realistic alternative for small employers.

There is no question that, on balance, the Pension Benefit Guaranty Corporation and the insurance program which it administers are giant steps forward in providing retirement security for employees.

Final Word on Allocation of Administrative Responsibilities

Table 5 summarizes the major responsibilities of the agencies which administer ERISA.

The following chapters describe in greater detail the implications of this agency regulation for your own retirement planning.

Table 5

Primary Administrative Responsibilities

Department of Labor	IRS	PBGC
(Qualified and nonqualified plans)	(Qualified plans and IRAs)	(Qualified defined benefit plans only)
–Reporting and disclosure (required reports to participants)	–Advance qualification –Minimum plan standards	–Plan termination insurance (guarantees vested benefits)
–Prohibited transactions	–Audits of plans and plan sponsors	–Plan mergers and divisions
–Regulation of fidiciary conduct	–Disqualification of plans which do not satisfy ERISA requirements –Plan mergers and divisions –Taxation of benefits –Penalty taxes	–Reportable events

Chapter 9

FINANCING RETIREMENT BENEFITS: A PRIMER OF FUND ECONOMICS

Your vested rights to a large monthly benefit would be meaningless if the pension plan of your employer or former employer did not have sufficient assets to pay you. Prior to ERISA there was no way to compel an employer to make the contributions to its retirement plan necessary to provide promised benefits. There was not even a requirement that the financial condition of the trust to which employer contributions were made be disclosed to participants. Due to this absence of regulation, the economic security of plan participants was dependent upon the financial health of their employer. An employee who had spent his or her entire lifetime working for a company and who had done long-term financial planning based upon an anticipated pension benefit could lose a substantial portion of that pension without warning if the employer went out of business or suffered a series of business losses.

The pension reform movement, spurred on by a number of publicized instances in which employees were denied vested pensions, succeeded ultimately in tightening the rules for plan funding and the investment of plan assets. Investment regulation is of particular importance because the management of retirement plan funds has become "big business." Many companies now maintain funds whose assets are 50 percent or more of their net worth.

The retirement security and peace of mind of defined benefit plan participants is, of course, also guaranteed by the PBGC insurance program which was created by ERISA.

Although the new rules governing the financing of retirement funds, and of retirement benefits, are quite complicated, they can be grouped into a number of understandable sets of rules—

1. Determining the rate at which contributions must be made.
2. Specifying where contributions are deposited.
3. Fixing responsibility for making investment decisions.
4. Regulating investment of plan assets.

DETERMINING COSTS AND REQUIRED CONTRIBUTIONS

Under ERISA, all qualified pension plans, whether they are defined benefit or defined contribution plans, must be funded. This simply means that monies contributed in advance over the working lifetime of the participants are accumulated to provide the benefits for which the participants are eligible on retirement or other termination of employment.

In the case of a defined contribution plan, contributions are made either in the discretion of the employer or in accordance with a contribution formula contained in the plan. Some defined contribution plans expressly provide for a combination of fixed and discretionary contributions.

The rules governing contributions under a defined benefit pension plan are much more complex. Nevertheless, it is especially important to ascertain the funded status of a defined benefit plan under which you are covered because you may receive as little as the PBGC guaranteed benefit, even if your vested benefit is substantially greater, when an underfunded defined benefit plan is terminated.

Minimum Funding Standards

Defined benefit pension plans are required to satisfy detailed *minimum* funding standards under ERISA. Although money purchase pension plans are technically subject to these funding rules, the funding requirements are satisfied simply by making the contributions specified by the terms of the plan.

Required funding of defined benefit plans is based on amortizing projected pension costs. Plan costs are divided into "normal costs," which are prorated annual costs of future benefits and "past service costs," which are the costs of benefits attributable to service rendered prior to the adoption of the plan or of an amendment increasing benefits. Normal costs may be calculated and allocated over a period of years under different methods, some of which are analogous to accelerated and straight line depreciation and which, like accelerated and straight line depreciation, can result in either level annual contributions or skewed contributions which are higher in some years of plan operation than in others. However, there is generally a sharp drop in the required contribution level under most actuarial methods when past service costs have been fully funded.

ERISA requires that an employer's annual contribution be large enough to pay a ratable portion of normal plan costs and to amortize its unfunded past service liability. The amortization period for unfunded past service costs may not exceed 40 years for liabilities in existence on or prior to the effective date of ERISA and 30 years for all other defined benefit plan liabilities. "Experience gains and losses," which result from investment performance or mortality and turnover which are better or worse than the assumptions used in determining contributions, must be amortized over a 15 year period.

Contributions needed to fund promised benefits under a defined benefit plan at a rate which satisfies these requirements are calculated each year by the plan's actuary who is retained by the employer sponsoring the plan. An actuary is a mathematician with special training in statistics and pension concepts whose job it is to devise a program for funding the pension benefits provided under the terms of the defined benefit plan. Defined contribution plans do not need the services of actuaries.

Actuarial Assumptions

In determining the funding required to provide pension benefits, an actuary must make assumptions which are only educated guesses as to the following:

1. Interest Rate

The actuary must assume or predict the average interest rate that will be earned by plan assets over a very long period of time. The interest rate assumption has a very great effect on an employer's contribution. Generally, the higher the interest rate assumed, the lower an employer's contribution, since interest anticipated to be earned on plan assets will constitute a greater proportion of the money needed to provide benefits when the interest rate is higher. A difference in the interest rate assumption of 1 percent could increase or decrease the amount of the employer's annual contribution by 20 percent or more, depending on the age composition of the employee group which participates in the plan.

Interest rates assumed by actuaries have been rising gradually since the end of the Second World War. Although an actuary would typically assume a 2½ percent interest rate at that time, he or she will now usually assume at least a 6 percent interest rate.

If the fiduciaries who invest fund assets are unable to produce earnings sufficient to match the interest assumption, contributions to the plan will eventually have to be increased.

2. Mortality

The actuary must make assumptions regarding the life expectancy of plan participants, since pensions are generally paid over a period which is measured, at least in part, by the participant's life or projected life expectancy. The most significant mortality difference which is taken into account when determining funding is that women as a group outlive men the same age. It is therefore more expensive to fund an equal monthly benefit for a woman than for a similarly-situated man. Variations in mortality tables, however, are not nearly as significant as variations in the interest rate in determining the size of the employer contributions to a defined benefit plan.

3. Turnover

The actuary must predict how many participants will remain employees at the time their benefits vest. If an employee leaves before becoming vested and thereby forfeits the pension which he or she accrued during the period of employment, the employer's contributions will be reduced because that employee is not entitled to a future plan benefit. The forfeiture will be applied towards funding the benefits of the remaining participants.

4. Salary Scales

The actuary must anticipate the effect of inflation on wage levels. If the plan provides the benefits based upon the employee's salary in the five years preceding retirement, the actuary must project a realistic future final salary. An employee aged 30 who is earning $10,000 a year may be earning $50,000 during the five years preceding his or her retirement at age 65. Even in a career average plan it is necessary to project future salary levels because benefits are based on each year's salary.

5. Retirement Age

The actuary must anticipate the average age at which participants will retire under the plan. If a substantial number of employees retire before their normal retirement dates, a plan will incur additional costs if it provides a subsidized early retirement benefit. Conversely, if a significant number of employees work beyond their normal retirement dates the plan will realize substantial savings if no additional benefits are given for service while on deferred retirement.

6. Valuation of Plan Assets

In order to determine future contributions, the actuary must also determine the actuarial value of the assets held by the plan. Actuaries have devised a large number of "averaging devices" to smooth out large changes in asset values so as to even out annual plan contributions. Of course, if a pension fund suffers continuing losses in asset values, the plan sponsor will have to make them up with additional contributions.

Actuarial Methods

After deciding upon these assumptions to estimate future experience under the plan, the actuary must select a permissible method of allocating pension costs over the years so that funds will be available when benefits become due.

Actuarial methods are quite complex and only an experienced actuary can describe them in any detail. Nevertheless, it is possible to illustrate an actuarial method in a simplified way.

Example 1. John Johnson incorporated PQR Corporation 15 years ago when he was 25 years old. PQR Corporation establishes a pension plan covering Johnson, its sole employee, when he is forty years old and earning $20,000 a year. The PQR pension plan provides a benefit equal to 50 percent of average compensation for the five-year period preceding retirement. In order to fund the benefit, PQR's actuary assumes a 6 percent interest rate, that Johnson will die at age 80, and will remain an employee until he retires at age 65 (a most likely outcome, since Johnson is his own boss). The actuary assumes that Johnson's average salary during the five year period ending at age 65 will be $50,000.

The lump sum value of Johnson's pension of $25,000 a year for the balance of his life beginning at age 65 is approximately $225,000. In other words, the cost to purchase an annuity at $25,000 a year for the remainder of the life of a male age 65 is $225,000.

The actuary then calculates how much to contribute each year so that the aggregate of the contributions, together with interest at 6 percent (the rate assumed) will amount to $225,000 in 25 years when Johnson reaches age 65. This amount would be approximately $4,100 per year.

You should note that this example is greatly simplified because the actuary can ignore mortality and turnover in such a "one-man" plan.

Under ERISA an actuary is required to make assumptions which are reasonably related to the actual experience of the plan and which represent his or her best estimate of the plan's anticipated experience. A pension plan must periodically file the certificate of its actuary attesting to the adequacy of its funding method. Actuaries tend to be conservative in selecting assumptions. By selecting conservative actuarial assumptions at the outset, actuaries can stabilize plan costs over a long period of time. When the rate of inflation is high, as at present, plan costs tend to increase steadily because the long term inflation rate is consistently higher than the actuarial profession projects. Benefit accruals then outstrip interest income.

Accounting Treatment of Pension Costs

Unfunded pension service costs are generally shown in a footnote to the employer's financial statements because they are not a liability. Only the minimum contribution which must be made in a particular year in order to meet ERISA's funding requirements is a legal obligation of the employer.

Another term often appearing in corporate financial statements is "unfunded vested liability." This amount represents the difference between the value of all of the benefits which are vested under the terms of the pension plan and the assets available to meet those liabilities. This amount need not be shown as a liability in the employer's financial statements because it is a contingent liability, since plan assets will be sufficient to pay benefits so long as the employer is meeting its funding obligations under ERISA. The unfunded vested liability becomes significant only when the plan is terminated. At that time plan assets may not be sufficient to provide for all vested benefits. In that case, the PBGC will provide all guaranteed benefits which cannot be provided from plan assets and the plan sponsor will be obligated to pay the PBGC the shortfall up to 30 percent of its net assets.

Funding Waivers

The IRS may waive part or all of the required contribution in any plan year if an employer cannot satisfy it without substantial business hardship and if the hardship is temporary. A waiver is made only in unusual circumstances. The theory behind the waiver rule is that it is in the long term interest of participants if employers are not forced to terminate their pension plans as a result of temporary business reverses.

Enforcement of Funding Standards

An employer which fails to meet funding standards for which compliance has not been waived is subject to a two-step penalty tax until the funding deficiency has been corrected. An initial 5 percent tax is imposed on the plan's accumulated funding deficiency as of the end of the plan year. The 5 percent tax is cumulative—that is, it may be imposed based on the same uncorrected deficiency in successive years and cannot be waived.

If the funding deficiency is not corrected after notification by the Internal Revenue Service, a second tax is imposed in the amount of 100 percent of the deficiency. The 100 percent penalty may be waived by the Internal Revenue Service in appropriate cases.

In addition to these sanctions imposed by the Service an employer found to be in violation of the minimum funding standards may be held accountable in legal proceedings instituted by both the Department of Labor and the PBGC. The Department of Labor may file a civil suit to bring about the correction of a funding deficiency, and, where the funding standards have been willfully violated, may even turn the matter over to the Justice Department for criminal prosecution.

The employer in such a case may also be made the subject of legal proceedings by the PBGC to terminate the plan. These involuntary terminations are discussed in Chapter 16.

WHERE ARE CONTRIBUTIONS INVESTED?

Contributions to a retirement plan are invested either in a trust fund or with an insurance company according to the terms of an annuity contract.

Since the development of pension plans, the banks (through trust arrangements) and the insurance companies (which sell annuity contracts) have been fierce competitors for control of the many billions of dollars in pension funds. Each of these funding vehicles has specific advantages and disadvantages which must be weighed by a plan sponsor. If a company establishes a trust fund, it maintains control over the investment of the retirement funds, although it may hire professional investment managers to make actual investment decisions.

Annuity contracts are a partial or complete alternative to the trust fund. There are many types of annuity contracts in use today. Traditionally, annuities were purchased annually for each participant based on the benefit which he or she accrued in that particular year. Since the insurance company guaranteed the annuity purchased each year it adopted very conservative interest and mortality assumptions. As interest rates rose these contracts were priced out of the market.

The insurance companies adjusted to rising interest rates by introducing more flexible annuity arrangements which more closely resembled trusteed funds. The principal new investment vehicle, called the deposit administration contract, provides that all contributions made by the sponsor together with interest at the annual rate earned by the insurance company on its investments in that year will be credited annually to the investment fund. No annuities are purchased until a participant retires.

In recent years a still more flexible method of insurance funding, called the immediate participation guaranteed annuity, has been offered. Under this type of contract no annuities are purchased *even after* the employee retires. Instead, pension payments are simply charged to the accumulated fund. However, a fund which is large enough to purchase annuities for all retired participants must be maintained. The immediate participation guaranteed annuity arrangements is closest to a trust fund because investment gains and losses are credited directly.

With these more flexible arrangements insurance companies won back a substantial amount of business which had been closed to them when they made available only the traditional deferred annuity contract method of funding. Indeed, today insurance contracts offer a particular advantage to participants in defined contribution plans (especially thrift plans) not available under trusteed plans. The insurance company *may guarantee the principal and interest* of each participant in the plan, much as a savings bank insures the accounts of its depositors.

Restrictions on the Handling and Investment of Plan Assets

ERISA regulates the behavior of all persons who administer retirement plans, who provide services to plans for a fee, or who handle plan assets.

Bonding

All persons who handle plan assets (except banks and insurance companies) must be bonded in an amount up to 10 percent of the funds handled (subject to statutory minimum and maximum amounts). The bonding requirement is administered by the Department of Labor and protects plan participants against the loss of plan funds due to the fraud and dishonesty of plan fiduciaries and other fund handlers.

General Fiduciary Standards

All persons or corporations having management or control over plan assets are called plan fiduciaries. Fiduciaries thus include trustees, investment managers, investment advisors, corporate plan administrative and investment committees, and usually the board of directors of the employer, which supervises plan operations and has authority to amend or terminate the plan. However, mere custodians of plan assets are not usually classified as fiduciaries.

The functions of trustee and custodian have become somewhat blurred. Traditionally, the trustee is charged with the responsibility for maintaining possession (or custody) of the trust funds and investing them in a prudent manner. The trustee also has the responsibility for paying benefits to plan participants and beneficiaries in accordance with the terms of the plan upon appropriate instructions from the plan sponsor.

In recent years, however, the investment management profession has taken over the investment of an increasingly large segment of pension funds. More and more employers sponsoring retirement plans have split custodial and investment responsibility by turning over investment management responsibilities to investment managers, and providing that bank trustees are to act only upon the instructions of these investment managers. Trustees of retirement funds and investment managers provide frequent reports of their investment activities and the results of their investment decisions to the plan sponsor. The plan sponsor, in turn, sets investment goals for the managers to teach. As a result of this bifurcation, many bank trustees have become, in effect, mere custodians (they are called "directed trustees") who receive contributions, hold them, and pay funds out only upon the specific instructions of others.

Fiduciaries are required to invest plan assets prudently for the exclusive benefit of participants and their beneficiaries. They are required to diversify plan assets, except if the plan is a tax credit ESOP, leveraged ESOP, or other Eligible Individual Account Plan, all of which are exempted from the diversification requirement. Fiduciaries must always act in accordance with the terms of the plan unless those terms are inconsistent with ERISA.

Prohibited Transactions

Fiduciaries are absolutely prohibited from benefiting personally from transactions with their plan and from representing parties with interests adverse to the plan's. ERISA also expressly prohibits certain transactions involving actual or potential conflicts of interest. These potential conflict of interest situations, called prohibited transactions, are based upon (but go beyond) traditional pre-ERISA restrictions on fiduciary conduct. The prohibited transaction rules also regulate the behavior of certain persons, called "Parties in Interest," who are not necessarily fiduciaries but who have relationships with the plan. Parties-in-interest include the plan sponsor, certain large shareholders, other related persons, and persons or organizations which provide services to the plan.

The prohibited transaction rules prevent a party in interest from lending money to the plan, unless the plan is an ESOP, or from selling to and exchanging assets with the plan.

ERISA has made it easier to hold fiduciaries responsible for breaches of the rules just discussed. The Internal Revenue Service imposes penalty taxes on parties in interest who engage in prohibited transactions. In addition, fiduciaries who engage in prohibited transactions may be held personally liable to make good to the plan losses caused by their improper conduct. ERISA, for the first time, provides that a participant or beneficiary may bring an action against a fiduciary in the federal courts regardless of the monetary amount at stake and gives the judge discretion to award legal fees of a victorious participant against the fiduciary.

In addition, ERISA has charged the Department of Labor with the responsibility of overseeing fiduciary conduct, a responsibility which that Department takes quite seriously. Where breaches of fiduciary responsibility have occurred, the Department of Labor has sought redress, for example, by compelling plans to appoint new investment managers and by bringing actions against the prior fiduciaries for violations of their obligation to administer plans solely in the interest of participants and their beneficiaries.

Although there have been a number of publicized situations of abuses in the management of retirement funds, it should be comforting to note that the bulk of retirement fund assets are honestly managed.

Chapter 10

REPORTING AND DISCLOSURE

AN OVERVIEW

ERISA contains very elaborate reporting and disclosure requirements which were intended to protect plan participants and their beneficiaries from being misinformed or simply kept in the dark about the rules under which their plans are operated. The safeguards established under ERISA can be compared to the registration requirements which protect investors under the federal securities laws or to the reporting requirements which safeguard purchasers of goods and services on credit under federal truth-in-lending legislation. These disclosure systems are all intended to ensure that "consumers" receive a balanced picture of the package being purchased.

The kind of abuse which the reporting and disclosure rules were designed to prevent is illustrated in the extreme by the facts in a recent lawsuit. John Daniel, an ex-truckdriver and teamster, sued both his plan and his union for failing to disclose to him a "Catch 22" rule of plan operation which ultimately cost him his pension. Although Daniel worked for 22½ years, and fully expected to receive a $400-a-month pension upon his termination of employment at age 63, he was shocked to learn that he was actually not entitled to receive a pension at all. Under the terms of his plan, 20 continuous years of service were required for vesting. Daniel's 22½ years of service had been interrupted when he was involuntarily laid off for four months. Although this layoff was considered a break in service under the terms of his pension plan, Daniel did not learn about this rule until he *actually applied* for pension payments.

Daniel's suit (which was lost shortly after his death) was based in part on the theory that if he had known how unlikely it was that he would qualify for a pension under the teamsters' plan, he would have looked for another job.

The substantive provisions of ERISA now bar plans from containing the specific rules which operated to deprive Daniel of his pension. In addition, future John Daniels are protected against a failure to disclose information which is essential to their retirement planning, such as delayed vesting provisions, since all pension plans are now subject to ERISA's rigorous reporting and disclosure rules. These rules would have required that Daniel be told about the "Catch 22" continuous service rule *soon after* he became a plan participant. They would have entitled him to an annual statement telling him whether or not he was vested and the number of years which he needed to work in order to become fully vested in his pension.

However, you will not find that all reporting and disclosure documents are equally protective or useful. The multiplicity and detail of reports and documents required to be filed with the Internal Revenue Service, the Department of Labor and the Pension Benefit Guaranty Corporation, and those required to be distributed to plan participants and beneficiaries have given rise to a good deal of justifiable criticism. In fact, the usefulness of the required reports to the sophisticated employee attempting to plan for retirement varies from those which are essential to effective planning (your Summary Plan Description) to those which are only marginally useful (the full Annual Report). In many cases, the schedule for updating information in these documents will result in a substantial delay between the time that a material amendment is made to your plan (for example, the addition of a new payment option or an increase in benefits) and the time at which you are required to be notified of the change. This is a specific example of a recurring problem—you will become more aware of these ERISA timing problems as you read further in this introduction to reporting and disclosure. For the moment, it is sufficient to say that ERISA often will not require that you receive relevant information when you actually need it. You may have to request it or ask specific questions of your administrator.

The remainder of this chapter contains a more detailed outline and a checklist-chart describing both the reports which must be furnished automatically to each plan participant, and those to

Plan Participant's Reporting and Disclosure Checklist

A. Documents Available to All Participants	Available Automatically?	Distribution Deadline	Planning Information
Summary Plan Description (SPD)	Yes	Later of: 1. 120 days after the plan's adoption, or 2. 90 days after participation begins.	1) Payment options. 2) Eligibility Requirements. 3) Benefit Formula. 4) Vesting Schedule. 5) Your rights under ERISA. 6) Conditions and Limitations on Benefits.
Plan, Trust Agreements, Insurance Contracts	Upon request only. You may be assessed duplicating costs.	30 days from request.	May be utilized by your tax planner/ adviser.
Summary Annual Report	Yes	Ninth month after end of plan year	Plan assets and liabilities; receipts and disbursements.
Annual Report	Upon request only.	30 days from request.	More particularized information re: plan investments, party-in-interest transactions.
Benefits Statement		180 days from start of plan year if automatic—otherwise, 30 days from request	Indicates accrued benefit at normal retirement date.

(continued)

Plan Participant's Reporting and Disclosure Checklist, cont.

B. Documents Available at Retirement Age or Receipt of Benefits	Available Automatically?	Distribution Deadline	Planning Information
Joint and Survivor Annuity Information (Married Participants)	*General Information*—Yes. *Individual Information*—Upon request only.	*General Information*—Generally, 9 months prior to plan's earliest retirement date. *Individual Information*—30 days from request, if request was made within 60 days of receiving general information.	*General Information*—Circumstances under which your benefit will be provided in this form. Election period during which you may decline this option. *Individual Information*—Dollar value of your adjusted benefit if joint and survivor option is elected.
Tax Form W-2P	Yes	By January 31 following end of the year in which payments are received.	Amount of your distribution and portion subject to tax.
Tax Form 1099R	Yes	By January 31 following end of the year in which payments are received.	1) Lump sum amount 2) Amount which is eligible for capital gains treatment.
Notification of suspension of benefits	Yes	By end of month in which normal retirement date is reached.	Informs you that payment of your pension is suspended until you actually retire.

which he or she is entitled only upon request, as well as suggestions as to their effective use in retirement planning.

It will be useful to study the participant's checklist which appears on the previous two pages before reading the more detailed descriptions which follow. You should also note that your employer must usually provide you with any document which you have requested within 30 days of that request or it risks the imposition of daily $100 fines until the document has been furnished.

The following documents must be distributed automatically to participating employees and beneficiaries, or are customarily distributed automatically by employers:

THE SUMMARY PLAN DESCRIPTION

The focal point of ERISA disclosure and the basic document for retirement planning is the Summary Plan Description (commonly called the SPD), which can be compared to a prospectus. Although the prospectus must be provided to prospective investors prior to their purchase of securities, the SPD is not legally required to be distributed sooner than 90 days after the date plan participation begins—under the operating rules of many plans, this would permit withholding the SPD until the *second* year of employment. However, most employers in fact distribute SPDs to new employees when they first report for work. It is unlikely that your request for an SPD prior to the time that your employer is legally required to provide you with one would ever be denied—even if you are merely considering accepting a job offer with that employer, you clearly have an interest in fully understanding the company benefit structure.

The concept of the SPD is hardly new—employers prior to ERISA would customarily distribute to retirement plan participants a booklet describing the provisions of the plan, but the booklet was far too often self-serving or incomplete. An employer, for example, might describe benefits in glowing terms, while failing to indicate in an equally prominent part of the booklet that an employee who left the job with fewer than 10 years of service would forfeit all benefits. The innovation in ERISA's reporting and disclosure regulations, apart from a formalization of the practice of distributing booklets, is the imposition of a clear set of rules which prohibits employers from describing their plans in an incomplete or self-serving manner. The SPD requirement is the main reason that there should not be many post-ERISA cases such as *Daniel* in which participants engage in financial planning under the mistaken assumption that they are entitled to benefits.

The Department of Labor requires that a Summary Plan Description be written in a manner "calculated to be understood by the average plan participant" and sufficiently comprehensive to apprise the plan's participants and beneficiaries of their rights and obligations under the plan. The preparer of the SPD must take into account the level of comprehension and education of typical participants in the plan and the complexity of the terms of the plan, so that an SPD for a plan covering university professors may probably be more complex than an SPD for a plan covering mostly blue collar workers. However, the SPD, regardless of the level of education of the participants, is not supposed to contain legalese, technical jargon or long complex sentences. It should use clarifying examples and illustrations, clear cross references and a table of contents. Indeed, a former Pension and Welfare Benefit Programs Administrator of the Department of Labor stated explicitly that SPDs which are "as lengthy and complex as the formal plan instruments" will not be considered to be in compliance with ERISA.

The format of the Summary Plan Description must not have the effect of misleading or failing to inform participants and beneficiaries of their rights and obligations under the plan. It may not omit information such as the fact that a participant in a defined contribution plan must be employed on the last day of the plan year in order to receive an allocation of his or her employer's contribution for that year. Limiting language must be described or summarized in a manner not less prominent than the type face used to describe the plan benefits—in other words, large type cannot confer benefits which type too small to be read without a magnifying glass takes away.

Most SPDs contain a disclaimer clause which reads somewhat as follows:

> This booklet is, necessarily, only a summary of the most important terms and provisions of the plan. The provisions of the plan are fully set forth in a legal document adopted by the Board of Directors. In the

case of any conflict between the provisions of this booklet and of the plan document, the latter must, of course, govern.

The extent to which such a disclaimer provision will be given effect under ERISA is not clear.

The courts will probably hold that if an SPD contains deliberate misstatements of fact or is carelessly prepared and contains material errors, or omits facts necessary to make the Summary Plan Description accurate, the plan sponsor is liable for benefits which the SPD appears to promise, especially if the employee has relied on those promises.

Your SPD is legally required to contain all of the following information:

- normal retirement age
- eligibility and vesting requirements
- the plan's benefit formula
- circumstances which can limit participation and vesting—rules for breaks in service, the rule of parity, etc.
- years credited for benefit accrual, including the manner in which benefits are prorated for employees failing to complete full years of service
- names and titles of plan trustees
- identity of agent for service of process if you wish to sue the plan
- the source of contributions (i.e., employer-payall) and identity of the insurance company, trust fund, or other entity which holds plan assets
- whether benefits are insured by the PBGC and if so, a general statement prepared by the Department of Labor which indicates that the PBGC does not, because of various limitations, insure all benefits under covered plans
- a description of the plan's claims procedure

–information on payment options and the situations in which joint and survivor annuities will be provided automatically

–a statement of ERISA rights (the Department of Labor sample is used by most plans) which describes, albeit in a much less comprehensive way, the rights discussed in this book.

The Department of Labor's statement of ERISA rights reads as follows:

> As a participant in the (name of plan) you are entitled to certain rights and protections under the Employee Retirement Income Security Act of 1974. ERISA provides that all plan participants shall be entitled to:
>
> Examine, without charge at the plan administrator's office and at other specified locations, such as work sites and union halls, all plan documents, including insurance contracts, and copies of all documents filed by the plan with the U.S. Department of Labor, such as detailed annual reports and plan descriptions.
>
> Obtain copies of all Plan documents and other Plan information upon written request to the Plan Administrator. The Administrator may make a reasonable charge for the copies.
>
> Receive a summary of the plan's annual financial report. The plan administrator is required by law to furnish each participant with a copy of this summary annual report.
>
> Obtain a statement telling you whether you have a right to receive a benefit at normal retirement age, and if so, what your benefits would be at normal retirement age if you stop working under the plan now. If you do not have a right to a pension, the statement will tell you how many more years you have to work to get a right to a pension. This statement must be requested in writing and is not required to be given more than once a year. The plan must provide the statement free of charge.
>
> In addition to creating rights for plan participants, ERISA imposes duties upon the people who are responsible for the operation of the employee benefit plan. The people who operate your plan, called "fiduciaries" of the plan, have a duty to do so prudently and in the interest of you and other plan participants and beneficiaries. No one, including your employer, your union, or any other person, may fire you or otherwise discriminate against you in any way to prevent you

from obtaining a (pension, welfare) benefit or exercising your rights under ERISA. If your claim for a (pension, welfare) benefit is denied in whole or in part you must receive a written explanation of the reason for the denial. You have the right to have the plan review and reconsider your claim.

Under ERISA, there are steps you can take to enforce the above rights. For instance, if you request materials from the plan and do not receive them within 30 days, you may file suit in a federal court. In such a case, the court may require the plan administrator to provide the materials and pay you up to $100 a day until you receive the materials, unless the materials were not sent because of reasons beyond the control of the administrator. If you have a claim for benefits which is denied or ignored, in whole or in part, you may file suit in a state or federal court. If it should happen that plan fiduciaries misuse the plan's money, or if you are discriminated against for asserting your rights, you may seek assistance from the U.S. Department of Labor, or you may file suit in a state or federal court. The court will decide who should pay court costs and legal fees. If you are successful the court may order the person you have sued to pay these costs and fees, for example, if it finds your claim is frivolous. If you have any questions about this statement or about your rights under ERISA, you should contact the nearest Area Office of the U.S. Labor-Management Services Administration, Department of Labor

The SPD is not required to contain individualized information—it will describe the general eligibility rules, but it won't tell you that you became a participant on January 1, 1976 or the dollar amount of your monthly benefit. You may need to request such specific information from your benefits administrator. The SPD also need not indicate the actual probability of your receiving a pension.

Your SPD must be distributed to you within 90 days after you become a participant or, in the case of a beneficiary (such as a surviving spouse) or retired participant, within 90 days after benefits are first received. However, in the case of a newly-established plan, your plan administrator has an extension until 120 days after the plan is adopted to distribute the SPDs, if this is later. Vested former employees who have not yet begun to receive benefits are also entitled to an SPD. However, vested separated and retired participants may be given an abbreviated SPD which eliminates information they no longer need, such as eligibility requirements.

TO SUE OR NOT TO SUE

Summary Plan Descriptions must describe a procedure by which a plan participant or beneficiary may file a claim for benefits under the plan, the manner in which a claimant will be notified of the action taken on his claim and a procedure for appealing or obtaining a rehearing of any claim denial. This is another valuable protection for participants. Under most pension plans, benefits are automatic. You must file a formal request only if you elect an optional form of payment. However, you must also file a formal claim to correct a mistake which you believe was made in calculating the dollar amount of your benefit or your entitlement to particular benefits.

Generally speaking, a claim must be acted upon within 90 days after a notice of claim is filed. A 90-day extension is available to the employer if you are notified in writing *within* the original 90 day period why additional time is needed. If a claim is denied, the participant or beneficiary must be notified in writing and must be told the specific reasons for the denial. He or she must be referred to the exact plan provision on which the denial is based and must be told what (if anything) must be done by him or her in order to perfect the claim, i.e., if failure to provide proof of age is the reason for denying the claim, he or she must be told that the benefits will be granted if appropriate proof of age, such as a copy of the participant's birth certificate, is provided.

Each retirement plan must provide that any request for a review of claim denial made within 60 days of the denial will generally be acted upon within 60 days. A 60 day extension is available, again only if *within* the original 60 day period you receive written notification of the reason it is needed. Some plans provide that the same fiduciary (usually the trustees or an administrative committee) who originally denied your claim will rule on your appeal. Others refer your appeal to a second fiduciary, which is often the Board of Directors.

It is questionable whether a plan participant may sue to obtain benefits denied him or her by the plan administrator without going through the plan's internal claims structure, unless it is clear that the claim would not be entertained in good faith. In any event, bypassing the plan's review procedure is rarely a good idea.

In fact, you have nothing to lose and everything to gain by *first* presenting your grievance to plan officials. Although there will be long delays before your claim is heard in the courts, the ERISA rules on claims outlined in your SPD require your plan administrator to process your claim quickly within the established deadlines. You can always go to court later. Furthermore, it doesn't cost you anything to use the plan's claims mechanism. Lawyers are expensive. If you go to court and lose, not only will you not recover your own legal fees (your opponent may have to pay your fees if you win) but you may, if the court decides that your claim is frivolous, actually have to pay your *opponent's* legal fees, too.

Finally, most plan administrators will make a genuine attempt to process your request for benefits in a fair manner. Even if the original decision made with respect to your claim is incorrect, the error may well be remedied on appeal.

In short, unless you have reason to believe that your plan officials would not consider or are not considering your claim objectively (which is a rare situation), it makes no sense for you to beat a path to the courtroom door. Use the procedure outlined in your SPD.

UPDATING THE SPD

The Summary Plan Description must be furnished without charge. The plan administrator is required to distribute a new SPD every five years (ten years if no material amendments to the plan have been made in the interim).

In addition, if there have been any material amendments to the plan, an employer is required to distribute a description of those changes within 210 days after the end of the plan year in which those plan amendments are adopted.

This is another example of a deadline which is too late to be really helpful to participants–although with John Daniel in mind we should generally agree that this is a case of "better late than never." If, for example, your calendar year plan is amended on January 1, 1982 to provide you with a new payment option, your plan will not be required to provide you with an SPD summary of the change until *July 28, 1983.* Presumably, employers will voluntarily notify employees about a new payment option prior to that time. The "moral" is simply that you should pay careful attention to all news about changes in your plan, and not rely upon SPD descriptions of plan changes.

INDIVIDUAL STATEMENT OF ACCRUED AND VESTED BENEFIT

A plan administrator is obligated to supply, on request, not more often than once each year, a statement to each plan participant or beneficiary setting forth the amount of his or her accrued benefit under the plan, whether and to what extent he or she is vested in that accrued benefit, and how long it will take that participant to become fully vested. Alternatively, a plan administrator may choose to distribute this statement automatically once a year.

It is becoming more and more common for employees to receive an elaborate statement which is individually calculated for each plan participant by computer and which clearly sets forth the value of their accrued benefits under their employer's retirement plans.

Although ERISA merely requires that this statement be furnished on the request of the plan participant, most employers furnish it automatically. In the unlikely event that your employer does not, it will be to your benefit to submit an annual request.

In addition, the Internal Revenue Service requires employers (prior to 7 months after the close of each plan year) to send former employees with vested benefits a benefit statement (Form SSA) and to file a copy with the Service which, in turn, forwards it to the Social Security Administration. Since the Social Security Administration keeps a record of the information which appears on this statement, it serves as a central source of information about your deferred vested benefits from all of your past employers.

WRITTEN EXPLANATION OF JOINT AND SURVIVOR ANNUITY

ERISA requires that every retirement plan that provides benefits in the form of a life annuity, must provide benefits for married participants in the form of a joint and survivor annuity unless the participant declines the joint and survivor annuity and elects another form of benefit.

Joint and survivor annuities are discussed more fully in Chapter 6.

A plan administrator is required to distribute to each employee about nine months before he or she is first eligible for retirement, a statement setting forth in simplified terms how the joint and survivor annuity option works and what the effect would be to him or her if the pension were paid in that manner.

The statement must also provide that if the employee desires individualized information as to the effect of the joint and survivor option in his or her case, that employee must be furnished with the additional information. Most employers automatically furnish individualized information to each participant without requiring him or her to request it. But make this request if you need to, since it will tell you the individual dollar effect on your pension—the actual reduction in *your* life benefits which will be made to provide the survivor benefit, and the dollar amount of that survivor benefit.

Here is another example of how ERISA's reporting and disclosure schedules may not dovetail with your individual needs. If your plan provides for early retirement at age 55, you will be entitled as a matter of right to get your joint and survivor information *only once*—9 months before your 55th birthday—even if you don't retire until age 65. Although the Regulations were obviously not drafted to protect employees who cease work after early retirement age under plans with early retirement options, most employers will voluntarily furnish this information again as you approach actual retirement. In any event, it is always useful to keep this information safely on file, and to read it carefully when it is received.

ANNUAL REPORT

ERISA requires each plan administrator to file an annual report (Form 5500) containing a statement of assets and liabilities of the plan as of the beginning and end of the plan year, and a statement of receipts and disbursements during the plan year. The annual report contains substantial additional information.

The administrator of a retirement plan covering more than 100 participants is required to engage an independent public accountant to audit the books and records of the plan and to render an opinion as to whether the plan's financial statements are presented fairly in conformity with generally accepted accounting principles applied on a basis consistent with that of the preceding year.

The audit by an independent public accountant is, of course, an important protection for plan participants. It is unfortunate that plans covering fewer than 100 participants are exempt from this requirement. The requirement for an annual audit was omitted in the case of these smaller plans since it was felt that the cost of such an audit would be high enough to cause many small employers to terminate their retirement plans.

Defined benefit pension plans are also required to retain an actuary to value plan assets and liabilities at least every third year, or more often if the actuary determines that it is necessary. He or she must also render, no more infrequently than once every three years, an opinion that the actuarial assumptions are in the aggregate reasonably related to the experience of the plan and to reasonable expectations and that they represent the actuary's best estimate of anticipated experience under the plan. The actuary's opinion is an additional valuable safeguard for a defined benefit plan participant.

SUMMARY ANNUAL REPORT

Each plan administrator is also required to distribute to each plan participant or beneficiary receiving benefits a summary of the annual report. The Summary Annual Report is a form which indicates the value of plan assets, plan expenses, and changes in net assets (for example, unrealized appreciation) during the year. It must also indicate whether applicable funding requirements have been met.

The Summary Annual Report is required to contain the following statement:

> You have the right to receive a copy of the full annual report, or any part thereof, on request. The items listed below are included in that report:
>
> 1. An accountant's report;
> 2. Assets held for investment;
> 3. Transactions between the plan and parties in interest (that is, persons who have certain relationships with the plan);
> 4. Loans or other obligations in default;
> 5. Leases in default;
> 6. Transactions in excess of 3 percent of plan assets;
> 7. Insurance information including sales commissions paid to insurance carriers; and
> 8. Actuarial information regarding the funding of the plan.

> To obtain a copy of the full annual report, or any part thereof, write or call the office of (name), who is (state title; e.g., the plan administrator), (business address and telephone number). The charge to cover copying costs will be ($) for the full annual report, or ($) per page for any part thereof.
>
> You also have the right to receive from the plan administrator, on request and at no charge, a statement of the assets and liabilities of the plan and accompanying notes, or a statement of income and expenses of the plan and accompanying notes, or both. If you request a copy of the full annual report from the plan administrator, these two statements and accompanying notes will be included as part of that report. The charge to cover copying costs given above does not include a charge for the copying of these portions of the report because these portions are furnished without charge.
>
> You also have the legally protected right to examine the annual report at the main office of the plan (address), (at any other location where the report is available for examination), and at the U.S. Department of Labor in Washington, D.C., or to obtain a copy from the U.S. Department of Labor upon payment of copying costs. Requests to the Department should be addressed to: Public Disclosure Room, N4677, Pension and Welfare Benefit Programs, Department of Labor, 200 Constitution Avenue, N.W., Washington, D.C. 20216.

A full report may be useful to you if you suspect that the trustees are mismanaging plan assets or have engaged in prohibited transactions (see discussion beginning in Chapter 9) and/or imprudent investments. It may also be useful if you are a participant in a defined contribution plan. Since your benefits will be determined by the fund's performance, and no particular benefits are guaranteed, you may want to see what the performance record of the trustees has been. However, the most important plan financial information is all concisely presented in the Summary Annual Report.

PLAN DOCUMENTS AND CONTRACTS

ERISA provides that an employer must also make available, upon request, copies of all plan documents such as the plan itself, trust agreements, insurance contracts and any other agreements relating to the plan or the manner in which plan assets are accumulated, although reasonable duplicating charges may be assessed if you make this request. Unless you have an attorney or accountant capable of utilizing these documents in planning, or are prepared to struggle through a web of provisions which even nonspecialist lawyers need time to untangle, these requests are not likely to be helpful to you. Such documents are most often written in complicated legalese rather than in vernacular. Indeed, you will understand why the Department of Labor insists that SPDs be written in simple English if you attempt to read selected provisions of your plan. While such trust agreements and insurance contracts are not recommended leisure-time reading, you should obtain copies of the plan documents if you have specific questions about benefits which are not answered to your satisfaction by your benefits administrator or your SPD.

TAX INFORMATION RETURNS

A terminated participant, or beneficiary who receives benefits from a retirement plan must generally be given (not later than January 31 of the year following the year in which distributions are made) a statement containing information which he or she will need in preparing the prior year's tax return.

If the participant or beneficiary is receiving benefits in the form of an annuity or installments, he or she is required to be given Form W-2P which sets forth the amount of the distribution and identifies the portion which is subject to tax (i.e., everything but the portion of the distribution attributable to your actual nondeductible voluntary contributions, exclusive of earnings).

Participants or beneficiaries who receive lump sum distributions are required to be given Form 1099-R which discloses the total amount of the distribution, the portion which is taxable and the part which represents a return of the employee's contributions.

The taxable portion must also be broken down to indicate the part (if any) that qualifies for capital gains treatment and the ordinary income element. Taxability of plan distributions is discussed more fully in Chapter 11.

Chapter 11

TAXATION OF DISTRIBUTIONS FROM QUALIFIED PLANS

This chapter describes the rules governing the manner in which distributions from retirement plans are taxed. These rules can be relatively simple if all you are entitled to receive is a series of periodic distributions from a single retirement plan. The rules could become exceedingly complex if you are offered the choice of a lump sum distribution or periodic payments, if you receive benefits from more than one plan, if part of the distribution consists of the return of your own contributions, or if a portion of the distribution consists of shares of stock of your employer or other noncash property.

PERIODIC DISTRIBUTIONS

Income Tax Treatment

All distributions from defined benefit or defined contribution plans, unless they are eligible for lump sum treatment (to be discussed further on in this chapter), or unless a special exception is applicable, are subject to tax as ordinary income. Beginning in 1982, the maximum federal income tax rate on ordinary income is 50%.

Periodic distributions are subject to tax in the same way regardless of which option (other than the lump sum) is chosen. Therefore, it is immaterial for purposes of taxation whether you choose to receive a pension for your life only, whether it is payable in the form of a qualified joint and survivor annuity, or whether it is paid over a period certain, such as in ten equal annual installments.

Distributions from qualified pension or profit sharing plans are not subject to withholding tax. However, an employee is permitted to enter into an agreement with his or her employer for voluntary withholding from pension plan payments.

If you receive periodic distributions from a pension or profit sharing plan, you will receive a form W-2P from your employer or from the plan each year listing the amount which you have received in that year and on which you must pay income tax.

Special Estate Tax Exclusion

If you choose to have your pension benefits payable during your lifetime only, there will be, by definition, no payments to be made to any person after your death and therefore no special estate tax problems. However, if you choose to have payments made under a periodic payment option which *does* provide a death benefit–such as a joint and survivor annuity, or over a period certain which may end after your death–the remaining payments which are made after your death to your spouse or any designated beneficiary other than your estate are not subject to estate tax.

> *Example 1.* John Reed elects to receive a pension of $500 a month payable for the remainder of his life. He is subject to tax on the $6,000 ($500 x 12) which he receives each year as if it were compensation, i.e., up to the 50 percent maximum federal income tax rate.
>
> *Example 2.* Mary Jones elects to receive a pension of $1,000 per month payable for the remainder of her life or for 10 years certain. She names her husband, William, as her beneficiary if he is then alive, and her son, Mark, as contingent beneficiary.
>
> Mary dies after four years, having received 48 monthly payments. During her lifetime, she had paid income tax on these payments in the same manner as did John in the

previous example. Since she elected a 10-year certain option, there are 72 installments remaining unpaid on her death. These payments are not subject to tax in her estate since they will be paid over more than one taxable year (that is, they are *not* lump sum payments) and she designated her husband, William, as her beneficiary.

Assume William lives another 5 years and receives 60 monthly payments. He will pay income tax on these amounts subject to the same rules as Mary. On William's death, 12 monthly installments remain unpaid. These payments will be made to Mary's son, Mark, who will pay income tax on them.

Note that the 12 unpaid installments were not includible in William's estate. This is because William had no right to designate that his estate would receive any installments remaining unpaid on his death.

Example 3. Assume the same facts as in the previous example, except that Mary did not name a beneficiary. The remaining 72 installments will be payable to her estate under the terms of her plan and therefore will be subject to estate tax.

It is very important that each participant in a qualified plan which provides a periodic death benefit who desires to take advantage of the estate tax exclusion, designate a beneficiary and contingent beneficiaries other than his or her estate to receive the death benefits payable under the plan. Unless this is done, the death benefits will not qualify for the special estate tax exclusion applicable to distributions from qualified plans.

Example 4. Assume the same facts as in Example 2. Mary empowered her husband, William, to designate a contingent beneficiary if any installments remain unpaid on William's death. There were no limitations placed upon William's choice. William designated their son, Mark, as contingent beneficiary. Under these circumstances, the 12 remaining unpaid installments on William's death will be included in his estate since William *could* have named his own estate as the beneficiary

> of these unpaid installments. It is immaterial that William actually exercised the power to name a person other than his estate as contingent beneficiary.

The special estate tax exclusion relating to death benefits payable from qualified plans is available only to the estate of the participant in the pension plan. It is not available to the estate of the spouse or other designated beneficiary of the participant. A participant may retain the right to designate any beneficiary without causing the value of the death benefit to be included in his or her estate. However, if the participant assigns to any other person the unlimited right to designate contingent beneficiaries, any remaining benefits payable after the death of that second individual will be included in the latter's estate.

LUMP SUM DISTRIBUTIONS

A lump sum distribution is defined as a distribution that consists of the entire balance to a participant's credit under a plan and which is payable either in a single sum or in installments during a single calendar year. Lump sum distributions are available under virtually all defined contribution plans and an increasing number of defined benefit plans. Lump sum distributions are entitled to more favorable income tax treatment than periodic distributions. However, the "tradeoff" is that lump sum distributions are not entitled to the special estate tax exclusion if this favorable income tax treatment is elected.

Income Tax Treatment—Qualifying for Special Treatment

In order to qualify for the special tax treatment described in the next section, the lump sum distribution must be:

1. Made in respect of an employee who has been a participant in the plan for at least 5 years and;
2. Payable after he or she has attained the age of 59½ years or by reason of separation from service or death.

In addition:

3. The recipient must affirmatively elect favorable income tax treatment; and

4. If the recipient is over age 59½, he or she must not have made a similar prior election after he or she attained age 59½. Otherwise, there is no limit on the number of elections which may be made by a recipient except that if a prior election had been made within the last 6 years, the prior distribution must be aggregated with the current year's distribution in calculating the tax.

Special rules apply when distributions are received in the same tax year from more than one plan. If the recipient receives lump sum distributions from more than one plan in a single taxable year, the election must be made as to all of the distributions received. Furthermore, in those rare cases in which an individual is covered by more than one pension plan, or by more than one profit sharing plan, he or she must receive lump sum distributions in the same year from all of the pension plans or from all of the profit sharing plans and make the election with respect to all such distributions.

Ten Year Forward Averaging

If all of these rules are complied with, the recipient may elect to have the lump sum distribution subject to tax under a favorable 10-year income averaging method. Under this method, the recipient first calculates the tax on one-tenth of the distribution, ignoring all other income and using the tax table applicable to a single individual even if he or she is married. The recipient then pays a tax equal to 10 times this amount.

This special method has the effect of widening the tax brackets by a multiple of 10. Another way of looking at it is that the use of this special 10-year income averaging produces the same result as if the recipient had received the lump sum distribution in 10 equal annual installments and had substantially no other taxable income during that ten year period.

In the case of lump sum distributions which are less than $70,000, a portion of the distribution is not subject to tax at all. This portion, called the "Minimum Distribution Allowance," is equal to the lesser of $10,000 or 50 percent of the distribution but is reduced if the distribution exceeds $20,000. If the distribution is $20,000 or less, one-half of the distribution is excluded from tax. If the distribution is more than $20,000 but less than

$70,000, the $10,000 exclusion is reduced by 20 percent of the amount by which the distribution exceeds $20,000. If the distribution is $70,000 or more, there is no minimum distribution allowance.

Example 5. Allen Brown receives a $50,000 distribution from the XYZ profit sharing plan. The minimum distribution allowance (i.e., the excluded portion of the distribution) is equal to the lesser of 50 percent of the distribution or $10,000–in this case, $10,000–reduced by 20 percent of the amount by which the distribution exceeds $20,000–in this case, $30,000. Thus, the exclusion is $10,000 less $6,000 (20 percent of $30,000), or $4,000. The remaining $46,000 is subject to the 10-year income averaging rule.

Capital Gains Election

A special rule is applicable to those employees who participated in a qualified pension or profit sharing plan prior to 1974. The portion of a lump sum distribution which is attributable to participation in a qualified plan prior to 1974 is subject to tax as a long-term capital gain unless the participant elects to have the entire distribution subject to tax under the 10-year income averaging rule. Sixty percent of a long-term capital gain is excluded from a recipient's taxable income and the remaining 40 percent is subject to tax as ordinary income. Taxation of a portion of a lump sum distribution at capital gains rates will usually (but not always) result in lower tax liability than if the entire distribution were subject to 10-year income averaging.

The portion of a lump sum distribution which is allocable to participation in a qualified plan prior to 1974 is calculated according to a set formula. The pre-1974 segment of a distribution is a percentage of the distribution equal to the ratio of the period of participation in the plan prior to 1974 to the entire period of participation in the plan, regardless of the weighting of the actual contributions made on an employee's behalf during those years.

Example 6. Ronald Knight became a participant in the XYZ profit sharing plan on January 1, 1970 and terminated his employment with XYZ on December 31, 1979. He received a lump sum distribution of $50,000 in 1981. Knight is in the 50 percent tax bracket. He had no capital gains or losses in 1981.

Knight was a participant in the plan for 10 years, 4 of them prior to 1974. Therefore, 40 percent of the distribution, or $20,000, will be subject to tax as a long-term capital gain unless he elects to have the entire distribution subject to tax under the 10-year income averaging rule. Since Knight is in the 50 percent tax bracket, he will do better to elect 10 year averaging for the entire distribution. A completed tax form 4972 for Knight, which illustrates how his special tax would be computed if no capital gains election were made, is printed on page 172. You should note that the effective rate of tax on Knight's lump sum is about 15 percent whereas he would have paid a 20 percent tax on the capital gains portion if he had not elected 10 year averaging for his entire distribution (i.e., 50 percent of the 40 percent of the capital gain which is subject to tax).

Under certain circumstances not present for Knight in Example 6, the treatment of the eligible portion of a distribution as a long-term capital gain will result in a lower effective income tax rate than under the 10-year income averaging method. This could occur, for example, if the recipient has little taxable income from other sources, if he or she has capital losses which may be offset against the long-term capital gain so that the effective rate of tax on the capital gain is relatively low or if the lump sum distribution is relatively large so that the effective rate of tax, even under 10-year income averaging, is relatively high.

No general rule can be given as to which method produces the better results. It is therefore advisable for any recipient of a lump sum distribution to calculate whether choosing to have the pre-1974 portion of the distribution subject to tax as a long-term capital gain produces a better tax result than having it taxed under the 10-year income averaging provision.

If the capital gain alternative is chosen, this does not reduce the effective rate of tax on the post-1973 segment of the lump sum distribution. The reason for this is that the 10-year income averaging tax is first calculated on the entire distribution and the tax is then multiplied by a decimal representing that portion of the

Form **4972**
Department of the Treasury
Internal Revenue Service

Special 10-Year Averaging Method

(For Total Distribution from Qualified Retirement Plan)

▶ Attach to Form 1040 or Form 1041. ▶ See separate instructions.

OMB No. 1545–0193

1981

Name(s) as shown on return: Ronald Knight

Identifying number: 000-00-0000

By checking this box ▶ ☐, I agree, for this and all other lump-sum distributions I receive for the same employee, not to treat any part as capital gain. I know this decision cannot be changed. (See Instruction F.)

Part I Use Part I if You Have Not Filed Form 4972 for Any Year after 1975

1	Capital gain part from payer's statement (Form 1099R, box 2)	1	0
	If you are using the 10-year averaging method for the capital gain from the distribution as well as for the ordinary income, leave line 1 blank and include the capital gain on line 2 (see instruction F). Otherwise, enter the capital gain from your payer's statement (Form 1099R, box 2). If you are filing Schedule D and cannot take the exclusion on line 4 below or do not have to decrease the capital gain for Federal estate tax, enter the capital gain on your Schedule D also. See the separate instructions for line 1.		
2	Ordinary income part from payer's statement (Form 1099R, box 3). Enter here instead of on Form 1040 or Form 1041	2	50,000
3	Add lines 1 and 2	3	50,000
4	Death benefit exclusion (see instructions for line 4)	4	N/A
5	Total taxable amount (subtract line 4 from line 3)	5	50,000
6	Current actuarial value of annuity, if applicable (from Form 1099R, box 9)	6	N/A
7	Adjusted total taxable amount (add lines 5 and 6). If this amount is $70,000 or more, skip lines 8 through 11, and enter this amount on line 12 also	7	50,000
8	50% of line 7, but not more than $10,000 — 8: 10,000		
9	Subtract $20,000 from line 7. Enter difference. If line 7 is $20,000 or less, enter zero — 9: 30,000		
10	20% of line 9 — 10: 6,000		
11	Minimum distribution allowance (subtract line 10 from line 8)	11	4,000
12	Subtract line 11 from line 7	12	46.000
13	Federal estate tax attributable to lump-sum distribution. Do not deduct on Form 1040 or Form 1041 the amount entered on this line that is attributable to the ordinary income entered on line 2. (See instructions for line 13)	13	N/A
14	Subtract line 13 from line 12	14	46,000
15	$2,300 plus 10% of line 14	15	6,900
16	Tax on amount on line 15. Use Tax Rate Schedule X (Single Taxpayer Rate) in Form 1040 Instructions	16	768
17	Multiply line 16 by 10. If no entry on line 6, skip lines 18 through 23, and enter this amount on line 24 also	17	7,630
18	Divide line 6 by line 7 (carry percentage to four places)	18	N/A %
19	Multiply line 11 by percentage on line 18	19	N/A
20	Subtract line 19 from line 6	20	N/A
21	$2,300 plus 10% of line 20	21	N/A
22	Tax on amount on line 21. Use Tax Rate Schedule X (Single Taxpayer Rate) in Form 1040 Instructions	22	N/A
23	Multiply line 22 by 10	23	N/A
24	Subtract line 23 from line 17	24	7,680
25	Divide line 2 by line 3 (carry percentage to four places)	25	100 %
26	Multiply line 24 by percentage on line 25	26	7,680
27	Tax rate reduction credit for 1981 (multiply line 26 by .0125)	27	96
28	Tax on ordinary income part of lump-sum distribution (subtract line 27 from line 26). Show this amount on Form 1040, line 36, or Form 1041, line 26b	28	7,584

For Paperwork Reduction Act Notice, see separate instructions. Form **4972** (1981)

total distribution which the pre-1974 portion constitutes. The pre-1974 remainder is then treated as a capital gain.

Example 7. Assume the tax on a $200,000 lump sum distribution calculated under the 10-year income averaging method is $49,250 and that 40 percent of this distribution is allocable to participation in the plan prior to 1974. The tax on the post-1973 segment ($120,000) will be $29,550 (60 percent of $49,250). The remaining $80,000, capital gain will be taxed pursuant to the rates applicable to all long-term capital gains–that is, it will be offset against long-term capital losses in excess of other long-term capital gains and then against short-term capital losses in excess of short-term capital gains; 40 percent of any excess will be taxed as ordinary income. The 10-year forward averaging tax on the remaining portion of the distribution will be calculated based on a $200,000 distribution (and not $120,000). The percentage represented by the post-1973 segment will be multiplied by the total liability calculated using the 10-year forward averaging method to determine the tax on the post-1973 portion of the distribution.

Lump Sum Death Benefits

The favorable lump sum tax rates are also applicable where a lump sum distribution is made by reason of the death of a participant.

The requirements which must be met in order for a lump sum distribution to qualify for the special lump sum income tax treatment are also applicable to death benefit distributions made to survivors by reason of a participant's death with one exception: the requirement that he or she have been a member of the plan for a five-year period does not apply under those circumstances.

Example 8. Harold Levine dies and his wife Helen receives a lump sum death benefit of $100,000 from the EFG Profit Sharing Trust. If Helen does not elect to delay taxation by rolling the death benefit into an IRA, she pays income tax on the distribution calculated as if she had been the plan participant instead of Harold. It does not matter whether Harold had participated in the plan for 5 years prior to his death.

Example 9. Assume, alternatively, that Harold's children, Leonard and Gloria, each receive 50 percent of the distribution of $50,000. Each child pays the tax on the portion of the distribution which he or she receives. The tax is calculated as if a single individual received the entire distribution and is then apportioned between the recipients. This means that each recipient gets the benefit of a ratable portion of the minimum distribution allowance, but only if the total distribution is less than $70,000. Where more than one recipient receives a distribution, the same election as to the manner in which the distribution is to be taxed need not be made by all of the recipients. Each recipient is free to determine the tax treatment (i.e., capital gains for the pre-1974 portion) which is best for him or her.

Example 10. Warren Brown elected to have benefits payable under a qualified plan at the rate of $1,000 a month, with any balance remaining in his account on his death payable in lump sum to his children, Adam and Lawrence. Warren died when there was $40,000 left in his account, and each child received $20,000. The lump sum distribution is eligible for the special tax treatment.

Aid in Calculating the Lump Sum Income Tax

An employee or other recipient of a lump sum distribution will receive a form 1099R from the employer or the plan which will list the total amount of the distribution, the portion (if any) that qualified for capital gains treatment, and the portion which is eligible for 10-year income averaging.

If a recipient of a lump sum distribution does not elect the special 10-year income averaging or capital gains tax treatment, the distribution will be subject to tax in the same way as a periodic distribution would be taxed. The election to choose 10-year income averaging (or long-term capital gains treatment, where applicable) is made by completing form 4972 and attaching it to the recipient's tax return for the year in which the distribution is received. If the distribution is made to multiple recipients, form 5544 is used by the recipient.

Loss of Estate Tax Exclusion

Whenever the special income tax treatment (10-year income averaging and/or capital gains treatment) is elected with respect to a lump sum distribution, the estate tax exclusion is lost. Therefore, in the case of large distributions from pension or profit sharing plans, you or your tax advisor must carefully calculate whether the overall best advantage is obtained by choosing to receive your benefits in the form of a lump sum distribution, thereby forfeiting the estate tax exclusion, or whether a better result would be obtained by electing to have distributions made in installments over a long period of time, giving up the favorable income tax treatment but retaining the estate tax exclusion.

Marital Deduction

Beginning in 1982, the Federal estate tax rules were changed to increase the maximum marital deduction for bequests to a spouse from 50% to 100% of the estate. For small and moderate sized estates this change offsets the loss of the estate tax exclusion and permits the special income tax treatments to be elected, where it formerly was undesirable. In the case of larger estates the choice between the election of favorable income and estate tax treatment is frequently so complicated that it is necessary to obtain professional advice in order to make a fully informed decision.

ROLLOVERS

As discussed in Chapter 4, an employee who receives a lump sum distribution from a qualified pension or profit sharing plan may postpone taxation of the distribution by rolling it over within 60 days after he or she receives it. The rollover may be made into an individual retirement account or into the qualified plan of a subsequent employer (if that plan authorizes rollover contributions). A number of requirements for 10-year income averaging are inapplicable to rollovers:

1. The employee need not have been a participant for a five-year period.
2. The rules concerning aggregation of distributions from more than one plan are inapplicable.
3. It is immaterial whether the employee had previously elected 10-year income averaging within the last 6 years or after he or she reached age 59½.
4. If the distribution results from the termination of the plan, it is immaterial whether he or she terminated employment.

Example 11. Fred Lyons receives a lump sum distribution of $75,000 from the Acme Products pension plan. If he elects to forego the favorable 10-year income averaging or long term capital gains treatment, he may roll over the distribution into an individual retirement account within 60 days after he receives it.

A recipient of a distribution which qualifies for rollover treatment may elect to roll over all or a *portion* of the distribution. The portion which is not rolled over will not be eligible for the favorable 10-year income averaging or capital gains treatment but will be subject to tax as ordinary income. If a distribution from a pension plan consists of securities or other property, the securities or other property may be rolled over or sold and the cash proceeds (or any portion thereof) may instead be rolled over.

Spousal Rollovers

If a death benefit is payable from a qualified plan to an employee's spouse, the spouse has the same rollover privilege as did the employee. However, neither the estate of the employee nor any recipient of a lump sum death benefit distribution who is not a spouse may roll it over into an individual retirement account.

Subsequent Rollovers

A distribution which is rolled over from a qualified plan to an individual retirement account may subsequently be rolled over to another individual retirement account without subjecting the transferred amount to tax. Distributions may also be rolled over from one individual retirement account to another on a tax-free basis provided that subsequent rollovers may not be made more frequently than at one-year intervals. Tax free rollovers may also be made from one qualified plan directly to another qualified plan or from an individual retirement account to another qualified plan.

Example 12. Peter Martin received a lump sum distribution of $100,000 from the ABC Profit Sharing plan and rolled it over into an individual retirement account within 60 days after he received it. He then rolled it over into a second individual account six months later. The one year waiting period was inapplicable since the first rollover was from a qualified profit sharing plan rather than from an IRA.

One year after the date of the first rollover he became dissatisfied with the manner in which his monies were invested. The individual retirement account had been maintained by a savings bank and he thought he could do better if it were rolled over into an individual retirement account maintained by a brokerage firm and invested in shares of stock. Therefore, Martin rolled over the balance of his account in the savings bank's individual retirement account into an individual retirement account maintained by a brokerage house. Martin did not subject his distribution to tax by virtue of transferring it.

Three months later, Martin's new employer amended its profit sharing plan to allow participants in that plan to roll-over amounts accumulated under any prior employer's qualified plan. He thereupon rolled over the balance in his individual retirement account into his new employer's profit sharing plan without subjecting the balance to income tax. The one year waiting period was inapplicable since the roll-over was to a profit sharing plan rather than to an IRA.

Taxation of Amounts Rolled Over into Individual Retirement Accounts

An individual retirement account is a tax exempt entity. Interest, dividends and capital gains earned on funds held in an individual retirement account are not subject to tax. The depositor of an individual retirement account is, however, subject to tax under *ordinary* tax rules on amounts withdrawn from the account in the year in which the withdrawal is made. *This means that the right to elect favorable income tax treatment is permanently lost when distributions are rolled over.* However, there is a special IRA estate tax exclusion which will become available.

Because individual retirement accounts, as the name implies, are intended to accumulate funds for retirement, withdrawals must be made only at specified times and rates (which were discussed in Chapter 4). Otherwise, special penalty taxes are imposed. These penalties are imposed if withdrawals are made prior to the date on which the depositor has attained age 59½ unless the depositor is disabled. From the time the depositor to an individual retirement account reaches the age of 59½ years until he or she reaches 70½ years, there is full discretion to make any withdrawals from the individual retirement account. The depositor will be taxed only on the withdrawals actually made. In the meantime, the amounts not withdrawn continue to build up tax free.

Beginning with the taxable year in which the depositor of the individual retirement account attains the age of 70½ years, the law requires that minimum distributions be made over a period not exceeding the depositor's life expectancy, or, if the depositor is married, the joint life expectancy of the depositor and his or her spouse, as discussed in Chapter 4.

Life expectancies used in calculating the minimum distributions are determined in accordance with tables published by the Internal Revenue Service.

> *Example 13.* James Jones made a rollover contribution of $100,000 into an individual retirement account maintained by the Fidelity Savings Bank when he was 58 years old. The funds accumulated with interest so that when he reached 70½ years the balance in the individual retirement account was $200,000. At that time, Jones' wife, Sarah, was 66 years old.
>
> The joint life and last survivor expectancy of Jones and his wife, determined in the taxable year in which Jones attained age 70½, is 20 years. Therefore, one-twentieth of the $200,000 balance in the individual retirement account, or $10,000 must be distributed in that taxable year. In the next year, one-nineteenth of the balance at the beginning of the second year must be distributed, and so on.

It should be noted that the amount of the annual distribution will probably increase each year since the interest rate (probably around 12 percent) which can be obtained on the balance in the IRA exceeds the percentage required to be distributed in the early years (i.e., 1/20 or 5 percent in year one, 1/19 or 5.26 percent in year two, etc.).

If the depositor to the individual retirement account takes out more than required in a particular year, he or she will be required to withdraw correspondingly less in future years.

If amounts are withdrawn from an individual retirement account over a period certain, and both the employee and his or her spouse die prior to the end of the period certain, the remaining payments may be made to contingent beneficiaries during the balance of the period certain.

If the depositor to the individual retirement account dies before payments have commenced, the balance in the individual retirement account must be fully distributed within 5 years after his or her death. Alternatively, within this 5-year period, the balance in the individual retirement account may be used to provide immediate annuities for the beneficiary or beneficiaries of the depositor to the individual retirement account. This rule does not apply if period certain payments were begun prior to death.

Although the rules applicable to the required minimum distributions from individual retirement accounts have been simplified here, they are quite complex and there are a number of gaps in the regulations published by the Internal Revenue Service. Accordingly, it is advisable to obtain legal advice if the amounts involved are substantial.

If the depositor to an individual retirement account fails to withdraw at least the minimum amount required after he or she attains the age of 70½, a penalty equal to 50 percent of the difference between the amount required to be withdrawn and the amount actually withdrawn is imposed. However, if the person making the withdrawal can show that failure to withdraw the required amount was due to a good faith error,—such as the result of incorrect advice—the Internal Revenue Service has the discretion to waive the penalty.

IRA Estate Tax Exclusion

The balance in the account of a depositor to an individual

retirement account on his or her death is excluded from the depositor's estate if that balance is payable to his or her spouse or other beneficiary over a period of at least 36 months in relatively equal installments. In addition, no more than 40 percent of the balance in the individual retirement account at the time of the depositor's death may be payable in any single year if there is a desire to take advantage of the estate tax exclusion.

SPECIAL SITUATIONS

Nondeductible Employee Contributions

This discussion of the taxation of distributions from qualified plans has, until now, assumed that the entire distribution is derived from employer contributions, which is usually the case. There are, however, many plans which provide for voluntary or required employee contributions.

Employee contributions, whether voluntary or compulsory, may be recovered tax free when received in a distribution since they are not deductible when contributed, i.e., they have already been subject to tax. Often plans permit withdrawal of voluntary contributions in a lump sum upon termination of employment or even while employed. However, when a distribution is made in periodic installments, employee contributions which are not withdrawn prior to the commencement of the distribution are generally recovered proportionately as the payments are made.

> *Example 14.* Frank Jones elected to receive a distribution from a qualified plan in equal annual installments over a 10-year period. He contributed $10,000 to the plan while employed. One thousand dollars of each installment is deemed a return of his own contributions and will not be subject to tax.

In the case of a pension plan where benefits are payable in the form of a life annuity—that is, over the employee's life or over the lives of the employee and his or her spouse—the return of the employee's own contributions is calculated in accordance with life expectancy tables published by the Internal Revenue Service.

There is a special rule applicable to the recovery of an employee's own contributions under a qualified plan. If the aggregate of the distributions which an employee is expected to receive within the three years following his or her retirement exceeds the sum or his or her own contributions to the plan, then all of the initial payments made by the plan are considered the return of the employee's own contributions. This means that they are tax free to him or her until all of these contributions have been recovered. Thereafter, all of the payments are fully taxable.

> *Example 15.* Samuel Barber retired under his employer's pension plan and elected to receive a pension of $500 a month for the balance of his life. He had contributed $12,000 to the plan. Since he is expected to receive $12,000 during the two years following his retirement, the first $12,000 of pension payments will be tax free to him. The remaining payments will be fully taxable.

If the employee dies before he or she receives all employee contributions made to the plan, that employee's estate does not receive any sort of a deduction for the unrecovered payments. Similarly, if the employee lives longer than his or her life expectancy and the special three-year rule is not applicable, he or she may recover tax free more than the amount of his or her own contributions. A portion of each contribution will continue to be tax free.

In the case of a lump sum distribution from a qualified plan, the portion of the distribution consisting of the employee's own nondeductible contribution will not be subject to tax, and may therefore not be rolled over into an individual retirement account.

Deductible Employee Contributions

As discussed in Chapter 4, a retirement plan may permit employees to make voluntary deductible contributions of up to $2,000 per year, beginning in 1982. These contributions, together with any accumulated income attributable thereto are subject to the same rules as those governing the taxation of distributions from IRAs. These rules are discussed at length in Chapter 4. You should note that the rules governing the taxation of distributions consisting of or funded by employer contributions, and distributions of nondeductible employee contributions are not affected by the simultaneous distribution of all or a portion of the balance in an employee's deductible voluntary contribution account.

Annuity Contracts

Occasionally, a plan provides that on termination of employment an employee will receive a nontransferable annuity contract from an insurance company which will then pay the benefits to which he or she is entitled. The recipient of such an annuity contract is not taxed upon receipt of the annuity contract. Instead, he or she is subject to tax in the year of payment on the payments actually received under that contract. If the contract is surrendered, the cash proceeds are subject to tax.

You should note that the rule that an employee is not taxed upon receipt of a nontransferable annuity contract is applicable only to annuity contracts received under a qualified plan. An employee who receives a nontransferable annuity contract directly from an employer and not as part of a qualified plan is subject to immediate tax on the value of that annuity contract.

An employee who receives a lump sum distribution from a qualified plan consisting in part of cash and in part of a nontransferable annuity contract may elect the favorable 10-year income averaging and capital gain tax treatment with respect to the cash received but will not pay tax on the annuity contract until benefits are received under the contract. At that time, those benefits will be subject to tax as ordinary income.

If favorable 10-year income averaging treatment is elected in a situation where a combination of cash and a nontransferable annuity contract is distributed, the tax is first calculated on the basis of the combined value of the annuity contract and the cash, and then multiplied by the percentage of the distribution which constitutes the cash.

> *Example 16.* Adam Roberts receives a lump sum distribution from the Acme Widget profit sharing plan consisting of $40,000 in cash and an annuity contract worth $60,000. The

tax using the 10-year income averaging is calculated on the distribution of $100,000 and 40 percent of that amount (the portion of the distribution represented by the cash) will constitute the immediate tax liability. When payments are made under the annuity contract, they will be taxable to the recipient as ordinary income.

Employer Securities

Distributions from qualified plans occasionally consist in whole or in part of shares of stock of the employer sponsoring the plan. This is especially common in the case of leveraged employee stock ownership plans, tax credit ESOPs (TRASOPs) or other eligible individual account plans.

If a lump sum distribution from a qualified plan consists in whole or in part of employer securities, the unrealized appreciation in the employer securities is not subject to tax until the securities are sold.

Example 17. Annette Rand receives an ESOP distribution of 1,000 shares of Fultran Computer Corporation worth $100,000. These shares were acquired by the trust for only $20,000. Rand will pay a tax only on the $20,000 which represents the cost of the shares to the trust. You will recall that under the rules applicable to lump sum distributions, $10,000 of this $20,000 distribution is exempt as a minimum distribution allowance and the remaining $10,000 is subject to tax under the 10-year income averaging rules.

The remaining $80,000 of unrealized appreciation will not be subject to tax until the shares are sold. At that time, the difference between the selling price and the cost of the shares ($20,000) will be subject to tax as a long-term capital gain. Of course, at that time the appreciation may be more or less than $80,000, or, in fact, the selling price may be less than $20,000.

In some cases, distributions consisting in whole or in part of employer securities are made in installments rather than in a lump sum. In such cases, only the portion of the appreciation in employer securities applicable to the employee's own contribution is received free from tax at the time the distribution is made.

STATE AND LOCAL TAXES

This chapter has been confined to the federal income and estate tax treatment of distributions from qualified plans. Many plan distributions are, in addition, subject to state and local tax.

Local rules differ from state to state. Some states, such as New York, generally treat distributions from qualified plans in the same way as does the Internal Revenue Code. However, this is not always the case under state tax laws.

Additional problems may develop in situations where, for example, an employee worked in state A all of his or her life and earned a pension while working for an employer located there, and then retired and went to live in state B and collected a pension while a resident of the latter state. It sometimes happens under those circumstances that both state A and state B take the position that the pensions are taxable in that state (in state A because the pension was earned there and in state B because the pension was received there). A recipient of pension benefits under these circumstances should get professional advice as to his or her liabilities.

Part Two

PLANNING ALTERNATIVES

Chapter 12

BEGINNING A NEW JOB

The significance to you of a prospective employer's retirement plans depends almost entirely on your age at the time you consider accepting a position with a new employer. If this is your first job right out of school, you will be primarily interested in establishing a successful career, rather than qualifying for a pension thirty or forty years down the road. On the other hand, if your new job represents a mid-career change in employment, or if you have two or more job offers presenting equal opportunities for current compensation and for advancement, your pension prospects become a real concern in deciding whether to accept a particular position. This chapter is arranged in the form of a checklist of pension factors to be considered by the employee beginning a new job. However, the first step in evaluating any employee benefit package is to analyze available summary plan descriptions.

Summary Plan Descriptions

As indicated in Chapter 10, an employer is required to furnish you with a summary plan description (*SPD*) of each plan which it maintains within 90 days after you first participate in that plan. Most employers distribute summary plan descriptions to new employees automatically upon employment. Obviously, this will be too late for preemployment retirement planning. However, most employers will honor preemployment requests by job applicants for summary plan descriptions so that the applicants can review the adequacy of the plans and make requests for relevant supplementary data (such as the past record of contributions under a discretionary profit-sharing plan) prior to making a decision as to whether to accept a position. You should not hesitate to request copies of all summary plan descriptions of your prospective employer if the adequacy of its retirement plans will be a factor in your decision. In light of the long delay between the time a plan modification becomes effective and the date at which it must be described in the SPD, you should also remember to ask if there have been any plan amendments which are not yet reflected in the SPD.

CONCERNS OF THE YOUNGER EMPLOYEE

Contributory Plan Features

Check to see whether your new employer maintains plans which permit matched employee contributions or unmatched voluntary contributions. As discussed in Chapter 3, thrift plans typically provide that employees may contribute from 1 to 6 percent of compensation which is matched by the employer in some fixed proportion—such as 25 or 50 percent. In addition, or alternatively, some retirement plans permit employees to contribute up to 10 percent of compensation which is not matched by the employer. These voluntary contributions are maintained and invested as part of a separate fund and often earn a favorable rate of return.

If your prospective employer's plan provides that your contribution will be matched, it is a good deal and you should probably join the plan even if you do not anticipate remaining on the job for any appreciable length of time. Even if your prospective employer's plan does not provide for such matching, you may still want to sign up for the maximum voluntary contributions which you can afford to make. Voluntary contributions constitute a type of "forced" savings. They therefore serve an important function quite aside from their tax shelter benefits.

As pointed out in Chapter 3, most employee contributions (even if matched) are not deductible. However, the income earned on such contributions is not subject to tax until withdrawn from the plan. At that time, the income earned on your contributions, if withdrawn in a lump sum by reason of termination of employment or after age 59½, is likely to be eligible for the favorable 10-year income averaging discussed in Chapter 11. In any event, you can roll over the income earned on your contributions (and any related employer contributions plus their income) into an individual retirement account and defer all tax until you actually withdraw and use the funds. Withdrawals must begin in the taxable year in which you reach age 70½ but may be spread out ratably over many years thereafter.

Contributions to IRA Compared to Participation in a Thrift Plan

As indicated in Chapter 4, active participants in qualified retirement plans may make deductible annual contributions to an IRA of up to $2,000 beginning in 1982.

Most younger employees, having just embarked on their careers, are earning relatively small salaries compared to what they expect to receive when they achieve more senior positions. Many of them will not be able to afford to make both maximum IRA contributions and maximum nondeductible voluntary contributions to their employers' thrift plans in which they are eligible to participate. These employees are confronted with the difficult choice of which program is most beneficial to them.

In general, if you do not expect to remain with your employer long enough to vest in your employer's matching contributions you are better off making deductible contributions to an IRA than participating in a contributory thrift plan. If you do expect to vest in your employer's matching contributions, you are probably better off participating in the thrift plan if the matching contributions are at the rate of about 50%. This is because your employer's matching contribution to the thrift plan is worth about as much as your tax deductions for contributions to the IRA and you have more flexibility in withdrawing your nondeductible contributions to the thrift plan.

> *Example 1.* Joseph Katz began working for the Swift Trucking Company in 1982. Swift maintains a thrift plan under which all employees are eligible, and all employee contributions up to 6% of salary are matched at the rate of 50%, and all employer contributions are fully vested.
>
> Katz earned $20,000 in 1982. If he contributes $1,000 to the thrift plan, (5% of his salary) his employer will add

$500. If he contributes $1,500 to an IRA, the tax deduction will result in a $500 reduction in his federal income tax liability.

Katz is better off participating in the thrift plan, since he can withdraw his own voluntary contribution free of tax under the terms of the plan, whereas, had he contributed $1,500 to the IRA, he could not withdraw it until age 59½ without paying a 10% penalty, in addition to being subject to federal income tax on the amount withdrawn.

Contributions to IRA Compared to Participation in a Cash or Deferred Plan

If you are eligible to participate in a cash or deferred plan under which you may withdraw a certain portion of the amount allocated to your account, and you can't afford both to defer the withdrawable amount and to make a contribution to an IRA, you generally would be better off leaving the money in the plan. Here the comparison is straightforward. In both cases the amount is not subject to tax but whereas amounts contributed to an IRA cannot be withdrawn without penalty until age 59½ (or prior disability), amounts left in cash or deferred plan may be withdrawn without penalty in the event of hardship, or upon termination of service. Moreover lump sum distributions from a cash or deferred plan are usually eligible for the special 10 year income averaging provision, while distributions from an IRA are not eligible for this advantageous treatment.

Beneficiary Designations

Many retirement plans provide preretirement death benefits for participants who die while in active employment. When you become eligible to participate in such a plan (or eligible for the death benefit, if this is later), you should execute a beneficiary designation indicating who is to receive the benefits payable by reason of your death and the form (lump sum, installments or other available death benefit option) in which such benefits are to be paid. Since many plans provide that your benefit will be paid in a lump sum to your estate if you have made no other election, you risk inadvertent inclusion of the death benefit in your estate if you fail to file a designation.

Segregated Accounts and Investment Funds

Some thrift or profit sharing plans permit you to designate the manner in which the funds in your account are to be invested. Typically, such plans allow you to choose whether your funds will be invested in a fixed income account guaranteed by an insurance company or in one or more common stock or bond funds. Some plans will even allow investment of the funds in a guaranteed savings bank account. If you are offered a number of funds for investment, you should make the choice carefully and review the investment performance and prospectuses of each of these funds prior to the deadline for making an investment designation so that the funds can continue to be invested most productively in light of your individual planning goals.

CHANGING YOUR JOB

If you are considering whether to change your job, you will of course wish to take into account the factors listed in the previous section. However, since you will be giving up rights under your present employer's retirement plans there are a number of new considerations which come into play.

Will You Forfeit Benefits?

You have by now undoubtedly become familiar with your current employer's retirement plans. You should carefully review these plans to determine what benefits you will forfeit by leaving your present position.

If you are covered by a profit sharing or thrift plan, or by an ESOP, the plan will probably provide that you will not receive an allocation of your employer's contribution in the year in which you leave your job, unless you are employed on the last day of the plan year. Assume, for example, that your employer's plan keeps its records on the calendar year basis. If you left your job on December 15th, you could lose your share of an entire year's contribution, which could be as much as 10 or 15 percent of your salary. If this is the case, you obviously should not leave until January.

You should also check to see whether by holding on to your present job for a relatively short period of time you could accumulate a meaningful additional vested interest.

For example, suppose you have been employed for 9½ years by an employer maintaining a pension plan that provides for full vesting upon the completion of 10 years of employment. Unless your prospective new position is extremely desirable or your new employer agrees to compensate you for the loss of pension benefits, you would be better advised to defer leaving your current job until after you have completed 10 years of service.

If you are covered under a profit sharing, thrift plan, or other defined contribution plan (which typically contain graduated vesting schedules) and are not yet fully vested, chances are you will also earn an additional incremental vested interest if you remain in your current position until after the end of the current plan year i.e., you may become 30 percent vested at the end of the year if you were 20 percent vested at the end of the previous year. You should carefully review your employer's plan to determine whether this is the case.

Effect of a Job Change on Your Aggregate Retirement Benefit

If you have completed a substantial number of years of employment with your current employer, you should consider the effect of switching jobs on the total pension you are likely to accumulate under the plans of both your present and your new employer at the time you reach retirement age. If you are more than 60 years old, you should first check carefully to see whether you are older than the maximum age for eligibility in the new plan. However, even if you are younger than the maximum age for plan participation you should note that job switching among nonaffiliated employers usually reduces total benefits.

Suppose, for example, that you are 40 years old and have completed 15 years of service with your present employer. You are fully vested in the pension which you have accrued to date. Of course, you will begin earning vesting credit under your new plan *only* from your date of employment. This means that you may well have to complete another ten years of service with your new employer in order to become vested in your second benefit.

It is important to note that even if your prospective employer maintains a pension plan which is identical to that of your present employer and you also become vested under that pension plan, you will probably wind up with a combined pension from the two employers which is substantially less than if you had continued on your present job.

This occurs because you may not complete a "full" period of service under either plan and thus will not have earned the benefit the employer has set as a replacement ratio goal for long term employees. For example, employers usually require 25 or 30 years of service to earn a full benefit and adopt a plan benefit formula with the 25 or 30 year employee in mind. Although you may have worked 25 to 30 years for both employers (combined), you will receive proportionately reduced benefits under both plans in the situation described above. (See Chapter 5 on Qualifying for Benefits for a more detailed discussion of this topic.)

Of course, pension benefits are not everything and your new position may have advantages over your current one which more than compensate for any lost pension credits. But all relevant factors should be taken into account before the decision is reached.

Negotiating for Special Benefits

Senior executives and other key employees are sometimes able to negotiate special pension benefits from prospective employers to compensate for benefits which they lost by reason of having resigned from their prior jobs. Your ability to negotiate such protection will depend entirely on how valuable you are to your prospective employer.

There are a number of ways to negotiate special pension protection. However, the most common method of compensating a transferee for the loss of pension benefits is for the new employer to provide him or her directly with a supplemental (nonqualified) pension. The supplement equals the difference between the pension which the transferee would have earned under the new employer's pension plan had the transferee been covered under that plan when the transferee began to work for the previous employer reduced by sum of the pension which the transferee will actually receive from the current employer upon attaining retirement age and the pension which he or she will actually receive from the new employer's pension plan at that time. Sometimes the new employer provides only the difference between what the transferee would have gotten under the prior employer's plan had he or she remained with that employer and the benefit earned by the transferee under the new employer's plan.

> *Example 1.* Allen Brown was employed by the ABC Corporation at age 25. He left the ABC Corporation to join the XYZ Corporation at age 40.
>
> The ABC Corporation pension plan provides a benefit equal to 1½ percent compensation for each year of employment multiplied by an employee's average compensation for the five years preceding termination of employment. XYZ Corporation maintains a similar plan except that the accrual rate is 2 percent a year.
>
> Assume Allen's average compensation between ages 35 and 40 is $20,000. He therefore will receive a pension beginning at age 65 from the ABC pension plan of $4,500 per year. Assume that Allen's compensation during the years 60 to 65 with XYZ Corporation is $50,000. Since he will have completed 20 years of service with XYZ Corporation if he remains with XYZ until age 65, he will be entitled to a pension of $20,000 from the XYZ Corporation pension plan.
>
> In order to induce him to join XYZ Corporation, XYZ agreed to pay Allen at age 65 an amount equal to the difference between the pension which he would have earned under that plan if he had begun working for XYZ Corporation at age 25 (when he started working for ABC Corporation) and his actual combined ABC and XYZ pension. If he had worked for XYZ Corporation for 40 years, he would have earned a pension of 80 percent of his $50,000 average final compensation, or $40,000. Since he will be receiving a total benefit of $24,500 ($20,000 from the XYZ Corporation pension plan and $4,500 from the ABC Corporation pension plan), XYZ Corporation will pay Allen an additional $15,500 per year. However, it is important to note that the supplemental payments to Allen will not qualify for the favorable tax

treatment described in Chapter 11, since they are not made through a qualified plan. Allen will not be fully compensated for the loss of benefits unless he is also reimbursed for any extra tax paid on benefits provided outside the qualified plans.

Transferring to Divisions or Subsidiaries

Occasionally an employee of a large corporation is offered an opportunity to transfer to a different division of that company either in the United States or abroad. If the new position is with a division which is not covered under the same plan, problems may arise which are similar to those which result when an employee leaves to take the position with an unrelated employer. However, your employer's plan by law must require that if you accept a transfer of employment to a division or subsidiary of an employer which is not covered by the same pension plan, service with that division or subsidiary will be recognized for the purpose of *vesting* in the benefit which you accrued prior to the transfer. Similarly, service with your present division or subsidiary will count for the purpose of determining vesting under the pension plans maintained by the division or subsidiary to which you are being transferred. That is, for vesting and eligibility purposes, you will be treated as if you had always been covered under one plan of a single employer.

Nevertheless, it may be that the aggregate of the benefits that you will accrue under the plans maintained by the two divisions will be less than that which you would have accrued if you had spent your entire working life in a single division, because service for *benefit accrual* purposes will be calculated as if you worked for two unrelated employers. Where this occurs an employer will typically agree to provide directly the difference in those benefits outside of the qualified plans. However, as previously noted, the supplement will not be eligible for preferential tax treatment.

Should You Elect to Receive an Immediate Payment?

If you have accumulated a vested benefit under your present employer's pension or profit sharing plan, you may have the choice of receiving your accrued benefit at the time you leave your current position or of postponing payment until you reach retirement age. This choice requires careful calculation on your part since the correct decision may substantially enhance the value of your benefits.

In the case of a defined contribution plan such as a thrift or profit sharing plan, it is generally best to accept a lump sum distribution of your entire account balance and roll it over into an individual retirement account. As previously discussed, if a rollover is made, tax on the distribution will be postponed, and the amount rolled over will continue to accumulate free of tax until withdrawn from the IRA many years later.

Many plans permit a participant to roll distributions received from a prior employer's plan directly over into the new employer's trust fund. If you are considering changing jobs, you should inquire whether your prospective employer's plans contain this feature. If you do have the choice of rolling a distribution from your current employer's plan over into that of your prospective employer, you should try to calculate whether you are likely to receive a better investment return from an individual retirement account or under your new employer's retirement plan by looking at the prior investment record of the plan and trust and comparing it with that of the IRA.

Although lump sum distributions are typically provided by defined contribution plans, many defined benefit pension plans also give a terminating participant the option of taking a lump sum distribution at the time he or she leaves the current position or of receiving a pension upon reaching retirement age. However, in order to determine which alternative produces the better result in the case of a defined benefit plan, you must become familiar with the actuarial factors which the defined benefit pension plan uses in calculating the value of a lump sum distribution. This topic is more fully discussed in Chapter 14 dealing with the considerations affecting the selection of an option at normal retirement age. However, it is illustrated in simplified form in Example 2.

> *Example 2.* Walter Weldon left the employ of the Wearever Washing Machine Corporation at the age of 45 years after having completed 20 years of service. He has been told that he has the choice of either receiving a lump sum of $34,000 or a pension of $1,000 per month beginning at age 65.

Weldon determines that if he establishes an individual retirement account at the Easy Money Brokerage House and invests the lump sum in high-grade bonds currently yielding well in excess of 9 percent, at age 65 the lump sum will amount to $190,000. On this basis, he could draw down annual interest which is larger than the pension he was told he would get if he left the lump sum with the company, and still preserve the principal. He should elect to receive an immediate distribution.

Distributions from ESOPs

Recipients should determine whether to insist upon a distribution wholly in employer securities. They should also decide whether to retain their shares with an eye towards future growth or exercise their statutory put option and resell the shares to the plan or the employer. One of the factors entering this decision is the price which the employer or the plan will pay to repurchase the shares.

Although ERISA does not require that these rights be given to participants in "ordinary" eligible individual account plans, many employers will voluntarily also provide put options to participants in those plans. The factors to be weighed in deciding whether to exercise the option are the same as under a leveraged or other ESOP.

Reemployment with a Former Employer

If you are covered by a defined contribution plan and should leave your current position but thereafter are rehired by your present employer, you may be able to qualify to have the benefits and service credit which you forfeited when you left your position reinstated by repaying before you incur a break in service the amounts that were distributed to you at the time you left your job. See discussion of breaks in service in Chapter 5.

However, even if you have not incurred a break in service, restoration of credit is possible only if you make the repayment within two years after your date of reemployment.

Example 3. Ruth Garrett receives a $4,000 distribution from the Spotless Cleaning Corp. profit sharing plan immediately upon her termination of employment in a year in which she has already completed 1,000 hours of service. Since she was only 40 percent vested at the end of the year, the remaining $6,000 in her account was forfeited on the last day of the plan year in which she resigned and allocated to the accounts of the remaining participants.

Six months later, but prior to the time she had incurred a break in service, Garrett was reemployed by Spotless. The Spotless plan must provide that the $6,000 which was forfeited from Garrett's account will be restored if Garrett repays the $4,000 distribution to the plan within two years of her reemployment (or prior to a break in service, if this would be earlier).

The amount restored will be unadjusted for trust fund investment performance after the date of distribution. This means that $6,000 must be restored to Garrett's account regardless of whether it would have been worth $5,000 or $7,000 as of the date of restoration, assuming that it had shared the fund's investment experience.

Plans which delay all forfeitures until participants have incurred a break in service do not need to provide for the buyback arrangement illustrated in Example 3. Defined benefit plans rarely contain buyback features.

Even if you return to your former employer too late to have the choice of repaying amounts distributed to you and thereby becoming reinstated in benefits which you had previously forfeited, or if your plan does not contain the buyback feature, you may still be entitled to credit for your prior period of service with your employer for the purpose of eligibility to participate in the retirement plans which it maintains and for the purpose of being vested in future benefits. As discussed more fully in Chapter 5, you must be credited upon reemployment with all prior service with your current employer for the purpose of eligibility and vesting if you had a vested interest in your employer's retirement plans at the time you terminated your employment. If you did not have such a vested interest but the period of your prior employment was longer than the period between the time you quit your job and the time you returned, your prior period of service must also be restored.

Prior service may be ignored only if you were not vested and the period of your break in service was longer than the pre-break period of service.

If you are covered under a defined benefit plan and are reemployed after having received a lump sum distribution, you may be entitled to have prior service for benefit accrual restored without making a repayment if your plan offsets the actuarial equivalent of the benefits already received against your total benefit payable at retirement.

> *Example 4.* Jack Landow terminated employment with the Sunspot Solar Heating Company in 1978 at age 50 after having completed 10 years of service with Sunspot and becoming vested under the Sunspot Pension Plan. Landow was permitted to receive an immediate lump sum payment of $20,000 equal to the actuarial equivalent of his accrued benefit at termination. (See Chapter 13, Actuarial Reductions.)
>
> Nine months later, Landow returned to Sunspot. The Sunspot plan provides that Landow's 10 prior years of service will be recognized automatically for all purposes upon his reemployment. However, in order to prevent Landow from receiving a double payment based upon his pretermination service, the $20,000 received by him plus 6 percent interest which it would have earned in the plan will be deducted from the lump sum value of the benefit payable to him at normal retirement age. If the lump sum value of this benefit were $240,000, for example, only $192,000–or 240,000 minus 48,000 (48,000 = 20,000 plus 6 percent interest over 15 years) – would be paid out (or used to calculate an actuarially equivalent option) at Landow's normal retirement age.

Chapter 13

EARLY RETIREMENT

Most qualified plans permit participants to retire or collect benefits prior to attaining the plan's normal retirement age (generally age 65), a practice which is known as early retirement. This chapter serves as a checklist of factors to be weighed by the employee contemplating whether to retire early. There are two particularly significant factors which must be evaluated when contemplating early retirement—the adequacy of early retirement income and the availability or loss of death benefit protection.

DEFINED BENEFIT PLANS

What Is the Plans' Early Retirement Age?

The most common age at which early retirement is permitted is age 55. Many plans permit early retirement only upon reaching age 60, and a few only at age 62. However, it is rare for a plan to permit early retirement based upon age alone. The service period required ranges from 10 to 25 years. The most common plan requirement for early retirement is reaching age 55 and completing 10 years of service.

What If I Continue to Work?

Death Benefits Available to Employees Who Work Past Early Retirement Age

Most pension plans do not provide for vesting in the event of death. Thus, if a participant in a pension plan dies after having completed 10 years of service, but before reaching early retirement age, his or her spouse will not receive any benefits from the plan even though that participant would have been entitled to a vested benefit under the plan if he or she had resigned rather than died. While this seems unfair, there is a historical reason why pension plans do not provide for vesting in the event of death–pension plans were established to provide retirement income to pensioners during their *lifetime*. In addition, most employers provide substantial death benefits through group insurance programs.

However, as explained in Chapter 5, pension plans are now required to allow participants who continue to work past early retirement age to elect or to make available automatic death benefit protection in the form of an early survivor annuity for their spouses after they reach early retirement age. The early survivor annuity must be at least 50 percent of the life annuity which would have been payable had the participant elected a qualified joint and survivor annuity and retired on the day preceding death. At this point, you may wish to refer to the discussion in Chapter 5 of the accompanying benefit reductions which may be imposed as a result of selecting an early survivor annuity election.

Should You Retire Early (Before Reaching Age 65)?

Will Retirement Income Be Adequate?

The early survivor annuity will be available if you do not elect to retire at the time you are first eligible to do so but, instead, continue to work, perhaps until you reach your normal retirement age. However, increasing numbers of plan participants do elect to retire early. Of course, many factors enter into the decision as to the age at which you will choose to retire. Among the factors generally considered are the degree of job satisfaction, other financial resources, and, if the employee is married and his or her spouse is also working, that spouse's retirement plans. Nevertheless, the availability of an adequate retirement income is almost always the determinative factor in deciding whether to retire early. Each participant contemplating early retirement should therefore request an individual statement indicating the dollar amount of his or her benefit.

An employee who is considering retirement must also decide the form in which he or she wishes to receive the pension. The choice of available forms of retirement benefits—called options—is fully discussed in the next chapter dealing with normal retirement. In most cases all of the options available at normal retirement age are also available at early retirement age. However, there are a number of special factors which must be considered at early retirement. In addition, there is one option—the Social Security Equalization Option—which is available only to early retirees.

Actuarial Reductions

Most pension plans provide that monthly benefits are actuarially reduced in the event of early retirement. This means that the monthly pension to which a participant is entitled will be reduced to compensate for the fact that it begins before the participant reaches normal retirement age and thus will be payable over a greater number of years than a benefit payable at and after age 65.

> *Example 1.* Alan Bradley is covered under the Universal Products pension plan, which provides a benefit equal to 2 percent of average compensation for the five year period preceding retirement multiplied by the number of complete years of credited service. Bradley is 55 years old, has completed 20 years of service, and his average compensation in the last 5 years was $30,000. He is therefore entitled to a pension of $1,000 per month beginning at age 65. (2 percent x 20 years equals 40 percent) x ($30,000) = $12,000 per year (or $1,000 per month). If Bradley elects to retire at age 55 and have his pension begin at that time, he will receive only $500 per month, since he will receive his pension for 10 years longer if he retires at age 55 rather than at age 65.

Most people who retire early elect to have their pensions begin immediately, since they need the money to pay current expenses. However, in some cases, employees retire early and then obtain a second job, perhaps earning a second pension with the new employer prior to finally retiring.

Usually, a person who chooses to retire early and move to another job does not elect to have the pension begin until he or she ceases to be actively employed. An employee who retires early and elects to postpone the commencement of a pension until normal retirement age can usually change his or her mind and elect to have the pension begin prior to normal retirement age if circumstances change because most plans do not limit employees to a choice between beginning to receive benefits at the early retirement date or the normal retirement date. The majority of plans permit them also to elect to begin receiving benefits as of the first day of any month in between those two dates. However, you should check to make sure that your plan does not impose a waiting period before your new election may become effective.

> *Example 2.* Assume in Example 1 above that Bradley elects not to have his pension begin when he retires at age 55 because he has found another job. At age 62, when he becomes eligible to receive Social Security benefits, he decides that he would like to move to Florida and play golf rather than continue to work. He is then entitled to receive a pension of $800 per month–less than the $1,000 per month to which he would have been entitled had his pension begun at age 65 but more than the $500 per month that he would have received had he decided to have his pension begin when he retired at age 55. Obviously, the closer Bradley is to age 65 at the time he elects to have his pension begin, the greater will be his monthly benefit. Like Social Security, Bradley's plan imposes a 20 percent reduction where benefits begin to be paid at age 62.

Calculation of Actuarially Equivalent Benefits

Even if two similarly situated (in terms of age, service, and compensation history) employees are eligible for early retirement under two plans with identical benefit formulas, both of which state that the early retirement benefits shall be the "actuarial equivalent" of the normal retirement benefit, those employees will not necessarily receive the same number of dollars per month. This is true whether they choose to receive payments in the normal form or under an option. The difference may occur because even though both benefits are being reduced to compensate for the same projected longer payout period, the actual reduction used will depend on the mortality and interest factors used by the plan's actuary to calculate the reduction.

In general, the older the mortality table used, the greater the reduction made to calculate early retirement benefits because life expectancies have been consistently increasing. Rather than using special tables which make exact actuarial reductions, some actuaries will reduce the benefit by a flat 1/15 for each of the first five years and 1/30 for each of the next five years, that the benefit commencement date of an employee precedes the normal retirement date. This formula produces a rough approximation of the result which would be obtained if an actuarial table were used—but it is much easier to understand and apply.

Finding Out About Your Plan's Reduction

Some plans and Summary Plan Descriptions expressly list the early retirement actuarial reductions. While at the moment there is no legal requirement that this be done, all plans will be required to list these factors by 1984. If the reductions are not mentioned in either document, they may be noted on your individual benefit statement. If you cannot find the reductions in any of these sources, you should not hesitate to discuss the question with your plan administrator.

Subsidized Early Retirement Benefits

Many employers offer subsidized early retirement pensions in order to induce their employees to retire early. If the early retirement pension is fully subsidized, this means that there is no reduction in the monthly benefit by reason of the fact that the pension begins prior to the time that the employee reaches age 65. In other cases, the pension is partially subsidized—this means that there is some reduction in the monthly pension by reason of its commencement prior to normal retirement age, but the reduction is less than the full amount called for actuarially.

> *Example 3.* Assume as in Example 1, that Bradley is entitled to a pension of $1,000 per month beginning at age 65. However, his plan provides that he is entitled to the same pension of $1,000 per month beginning at age 62. This is a fully subsidized early retirement benefit. If Bradley were instead entitled to receive $950 at age 62 (rather than the $800

resulting from a full actuarial reduction), the benefit would be only partially subsidized.

Virtually all plans which provide subsidized early retirement benefits list the manner in which the reductions are made. Otherwise, it would be impossible to calculate an early retiree's benefit. Therefore, it is possible to find out the amount of the subsidy by reading your plan or summary plan description or by asking your plan administrator to give you the amount of the subsidized benefit. The subsidized amount can then be compared with a benefit calculated using the 1/15 and 1/30 reductions to approximate the amount of the subsidy.

Obviously, an employee who wishes to retire prior to normal retirement age and who is entitled to a fully subsidized early retirement pension should not elect to postpone the commencement of his or her pension since he or she would lose the benefit of the entire subsidy in that case.

For the same reason, an employee who is entitled to a subsidized early retirement pension but who elects to continue to work until normal retirement age should view himself or herself as working for the difference between the sum of the nominal salary and any additional pension credits earned and the plan's subsidized pension which is being given up by not retiring.

> *Example 4.* Assume that Marsha Wilcox was earning $30,000 per year at age 62. She could have retired at age 62 and received a subsidized early retirement pension of $12,000 per year. Her company's plan bases benefits on an employee's compensation during his or her entire career. It provides a benefit of 2 percent of each year's compensation. In this situation, Wilcox's salary is really $18,000 per year plus the additional pension credit which she earns, since by continuing to work, she is giving up the pension of $12,000 per year.

Note, however, that by continuing to work an additional three years, Wilcox would earn a pension of an additional 6 percent (2 percent x 3 years). Moreover, if her plan were a final average pay plan and her salary in the five years preceding retirement at age 65 were to increase, her pension could be increased still further.

Death Protection for Early Retirees Who Defer Benefit Commencement

If an employee who is married retires early and elects to defer the commencement of his or her pension, and then dies prior to having received any pension benefits, that employee's spouse will be entitled to receive a survivor annuity which will generally be equal to 50 percent of the pension which the employee would have been entitled to receive had he or she elected to have the pension commence immediately before death on a joint and 50 percent survivor basis. This rule requires the "passing on" of any early retirement subsidy available to the employee—that is, the employer is legally required to pay the surviving spouse at least 50 percent of the subsidized benefit which would have been payable to the participant and may not pay 50 percent of a hypothetical actuarially reduced benefit if the plan provides for early retirement subsidies. However, if the employee had actually elected to have his or her pension payable pursuant to another option, the surviving spouse would be entitled to receive only the death benefit payable under the option that was elected rather than the survivor annuity. This subject is discussed more fully in the next chapter.

Social Security Equalization

There is one special option which is available *only* in the case of early retirement prior to age 62—the Social Security adjustment option, commonly called the Social Security equalization option.

As discussed in Chapter 7, Social Security benefits are not payable earlier than age 62. The goal of Social Security equalization is to provide a level aggregate monthly benefit from government sources and the employer. Ordinarily, an employee who retires prior to age 62 will receive a lower monthly income until his or her Social Security benefits begin and a higher combined income from the employer's pension plan and Social Security thereafter. This discourages employees from retiring prior to age 62. In order to overcome this disincentive, many plans offer an option under which an employee will receive a higher monthly pension from the date of his or her early retirement until reaching age 62 and a lower pension thereafter so that his or her monthly income before and after age 62 will remain approximately the same.

> *Example 5.* Arnold Blye intends to retire under the Reliable Products pension plan at age 60. He is entitled to a pension of $500 per month and he anticipates that at age 62 he will be entitled to a benefit from Social Security of $400 per month. Blye believes that with his savings he could live comfortably on $800–900 per month, the total of his pension and Social Security, though he would find it very difficult to live on only $500 per month for two years until his Social Security benefits begin. He therefore chooses the Social Security equalization option under which he will receive $850 per month from the Reliable pension plan for two years and $450 per month thereafter. Thus, Blye will receive income in the neighborhood of $850 per month for life: for the first two years solely from his employer's pension plan and thereafter from a combination of his employer's pension plan and from Social Security. However, since Social Security benefits now increase with cost of living, it is impossible to provide more than approximately equivalent benefits under the Social Security equalization option.

DEFINED CONTRIBUTION PLANS

In the case of defined contribution plans, early retirement is of very little significance. Most participants who are covered by both a defined contribution plan and a defined benefit plan (generally a profit sharing or thrift plan and a pension plan) are usually fully vested in their account balances by the time they reach early retirement age under their employer's pension plan, since defined contribution plans usually contain faster vesting schedules than defined benefit plans. Benefits under the defined contribution plan will generally be payable upon termination of employment either in a lump sum or in installments over a specified period. Since defined contribution plans usually provide for full vesting in the event of death, there is often no need even to worry about the availability of early survivor annuities. Where participants are given the choice of receiving benefits under a defined contribution plan either in a lump sum or in installments over a period of years, most participants choose the lump sum and either roll it over into an individual retirement account, thereby deferring income tax until actual withdrawal from the individual retirement account, or pay the tax on the lump sum distribution using the favorable income averaging described in Chapter 11.

Chapter 14

NORMAL RETIREMENT

DEFINED BENEFIT PLANS–CHECKLIST FOR THE RETIREE

The focal point of a defined benefit pension plan is the benefit available to an employee who retires at normal retirement age. All other benefits under the plan, such as the early retirement benefits which were discussed in the previous chapter and benefits payable on deferred retirement, which are discussed in the next chapter, are derived from the normal form of benefit. Even ancillary benefits such as death benefits are derived from the basic benefit payable at normal retirement age.

1. What Is the Plan's Normal Retirement Age?

Under most pension plans normal retirement age is defined as age 65. However, some plans require that the participant also complete a prescribed period of plan participation which may not exceed 10 years before he or she will be deemed to have attained normal retirement age. Attainment of normal retirement age is significant because ERISA requires all pension plans to provide for full vesting at normal retirement age. It is also the earliest age under most plans at which participants may retire and receive an immediate unreduced benefit.

The phrase "immediate unreduced benefit" is really a term of art. The feature that distinguishes normal retirement benefits from those payable at earlier or later ages is that a benefit payable at normal retirement age may not be actuarially reduced, as in the case of an early retirement benefit, nor may the value of the benefit be decreased on account of continued service, as in the case of a deferred retirement benefit which is not increased actuarially but is frozen at age 65. Therefore, the effect of a requirement that a specified period of participation be completed before normal retirement age is attained is to lengthen the period over which benefits may remain unvested and over which the accrued benefit may be reduced.

> *Example 1.* Melinda Graham has been a participant in the Festive Catering Corporation pension plan for four years. The Festive Plan has a 10 year cliff vesting schedule and defines normal retirement age as a participant's 65th birthday. Graham was 59 when she began working for Festive and is now 64. If she remains employed by Festive, Graham will be eligible to receive an immediate unreduced pension on her 65th birthday, even though she will not have completed 10 years of service at that time.

> *Example 2.* Arthur Willis became a participant in the Illuminated Lighting Corporation pension plan at age 61. His younger brother Jack became a participant in the plan on the same day, but at age 50. The Illuminated plan has 10 year cliff vesting and defines normal retirement age as *the later of* attainment of age 65 or the tenth anniversary of the commencement of plan participation. There are no early retirement benefits. Under the plan (assuming that Arthur and Jack both remain employed by Illuminated) Jack will be eligible to receive an immediate pension on his 65th birthday. However, Arthur must wait until he is 71 (the tenth anniversary of his commencement of plan participation) in order to receive an immediate pension.

As discussed in Chapter 6, the basic benefit payable under a defined benefit plan, which is also called the normal form of benefit, is an annuity payable for the life of the employee. Benefits are also payable in other forms, called options, which are derived from the normal form of benefit. At this point, you may wish to review the examples of the most common plan payment options in Chapter 6 before proceeding to the considerations involved in selecting an option, which are analyzed in the remainder of this chapter.

2. Is There One Preferred Payment Option?

As you will recall from Chapter 6, options are offered because there is a perceived unfairness when an employer fails to provide benefits for the spouse or other dependents of an employee merely because of that employee's untimely death. Options are alternative forms of payment which provide some form of death benefit. The availability of other income, and the size of the desired death benefit are important factors to be weighed by any employee selecting an option. Because these considerations are all highly personal, it is impossible to recommend one option which will best serve the needs of all plan participants. This chapter will concentrate on the factors which you, as a plan participant, must weigh in light of your personal financial circumstances when deciding which option to choose.

3. Should You Select the Qualified Joint and Survivor Annuity?

ERISA requires pension plans to provide benefits to all married employees in the form of a reduced pension for the life of the employee with a pension equal to at least 50 percent of that reduced pension payable to the employee's spouse if the spouse is alive on the date of the employee's death and the employee has not declined to be paid in that form. (See Chapter 6 for a discussion of the rules governing joint and survivor benefits.) In some plans there is also a requirement that the employee have been married to the spouse for a specified period of time prior to the date of retirement or death in order to qualify for the qualified joint and survivor annuity. This period may not exceed one year.

In some cases the benefits payable under the qualified joint and survivor annuity are fully or partially subsidized by the employer. Very few plans provide for full subsidization of the qualified joint and survivor annuity, since it is possible to increase the cost of funding a plan by 15–20 percent (or in some cases even more, depending on the composition of the employer's work force) by fully subsidizing this benefit. However, it is not uncommon for employers to partially subsidize the qualified joint and survivor annuity so that the monthly benefit is reduced below the benefit to which the employee would be entitled if it were paid in the form of a life annuity but not to a level which would make it actuarially equivalent.

4. Importance of the Statutory Election Period

The qualified joint and survivor annuity is required to be made available to all married employees who have made no other written payment elections under the plan and whose spouses qualify for benefits under the terms of the particular plan. The information pertaining to the statutory election should be made available approximately 180 days prior to a participant's early retirement date if an early survivor annuity may be elected, or nine months prior to a participant's early retirement date if the plan provides an automatic early survivor annuity. If the plan does not provide early retirement benefits, the information should be made available nine months prior to the normal retirement date. You must make sure to decline this benefit within the statutory election period if you are married and the qualified joint and survivor annuity does not serve your needs.

Bear in mind that ERISA guarantees that you will have at least until 90 days prior to the scheduled commencement of benefit payments to change your decision, although the specific terms of your plan regarding election and change of options may limit you to changing to an option with a lesser death benefit than that provided by the qualified joint and survivor annuity (plan provisions governing the changing of options are discussed later on in this chapter). You should also bear in mind that if your plan requires that you have been married for one year prior to the date on which you retire and if you have not yet been married to your spouse for that length of time, you should affirmatively elect the "ordinary" (defined below) joint and survivor annuity if you want to guarantee him or her appropriate death benefit protection and this alternative option is not subject to a one year waiting period. You may be able to elect back into the qualified joint and survivor annuity in order to take advantage of an available subsidy after the one year is over.

5. Choosing the "Ordinary" Joint and Survivor Annuity

The joint and survivor annuity operates in the same way as the qualified joint and survivor annuity except that (1) the employee may designate any beneficiary to receive the survivor portion of the benefit and (2) it must be affirmatively elected by the employee. Since the qualified joint and survivor annuity is provided only to a person to whom the employee is legally married, if the employee is living with a person to whom he or she is not married, and wishes to provide for his or her companion under the employer's pension plan, the employee must do so by affirmatively electing the "plain" joint and survivor annuity or another form of option.

You may also use this option to provide a different percentage survivor benefit to your spouse than that provided under the qualified joint and survivor annuity.

The joint and survivor annuity is frequently made available with a number of alternative continuations to the survivor-annuitant. Obviously, since it is necessary to keep the pension actuarially equivalent—that is, to make sure that the total value of the life benefit plus any survivor benefit under options is equal to the value of a single life annuity—the higher the percentage of the employee's pension which the survivor—annuitant is entitled to receive, the greater the reduction in the dollar amount of the pension which the employee will be entitled to receive. If, for example, an employee's pension must be reduced from $1,000 per month (payable for life only) to $800 per month in order to permit his or her surviving spouse to receive a pension of $400 per month (50 percent continuation), it may have to be reduced to about $700 per month in order to allow the same survivor-annuitant to receive a pension equal to that same $700 per month (100 percent continuation).

6. Effect of Death and Divorce on Joint and Survivor Options

It should be noted that both in the case of the qualified joint and survivor annuity and in the case of the "ordinary" joint and survivor annuity, if the survivor-annuitant dies before the employee does but after payments have begun, the employee's pension will not be increased.

In most cases, whether the qualified joint and survivor annuity or the regular joint and survivor annuity is chosen, the surviving annuitant will be the spouse to whom the employee was married when the pension payments began, even if there is a subsequent divorce. If the employee's spouse dies, or if they are divorced and the employee remarries, the second spouse will usually not be entitled to the survivor annuity if he or she survives the employee since the actuarial reduction was made based on the first spouse's age. Other plans provide that the employee within a specified period after the divorce may elect to have the pension payable to the former spouse or, alternatively, may elect to have the pension increased and thereafter payable for his or her life only, but with no spousal/survivor benefit at all.

Still other plans—all too many in light of the incidence of divorce—are unclear as to what happens under these circumstances. Because of the frequency of divorce, it is important that every employee understand the effect of divorce on any plan elections of the joint and survivor annuity.

Proposed Additional Protection for Spouses

There are a number of bills pending in Congress that would extend the protections available under the qualified joint and survivor annuity. For example, the law now provides that an employee can elect not to receive a pension in the form of a qualified joint and survivor annuity without the consent of his or her spouse (although a plan may legally require such consent and the practice of requiring spousal consent is common in community property states). One of these bills would change the law to *require* such consent in all cases. Another bill would make the early survivor annuity discussed in the previous chapter mandatory and available not only after an employee had reached early retirement age but after he or she had completed 10 years of service under any pension plan. Obviously, these bills express new social policies for the protection of spouses, and are very closely related to developments in the law governing the impact of separation and divorce on pension benefits which are discussed in Chapter 17.

7. Comparing the Period Certain and Life Options

The most common variant of this option provides that if an employee dies within 10 years after the commencement of payment of pension benefits, benefits will continue to be paid for the balance of the 10 year period to the employee's designated beneficiary. If the employee lives beyond the expiration of the 10 year period, payments will continue to be made to him or her for the balance of his or her life.

Pension plans commonly allow an employee to select other periods certain, such as five years, fifteen or twenty years, or in some cases even twenty-five or thirty years. Obviously, the longer the period certain, the larger the reduction in the monthly pension benefit which the employee would otherwise have been entitled to receive.

A male employee's life expectancy at age 65 is approximately 13 to 15 years, while a woman's is approximately 7 or 8 years longer than a man's. Thus, if an employee selects a period certain of twenty years or longer, the chances are that he or she will die before the expiration of that period. However, there is always the possibility that the employee and spouse or other dependents might outlive the period certain, in which case no benefits would be payable after the employee's death. Therefore, many pension plans permit an employee to combine the joint and survivor annuity with a period certain feature providing some death benefit protection.

> *Example 3.* Leonard Root selected a 100 percent joint and survivor annuity for his wife, Iris, with a twenty year certain feature. Under this option, Leonard and Iris will each receive the same monthly pension as long as either of them is alive. If they both die before the expiration of the twenty year period, Leonard's designated beneficiary, his son Larry, will receive pension benefits for the balance of the twenty year period.

Since the joint life and last survivor expectancy of an employee age 65 and his or her spouse of approximately the same age is well over 20 years, the additional reduction in the monthly joint and survivor benefits for adding the twenty year certain feature is not likely to be very large. If this combination of options is available to you, you may obtain information from your employer's personnel department describing the precise cost of this feature in your case.

You should note that if the joint and survivor annuity is partially or fully subsidized, you will probably not lose the benefit of this subsidy if you should combine it with the period certain feature.

8. Should You Elect a Period Certain With No Life Contingency?

In many cases, an employee is not concerned with outliving his or her pension since there are ample resources on which to live during his or her retirement. In this case, the employee may not be interested in assuming any "death gamble" at all since he or she is, in effect, in a position to self-insure against living too long. In such a situation, assuming that the option is available under the employer's pension plan, he or she may select a period certain option under which benefits are paid during a prescribed period without regard to how long the employee lives.

When an employee selects a period certain option with no life contingency, the effect is very similar to having a savings account and taking distributions from that account at prescribed periods. Some plans place limitations on the installment payout period, such as a maximum of ten years. However, the longest permissible payout period under ERISA is the greater of twice the participant's life expectancy at the benefit commencement date or, if the participant is married, the joint life and last survivor expectancy of the participant and his or her spouse.

> *Example 4.* Harry Archer is entitled to a pension of $1,000 per month for the balance of his life beginning at age 65. Instead, he chooses a twenty year certain option under which he will receive a benefit of $800 per month for twenty years. If he lives beyond the twenty year period, pension benefits automatically stop at the conclusion of that period regardless of how much longer Archer lives. If Archer dies prior to the end of the twenty year period, payments will continue for the balance of the period to his designated beneficiary.

Before selecting this option, it is important to compare it with the lump sum option which is discussed below and to recognize that, unlike a lump sum for which favorable income tax treatment has been elected, installment payments are not includible in the employee's gross estate. The period certain option should also be compared with the alternative of the lump sum option which is rolled over into an individual retirement account.

9. Evaluating Cash Refund Annuities

All pension benefits have a present lump sum value based upon the actuarial assumptions which the plan's actuary uses. For example, a pension of $1,000 per month payable for life beginning at age 65 may have a current lump sum value equal to $110,000. Under a cash refund annuity option, an employee entitled to receive $1,000 per month at age 65 might, instead, receive $700 per month with the condition that if he or she dies before the aggregate of all of the monthly pension benefits equals $110,000, monthly benefits will continue to be paid to his or her designated beneficiary until the total of all of the benefits received by the employee and that beneficiary equals $110,000.

The cash refund option produces much the same effect as the period certain and life option previously discussed. Thus, it would take 157 months for a $700 monthly pension to result in aggregate payments equaling $110,000. This is the same as electing a period certain option of approximately 13 years.

The only reason to consider a cash refund option is if it results in the equivalent of a period certain which is substantially longer than the maximum period certain permitted under your employer's pension plan and you are interested in providing maximum death benefit protection.

10. Evaluating the Lump Sum Option

Perhaps the most controversial option available under pension plans today is the lump sum option. Under this option, an employee may receive in one calendar year the actuarial equivalent of the normal form of benefit to which he or she would otherwise be entitled, i.e., the present value of $X per month for the remainder of his or her lifetime. Many employers feel that the lump sum option should not be provided as a matter of policy under defined benefit plans, since such pension plans are designed to provide a steady income during a person's retirement years rather than one time cash distributions. However, since rollovers to individual retirement accounts became permissible, there has been increasing pressure from participants to make the lump sum option available so that the taxation of payments may be deferred.

Even if the lump sum option is not specifically named in your plan document or in your summary plan description, your plan may contain a catch-all provision authorizing participants to request any form of payment permitted by the Internal Revenue Service, subject to the approval of the plan retirement committee or the trustees. The only significant Internal Revenue Service limitation on options is, as previously discussed in Chapter 6, that at least 50 percent of the actuarial value of a benefit must be payable during the participant's lifetime. The lump sum obviously satisfies this rule. Therefore, it may be possible for you to receive a lump sum upon special request even if it is not described in the materials you received summarizing the operation of your plan.

11. Calculating Actuarially Equivalent Options—Why Some Options May Be Bargains

All optional benefits are derived from the normal form of benefit, which is a life annuity beginning at the plan's normal retirement date. In order to make an option calculation, the normal form is first converted to a lump sum and the lump sum is subsequently converted into the option chosen. There are two actuarial assumptions which are fed into this calculation and which may vary from plan to plan—interest rate and life expectancies. Even though all options are called "actuarially equivalent," the effect of these actuarial factors is to make some options relatively more valuable than others for the same employee—that is, to make some options "bargains." It is therefore essential to inquire carefully about the actuarial assumptions used to calculate *each* option available under your plan.

Although actuarial assumptions are not usually listed in SPDs, under a new Internal Revenue Service rule all new plans are required to incorporate the actuarial assumptions used to calculate options. Plans in existence in March of 1979 have until 1984 to comply with this rule. It should therefore become easier for you, as a plan participant, to find out which assumptions will be used to calculate your benefit and thus which benefits will be relative bargains because of the relationships among those assumptions. There is a second Internal Revenue Service rule which may also provide protection for you. It may be unlawful to change actuarial assumptions in a way that reduced benefits which you have already accrued. You will better understand the significance of this rule after you have read Sections A and B.

A. The Effect of Interest Rates on the Calculation of Options

Actuaries generally use the same interest rate in calculating optional benefits as they do for calculating plan costs. (The interest assumption was previously discussed in Chapter 9.) Since interest rates have gradually been rising in recent years, the interest rate used for calculating options has also been rising. The effect of using a higher interest rate is to increase the value of optional benefits other than the lump sum. The reason for this is that in calculating the amount of an optional benefit an actuary first converts a life annuity to a lump sum by discounting at the applicable interest rate and then converts it to an option by adding interest at that same rate. Although discounting a normal form of benefit at a higher interest rate produces a smaller lump sum, adding interest for the longer period over which benefits are payable under any other option more than counter-balances this reduction.

Assume that an employee aged 65 and entitled to a pension of $1,000 per month has a life expectancy of 15 years. If discounted at an interest rate of 5 percent, this benefit has a lump sum value of $127,000, while at 7 percent it has a lump sum value of $112,000. However, if the employee chooses a twenty year certain option, at 5 percent he would receive $835.00 per month while at 7 percent he or she would receive $863.00 per month.

The general rule is therefore that the higher the interest rate used, the more favorable the monthly benefit payment to the employee. However, the lump sum is an exception to this rule.

As you can see from the example above, in the case of a lump sum option the higher the discount interest rate used, the lower the lump sum. There is no counterbalancing increase for a long payout period since the lump sum, by definition, is paid out immediately.

When Should You Elect the Lump Sum?

While the constantly increasing interest rates used in calculating pension costs have tended to reduce the size of lump sum benefits, these interest rates have nevertheless lagged behind current interest rates for high grade securities. Thus, under some plans employees can perform a type of arbitraging where they select the lump sum option which would be discounted at, say 6 percent, and roll it over into an individual retirement account and invest it at say 11 percent. This could result in an employee receiving a much larger benefit than he or she would receive if the employee had selected any option under the pension plan under which benefits are payable over a period of years.

In order to avoid this windfall to employees, many employers use a different–and under current economic conditions invariably higher–interest rate in calculating the lump sum option than is used for other purposes under the plan.

The Internal Revenue Service has taken the position that the interest rate used in calculating lump sums must be published (as part of its general rule which applies to other options) and that any rate incorporated in a plan document cannot be increased in such manner as to reduce the portion of a lump sum benefit earned prior to the date on which the interest rate is increased.

Always find out whether the interest rate used to calculate the lump sum option is different from the interest rate used to calculate other options under your plan. Does the plan use the long term interest assumption used by the actuary for funding purposes for most options, but a higher current market interest rate for the lump sum? Does the lump sum interest rate fluctuate from year to year or from quarter to quarter in response to changes in indices such as a long term bond interest rate index? If the interest rate is low or hasn't been changed for some time, the lump sum may be a bargain compared to the other options. On the other hand, employers desiring to discourage selection of the lump sum option often use high market interest rates which result in relatively lower lump sum benefits. You may suffer an economic loss if you elect the lump sum option under such circumstances unless the arbitraging just discussed is attractive to you.

Another factor which affects the value of a lump sum to you is whether the lump sum is calculated using sex-based mortality tables. Since females have substantially longer life expectancies than males, under plans using sex-based tables a female would be entitled to a larger lump sum than would a man of the same age and an identical earnings history. This problem has added to the controversy surrounding the lump sum option and will be discussed more fully in Section B.

B. Sex Discrimination in the Calculation of Optional Benefits

The second important factor which determines the relative value of an option for an individual employee is the mortality assumption—the projected life expectancy of the participant and/or the joint annuitant—which is used to make the calculation. Mortality tables are either sex-based or so-called unisex tables under which the same life expectancies are used for males and females of the same age.

Since females in reality have longer life expectancies than do males of the same age, under plans using sex-based tables the lump sum value of a life annuity for a female is substantially higher than the equivalent value for a male the same age. Since the lump sum value serves as the base figure for all other option calculations, this means that if a plan uses sex-based mortality tables, virtually all of the options are relatively more valuable for females than for males. Females lose out on this bonus if they elect life annuities under such traditional plans. Conversely, males gain by choosing the normal form of benefit.

> *Example 5.* Frances Williams and Harold Cane, two unrelated employees covered by the Acme Widget pension plan, were born on the same day and have identical employment histories and are therefore entitled to identical pensions of $1,000 per month for life under the Acme plan. Since Williams has a substantially longer life expectancy, it is anticipated that her pension will be payable for a longer period of time. It is therefore worth substantially more. In this case, the actuaries have calculated that the lump sum value of Williams' pension is $110,000 while the lump sum value of Cane's is only $95,000.

The disparity between the value of an identical life annuity of similarly situated male and female employees becomes even greater in the case of the joint and survivor annuity.

Assume that Williams and Cane are each married to spouses of the same age. In Williams's case she is likely to outlive her husband so that the reduction required for a joint and survivor annuity will be relatively moderate. On the other hand, Cane's wife is more likely to outlive him so that the reduction for a joint and survivor annuity will be substantially larger.

The result of this combination of factors is that a female employee's life annuity is worth substantially more than an equivalent annuity of a male employee and the reduction for a joint and survivor annuity is substantially less where the employee is the female and the survivor annuitant the male rather than vice versa. These differences in projected life expectancy result in the male-female combination receiving a *much* smaller joint and survivor annuity than similarly-situated female-male combinations.

> *Example 6.* In the above example, Williams and Cane were each entitled to receive an annuity of $1,000 per month for life beginning at age 65. Assume each selects a qualified joint and 100 percent survivor annuity and each has a spouse also aged 65.
>
> Williams and her spouse will receive a qualified joint and survivor annuity of approximately $900 per month (a 10 percent reduction) while Cane and his wife will receive a qualified joint and survivor annuity of $750 per month (a 25 percent reduction).

There is obviously a certain amount of unfairness in this situation. It has also been determined to constitute sex discrimination prohibited under Title VII of the Civil Rights Act of 1964.

The issue of sex discrimination was raised by Marie Manhart, who was covered under a relatively rare type of contributory pension plan maintained by the Los Angeles Bureau of Water Supply. Under that plan women employees were required to make larger contributions than similarly situated male employees in order to receive identical pensions. The United States Supreme Court in the now famous *Manhart* case held that that particular plan discriminated against female employees.

As you now know, having come this far in the book, most pension plans are noncontributory. Since the employer pays for all benefits, traditional pension plans which provide for greater monthly optional benefits for female employees discriminate against men.

Under the principle laid down by the United States Supreme Court in the *Manhart* case these pension plans will be required to adopt unisex actuarial factors so that similarly situated male and female employees will receive identical normal and optional monthly pension benefits.

Compliance with Manhart

The EEOC, which is charged with enforcing the sex discrimination provision of the Civil Rights Act, has not yet issued regulations determining precisely how unisex tables are to be created and this sex discrimination is to be cured. However, typical Title VII remedial principles generally require that the group previously discriminated against must always be raised to the level of the previously favored sex. This may mean that females must be raised to the monthly life annuity benefit levels of similarly situated males, and that in other situations males must be raised to the optional monthly benefit levels applicable to females. Furthermore, the Internal Revenue Code prohibits retroactive reductions in accrued benefits, at least where actuarial factors have been listed in the plan. As discussed earlier in this chapter, all plans may ultimately be required to list their actuarial assumptions. A change to an optional benefit level lower than the full benefit payable to a female with the same age and service history may therefore be illegal, at least insofar as it applies to benefits accrued, or earned, before the change.

For all these reasons, it is not clear whether employers (unless they are adopting new plans) have the choice of utilizing tables containing mortality factors weighed 50 percent between male and female life expectancies (i.e., which split the difference between the higher and lower monthly amounts) or, alternatively, of weighting male and female mortality characteristics based upon the composition of the employer's work force except for future (as yet unearned) benefits, since such unisex tables result in lesser benefits for female employees.

There are several alternative ways to adjust monthly benefit levels proportionately which will be available under new plans or plans which desire to use the new rules for future benefits. For example, if a particular employer has a work force which is 80 percent female, it might use mortality tables which contain life expectancies weighted 80 percent toward the female end of the range. Alternatively, a plan sponsor might use mortality tables containing life expectancies midway between those of male and female groups. Some actuaries want to use a "per option" weighting method which would be based on the percentage of males and females who have chosen that particular option in the past. This means that if 60 percent of the participants electing the lump sum have been women, the mortality table used to calculate the lump sum would be weighted 60 percent toward female life expectancies.

The result of these changing rules will be that no matter how weighting is accomplished, female employees will suffer something of a penalty, and male employees will get a corresponding bonus when they choose options, a result which was probably unintended by the plaintiffs in *Manhart*.

While female employees under plans with unisex tables would be better off from a strict actuarial standpoint in having their pensions payable in the normal form—that is, as a life annuity—personal and tax considerations may nevertheless dictate the choice of one of the available options.

Final Note on Actuarial Assumptions

The effect of the combination of the Internal Revenue Service's new position and the new rules relating to sex discrimination will combine to focus the interests of participants on the manner in which optional benefits are calculated. Such increased interest will cause employers to make information about the actuarial factors used more readily available to employees. While personal and tax considerations will remain the basic factors that govern an employee's choice of an option, the actuarial factors involved will become more meaningful once pension plans convert to unisex actuarial factors and employees learn to evaluate their significance.

12. Waiting Periods and Adverse Selection

Almost all pension plans require a waiting period before the choice of an option becomes effective. For example, many plans provide that if an employee wishes to choose a ten year certain and life option, he or she must do so at least one year before the pension payments are to start. Thus, if the employee wishes to retire at age 65, he or she must select an option not later than age

64. Employers normally notify participants sufficiently before the deadline for selecting an option so that they may do so and retire when scheduled.

Many plans, however, provide that the prescribed waiting period may be waived if the employee is in good health. Good health is normally determined by a physician acceptable to the pension plan's retirement committee. In most cases the retirement committee will rely on the employee's own personal physician.

Obviously, the reason for these safeguards is to avoid deathbed elections of options unrelated to life expectancy. The technical term for this is "adverse selection."

Pension plans are funded on the assumption that, on the average, employees will live to (but not beyond) their life expectancies. This means that approximately 50 percent of employees will die before their life expectancy while the remaining 50 percent will outlive their life expectancy. The reduction in the normal form of pension which is made in the case of employees selecting options containing death benefits is made on the assumption that the employees choosing such options are healthy and representative of the work force in general. Obviously, if seriously ill employees all chose lump sum or long period certain options in order to provide protection for their dependents (an extreme example of adverse selection), the cost of funding pension plans would go up substantially.

13. Changing an Election

Generally speaking, employees are given the right to revoke options already selected and choose new ones during the same period that they could have made an original choice of an option. The same waiting period applies for the selection of a replacement option after the revocation of a prior option as in the case of the selection of the original option. However, there is usually one important difference. If the employee previously selected an option with a larger death benefit than the option to which he or she wishes to move, the waiting period will normally be waived because the change cannot result in adverse selection.

Example 7. Richard Henkel selected the lump sum option under his employer's pension plan. He subsequently reconsidered and elected a twenty year certain option. His employer's pension plan did not impose a waiting period for election of the new twenty year certain option, since the risk to the plan sponsor would not have been increased if he died prematurely. There would be no additional risk because the employer was already obligated to pay out the lum sum (his entire accrued benefit, reduced to a present value) to him.

The lump sum option provides the greatest death benefit protection since the pension plan will pay out the entire benefit to which the employee is entitled and if, for some reason, the employee dies after retirement but prior to payment, the beneficiary is entitled to receive the entire amount that would have been payable to the employee. Generally speaking, in the case of the other options, the larger the reduction in the monthly pension payable, the larger the death benefit. Therefore, if an employee revokes an option and chooses a different option which provides a higher monthly benefit, he or she is switching over to an option with a lower death benefit.

14. Do ERISA Maximum Limitations Affect You?

ERISA contains certain limitations on the maximum pensions which may be payable from a qualified plan. These maximums are so high that very few people are affected by them—generally, only the senior executives of large or exceptionally profitable smaller corporations.

A pension plan may not usually pay a pension which is larger than an employee's compensation in the highest three consecutive year period of employment with the plan sponsor. In addition, the pension may not exceed a prescribed dollar amount. In 1982 this amount was $136,425. In subsequent years this maximum dollar amount will be increased in accordance with the rate of inflation. The pension against which this maximum is measured is the pension payable under the normal form of benefit even if payment under an option is elected. Therefore, if an employee is entitled to receive a pension for life in excess of $136,425 per year in 1982 (or the equivalent amount in later years) and he or she chooses a reduced amount payable for twenty years certain, the pension must be further reduced in order to comply with the statutory maximum. However, in the case of benefits payable under the qualified joint and survivor annuity, the maximum limitation is applied to benefits payable in this form *after* the reduction, and not prior to the reduction as in the case of the other options.

Example 8. Cheryl Jones, who retired in 1982, is entitled to a pension of $136,425 per year for life under her employer's pension plan. If she should choose any optional form of benefit other than the qualified joint and survivor annuity, the option must be calculated to be the equivalent of a normal form of benefit of $136,425 per year. On the other hand, if the benefit is payable in the form of a qualified joint and survivor annuity, the benefit may be the equivalent of a life annuity of more than $136,425 per year—provided that, after reduction, not more than $136,425 per year is payable to Jones.

Example 9. Robert Smith retires in 1981. He is entitled to a pension of $150,000 per year for life before the application of the maximum dollar limitation. Assume the dollar limitation ($124,500 in 1981) increases because of inflation, at the rate of approximately 10% as follows: 1982: 136,425; 1983: 146,500; 1984: 161,000. Smith will receive a pension of $124,500 in 1981, $136,425 in 1982, $146,500 in 1983, and $150,000 in 1984 and subsequent years (assuming, of course, that he is then alive). If Smith had elected the qualified joint and 100% survivor option and his pension had been reduced to $130,000 per year, he will receive $124,500 in 1981 and $130,000 in subsequent years (assuming, of course, that either he or his wife is then alive).

DEFINED CONTRIBUTION PLANS

Because benefits under defined contribution plans consist simply of the balance in a participant's account and benefits are unaffected by actuarial considerations, such as the participant's age, normal retirement date has limited significance for defined contribution plan participants. Usually, a normal retirement date has significance in a defined contribution plan for two purposes only. Participants must become fully vested, if they were not so previously, upon attaining normal retirement age. Furthermore, initial benefit payments may not be postponed without the participant's consent beyond 60 days following the end of the plan year in which occurs the later of a participant's termination of employment or his or her normal retirement date.

Even these rules have extremely limited impact, since most defined contribution plans pay out benefits at or shortly after termination of employment. However, you should be aware that a minority of defined contribution plans do not authorize any payments prior to the normal retirement date, regardless of whether an employee remains in service until that date. If your plan imposes such a rule, it should be clearly described in your summary plan description.

DEFERRAL AND COORDINATION OF BENEFITS

Although the same rules govern the definition of normal retirement date in defined contribution plans as in defined benefit plans, plan sponsors who maintain both a defined benefit plan and a defined contribution plan are not required to incorporate identical definitions of normal retirement date in each plan. It is therefore important to check to see whether different requirements are imposed under the defined contribution plan if you are an employee covered by such an arrangement.

Many employees who participate in both a defined contribution and a defined benefit plan and who choose to retire early, prefer to roll over a lump sum received from the defined contribution plan in the manner discussed in Chapter 13 on early retirement, regardless of the time and manner in which the benefit under the defined benefit plan is payable, and begin receiving payments from the IRA when the pension becomes payable. However, it may not be necessary to do so merely to coordinate the timing of benefit payments, since it is sometimes possible to achieve this result by taking advantage of the terms of the plans under which you are covered. For example, if you are a vested former participant in a pension plan who will not receive an initial pension check before attaining age 65, and you also wish to elect a fifteen year installment payout for your vested account balance under the defined contribution plan, you may be entitled to file a written election under that plan deferring the commencement of the first installment payment until age 65. However, there is no requirement that the plan sponsor insert identical payment provisions in all of the qualified plans which it sponsors. In fact, most profit sharing plans do not provide life annuity options. Nor is there any requirement that the participant coordinate elections under all of the plans under which he or she is covered. Most of the information that you will need to coordinate payments (or to determine whether coordination is possible) is required to be contained in your summary plan description.

Chapter 15

DEFERRED RETIREMENT

Deferred retirement is a term used by pension practitioners to describe any termination of employment following the normal retirement date (usually age 65).

NEW LEGAL RIGHTS

Deferred retirement used to be permitted at the employer's discretion. This practice was permissible prior to 1978, because federal law then prohibited most private employers who did not sponsor any pension plan from retiring employees mandatorily at an age younger than 65. However, all employees could be forced to retire on their 65th birthday. Employers who sponsored pension plans with normal retirement ages earlier than age 65 were even permitted to forcibly retire employees at the plan's normal retirement age. In 1978, by means of amendments to the federal Age Discrimination in Employment Act, ("ADEA") Congress denied employers the right to retire employees in accordance with the terms of a pension plan at normal retirement ages younger than 65. Effective January 1, 1979 Congress amended the ADEA and raised the federal mandatory retirement age applicable to private employers from 65 to 70.

Prior to the January 1, 1979 effective date of the 1978 amendments to the Age Discrimination in Employment Act, most pension plans provided that an employee had to retire at age 65 unless his or her employer consented to continued employment beyond that age. Although some plans specifically authorized deferred retirement without a need for special permission, in order to discourage most employees from working beyond age 65, many of these plans also provided that an employee would not accrue additional benefits by reason of continued employment beyond age 65. Although most employees now have a federally protected right to continued employment to age 70 without the need to obtain employer consent, freezing benefit credit in this manner is still perfectly permissible under ERISA and ADEA. However, neither statute prevents employers from voluntarily increasing benefits of deferred retirees to reflect increased compensation and service and/or to adjust for the fact that they are likely to receive monthly pension checks for a shorter period of time than similarly situated employees who retire at age 65.

The "Bona Fide" Executive Exemption

Although employers are now prohibited, as matter of federal law, from forcing most employees to retire at age 65 if they are capable of continuing to do their jobs, an important exception was written into ADEA.

Employers may still compel the retirement at the age of 65 of "bona fide" executives–that is, executives in high policy making positions–who are also entitled to annual pensions of at least $27,000 per year, calculated on a life annuity basis.

EFFECT OF FEDERAL AGE DISCRIMINATION LAW ON DEFERRED RETIREMENT DECISIONS

Defined Benefit Plans

The new legislation did not go beyond the scope of ERISA to require defined benefit pension plans to provide additional benefits related to continued employment beyond age 65, thus sanctioning prior practice. Age discrimination regulations appear to provide some relief for participants in integrated defined benefit plans by requiring that if benefits are otherwise frozen at the normal retirement date, the Social Security offset may not be increased to reflect increases in Social Security levels which go into effect after the normal retirement date. However, this is merely an application of the rule that benefits may not be decreased on account of continued service after the normal retirement date and is not comparable to earning an additional benefit. Furthermore, as indicated in Chapter 7, deferred retirees are shortchanged under the Social Security system as well as under many existing private pension plans.

It is therefore important for every employee contemplating deferred retirement (and who is not being forcibly retired under the bona fide executive exemption) to understand that the applicable legal rules make it financially disadvantageous for the majority of employees to continue to work beyond normal retirement age. Although other significant reasons, such as job satisfaction, living expenses which exceed the accrued pension payable to a particular employee, and fear of inflation may lead an employee to decide to continue working past age 65, each plan participant should carefully weigh the financial consequences of such a decision which are illustrated below.

Why Deferred Retirement Usually Results in Economic Penalties

FROZEN MONTHLY BENEFITS

Since the regulations issued by the Department of Labor interpreting the new age discrimination law and existing pension law clearly permit pension benefits to be suspended while an employee is on deferred retirement. However, in order to suspend the pension of a participant who elects to work past his normal retirement date, his employer must give him or her a notice of suspension of benefits not later than the end of the month in which the participant reaches his or her normal retirement date. If, for example, an employee would have been entitled to a pension of $1,000 per month beginning at age 65, but instead of retiring at that time elected to continue working until age 70, his or her pension could be suspended until that employee retired. At that time, he or she would begin receiving a pension of the same $1,000 a month for life, but payable over a substantially shorter projected life span.

It should be noted that under these circumstances when an employee works beyond age 65 and no additional pension credits are earned after that date, his or her true compensation is really the difference between the nominal salary paid and the pension which he or she is losing by reason of not having retired at age 65.

> *Example 1.* Norma Wallace is entitled to receive a pension of $1,000 per month beginning at age 65. She elects to continue working beyond age 65 at her salary of $4,000 per month. Since by not retiring she has given up her pension of $1,000 per month, her real salary is only $3,000 per month.

OPTION CALCULATIONS

Some plans provide that all options are calculated at the retirement pension starting date. Thus, the monthly benefits under the joint and survivor annuity option are calculated based on the employee's and survivor annuitant's ages when the employee retires at age 70 rather than based on their ages at the plan's normal retirement date. Although this is customary if service beyond the normal retirement date is recognized, if benefit credit is frozen at age 65 calculation of options at the retirement pension starting date could result in substantially lower optional benefits (the lump sum base figure being lower because it is based on a shorter projected payout period) than if options were calculated at the normal retirement date. It is usually advantageous to participants to have options frozen at the normal retirement date if benefit credit is frozen at that time.

> *Example 2.* Assume that Norma Wallace in the previous example elected a qualified joint and 50 percent survivor annuity covering her husband Joseph under which (based on their ages when she was 65) she would have been entitled to a monthly benefit of $900 for the remainder of her life and he would have been entitled to a monthly benefit of $450 per month if he survived her. However, Wallace did not retire until age 70.
>
> If the qualified joint and survivor annuity were calculated based upon Norma and Joseph's ages when she actually retired, her monthly benefit (and consequently, his) would have been substantially lower (say $750 and $375 respectively) because the Wallace's life expectancies would be shorter at age 70 than at age 65.

Freezing Elections–Can You Change Options After You are 65?

Some plans which freeze options at normal retirement age require an employee to elect an option prior to attaining normal retirement age and do not permit options to be revoked or changed after that time. Some plan sponsors believe this to be an unduly restrictive practice and, for that reason, many pension plans do permit an employee to revoke an option previously selected, and to select a new option as late as one year prior to actual retirement, or even immediately prior to actual retirement if he or she can demonstrate good health to the satisfaction of the retirement committee. However, if your plan "locks" you into an option at age 65, you should carefully consider whether continued service will be recognized when your employer makes that option calculation.

Actuarial Increases Under Defined Benefit Plans

Although there is no legal requirement that this be done, many pension plans do not provide that an employee's pension will be frozen if he or she elects not to retire at age 65. There are a number of techniques used under these plans to give an employee larger benefits by reason of employment beyond normal retirement age.

Some plans provide that an employee will continue to accrue credited service for employment beyond normal retirement age. Others provide for no additional credited service but that any increases in an employee's compensation after age 65 will be reflected in the compensation base by which his or her pension is measured. Still other plans incorporate both of these techniques, thereby treating employment beyond normal retirement age in much the same way as employment prior to that time (that is, thereby increasing benefits for each year of continued employment).

> *Example 3.* Ralph Baker was covered under the American Building Products pension plan which provides a benefit equal to 2 percent of average compensation in the five years preceding retirement multiplied by the number of years of credited service prior to retirement.

Baker began working for American Building Products at age 35 and had completed 30 years of service at age 65 and 35 years of service by the time that he retired at age 70.

The American Building Products pension plan recognizes all 35 years of service as years of credited service. In addition, since Baker's compensation increased each year after he reached age 65 to offset inflation, his higher compensation during the ages 66 through 70 was used to determine the amount of his pension.

A number of pension plans use an entirely different alternative technique for increasing the value of the pension of an employee who works beyond normal retirement age. These plans provide that annual interest at an appropriate rate is to be added to the lump sum value of an employee's pension at age 65 and the larger lump sum is to be converted into a monthly pension when the employee actually retires at age 70 based upon his or her life expectancy at age 70.

Example 4. Assume an employee is entitled to receive a pension of $1,000 per month at age 65 which, based upon a 7 percent interest rate and a mortality table used by the actuary, has a lump sum value at that time of $100,000. When the employee actually retires at age 70, interest at 7 percent will be added resulting in a lump sum at age 70 of approximately $140,000. Since the employee's life expectancy at age 70 is substantially shorter than it was at age 65, this larger lump sum will be sufficient to provide him or her with a monthly pension which is almost twice as large as that to which he or she was entitled at age 65.

Relatively few plans use this method since it results in a very large increase in an employee's pension benefit if he or she elects to continue working beyond age 65.

If your plan provides a method of recognizing employment after normal retirement date you may well be an exception to the general rule that deferred retirement is financially disadvantageous.

Cost of Living Adjustments

Another method which may be used to increase the benefits of deferred retirees is to adjust the pension, once it has commenced to be paid, for inflation by means of cost of living adjustments. Cost of living adjustments are usually made annually in accordance with changes in one of the Department of Labor's consumer price indices and are almost always subject to a cap, such as 3 percent or 5 percent a year, which is used to keep plan costs from escalating unreasonably.

However, because these adjustments are usually not applied until an employee retires, an employee who elects deferred retirement may suffer an initial financial penalty if his or her plan has an adjustment clause of the type just discussed, because of ineligibility for increases during the years of continued employment.

Defined Contribution Plans

Different standards govern the eligibility for continued plan participation after normal retirement age in the case of profit sharing plans or money purchase plans. If an employee is covered by both a pension and profit sharing plan, the profit sharing plan is considered to be "supplementary" and therefore the employer is required to continue allocating full contributions under the plan's formula to the accounts of employees who continue to work beyond age 65. On the other hand, if the employee is covered only by the profit sharing plan, that plan is not considered to be supplementary and therefore the employer is not required to continue making contributions on behalf of an employee who continues to work beyond his or her normal retirement age.

Pressures for Liberalization of These Rules

It is likely that pressures will develop to require employers to credit employees with additional benefits under *all* defined benefit and defined contribution plans for their service beyond normal retirement age. After all, there is an element of unfairness in not providing an employee with benefits based on compensation for service rendered after having attained normal retirement age, whether the participant is covered under a defined contribution plan or a defined benefit plan. The EEOC, which has assumed the Department of Labor's role of administering ADEA may adopt regulations requiring some form of recognition for postnormal retirement date employment.

ADDITIONAL PROTECTIONS UNDER STATE LAW

ADEA establishes a floor rather than a ceiling of required legal protection. States can and do enact their own age discrimination legislation which may cover employers with fewer than 20 employees (which are not covered under the federal law) and/or may establish mandatory retirement ages higher than 70. Some states, such as California, Alaska, and Maine, have even enacted statutes which abolish the concept of a mandatory retirement age altogether. This means that although employees may obviously be terminated for cause such as poor job performance, it is no longer generally permissible to retire employees at any fixed age, solely because of their age, in those states.

Since pension plans traditionally contain language authorizing the mandatory retirement of participants at a set age, and since ERISA contains language preempting the application of state law to pension plans, it is not yet clear whether plan participants will be entitled to rely on *state* laws to provide them with a right to continued employment beyond age 70. It seems that states do not have the right to require that plans provide that additional pension credits may be earned after normal retirement date, since states would then be dictating the specific terms of pension plans, a field set aside for federal control under ERISA. However, because ERISA does not *require* plans to fix a mandatory retirement age or even address the issue of a participant's right to continued employment beyond age 65, and a qualified plan need not incorporate any mandatory retirement policy, state laws such as California's may ultimately be found to expand the rights of pension plan participants.

Although it is still too early to draw any conclusions about whether state age discrimination legislation, insofar as it applies to pension plan participants, is preempted by ERISA, any participant contemplating deferred retirement should inquire not only about his or her employer's pension provisions relating to employment after normal retirement date, but also as to whether additional rights may be afforded him or her by state law.

Chapter 16

PLAN MERGERS AND TERMINATION

A persistent concern of plan participants is whether corporate actions such as bankruptcies, plant shutdowns, divestitures, mergers and acquisitions may result in a loss of their accrued benefits. Prior to the enactment of ERISA a number of highly publicized business failures resulted in substantial losses of accrued benefits. One of these failures, which precipitated the termination of the Studebaker pension plan and was highly publicized at the time, led to the enactment of the plan termination benefit insurance program which is administered by the Pension Benefit Guaranty Corporation.

This chapter describes a great many different types of business transactions which affect pension expectancies. You should note that no type of transaction leads unavoidably to a reduction in participant's benefits. In some mergers and terminations all participants can be paid their full accrued benefits. In others, participants will receive a lot less than their accrued benefit statements show. Whether a transaction affects benefit levels adversely depends on factors to be analyzed in the remainder of this chapter.

COMPLETE PLAN TERMINATIONS

Defined Benefit Plans

This is the classic situation the Pension Benefit Guaranty Corporation was created to regulate: A plan sponsor is in precarious financial shape, having reported large losses in recent years. Creditors are calling in their loans and suppliers are prepared to deal only on cash terms. Everyone is waiting for the other shoe to fall. Finally the dreaded announcement comes. The plan sponsor is filing for protection under the bankruptcy laws. An attempt to reorganize the corporation fails and the pension plan is terminated. What happens now?

ERISA contains detailed provisions for handling a plan termination. A plan termination is, in effect, a plan bankruptcy and the procedure for allocating assets has many similarities to the procedure in a business bankruptcy.

ERISA requires that plan assets be allocated in accordance with specified priorities. The plan's actuary is first required to calculate the cost of providing the benefits of all plan participants and then is required to classify them in the following order of priorities.

1. If employees contribute to the plan, benefits funded with those contributions are in the highest priority.

2. The benefits of retired employees and those who were eligible to retire at least three years prior to the plan termination are in the next priority.

3. Other vested benefits of active employees guaranteed by the Pension Benefit Guaranty Corporation are in the following priority.

The Pension Benefit Guaranty Corporation guaranties all vested benefits in effect for five years prior to the plan termination up to a maximum of almost $1,400 per month in 1981. (The maximum monthly guaranteed benefit increases with the cost of living in the same way as do Social Security benefits.) Benefits not in effect for five years prior to the plan termination date are phased in over a five year period at the rate of the greater of $20 or 20 percent per year.

4. Other vested benefits of active employees not guaranteed by the Pension Benefit Guaranty Corporation (because they are over the monthly maximum, or because they have not been in effect for five years) are in the next priority.

5. Benefits which were not vested prior to the termination are in the lowest priority and are not guaranteed.

Assets are then allocated to these classes of benefits in order of priority. If the assets are sufficient to pay all benefits in all categories, every employee will receive his or her full accrued benefit. If not, some of the benefits will be lost except to the extent they are guaranteed by the Pension Benefit Guaranty Corporation.

Example 1. The Wondrous Gizmo pension plan was terminated at a time when the cost of providing the accrued benefits was calculated and classified as follows:

1. Benefits provided by employee contributions	$ 100,000
2. Retirees' benefits	500,000
3. Other vested guaranteed benefits	1,000,000
4. Vested nonguaranteed benefits	400,000
5. Nonvested benefits	500,000
Total	$2,500,000

The plan has assets of $3,000,000. In this rare situation the plan has a surplus of $500,000. Each participant will receive his or her full accrued benefit. As the plan is overfunded, Wondrous Gizmo will receive a refund of $500,000 since, in retrospect, it overcontributed to the plan.

Example 2. Assume the same facts as in Example 1 except that the plan has assets of only $1,000,000. This is a more typical situation.

The assets are allocated in priority order. First $100,000 is set aside to provide the benefits related to employee contributions. Then $500,000 is allocated to fund the benefits of the retirees. Now $400,000 is left. The next priority—that of vested benefits of active employees for which the Pension Benefit Guaranty Corporation is responsible—would require $1,000,000 to satisfy in full. Since only $400,000 of plan assets are available, the plan sponsor must notify the Pension Benefit Guaranty Corporation that plan assets are insufficient to provide all benefits guaranteed by the Pension Benefit Guaranty Corporation.

The Pension Benefit Guaranty Corporation will then take over the plan and the entire $1,000,000 in plan assets and provide all benefits for which it is responsible–i.e., all those through the third priority. The Pension Benefit Guaranty Corporation will have to expend $1,600,000 to provide these benefits. Since the plan had assets of only $1,000,000 the Pension Benefit Guaranty Corporation will lose $600,000.

The benefits in the last two priority categories–worth $900,000–will be lost.

The Pension Benefit Guaranty Corporation, in order to recoup its $600,000 loss will assert a claim for this amount but may recover only 30 percent of the plan sponsor's net worth if that amount is less than its loss.

Example 3. Wondrous Gizmo had a net worth of $1,000,000 at the time it terminated the plan. The Pension Benefit Guaranty Corporation can recover only $300,000 (30% of $1,000,000) from Wondrous Gizmo. The balance of its loss ($300,000) is met through the premium payments of other pension plan sponsors.

Example 4. Assume the same facts as Example 1 except that plan assets are $1,800,000.

Since plan assets are more than sufficient to provide benefits for which the Pension Benefit Guaranty Corporation is responsible–i.e., they exceed $1,600,000 in this case–the Pension Benefit Guaranty Corporation will not take over the plan. Instead, Wondrous Gizmo will liquidate its plan.

Participants whose benefits are the first three priority categories will receive their full accrued benefits. Participants in the fourth priority category will receive 50 percent of their accrued benefits since $200,000 ($1,800,000 minus $1,600,000) is available to fund the $400,000 worth of benefits in this priority category. Participants whose benefits are in priority category 5 will receive nothing.

Mechanics of Plan Termination

An employer that wishes to terminate its defined benefit pension plan files a Notice of Termination with the Pension Benefit Guaranty Corporation and a request for a determination by the Internal Revenue Service that the proposed distribution of benefits does not discriminate in favor of officers, stockholders or highly compensated employees. Such discrimination would cause the plan to lose its qualified status.

The Internal Revenue Service sometimes requires the benefits of highly compensated employees to be reduced and those of lower paid employees to be correspondingly increased as a condition to issuing a favorable determination. Plan sponsors will not liquidate plan assets until after having received the approval of both the Service and the Pension Benefit Guaranty Corporation. Such approval often is obtained only after a lengthy period of time thus resulting in extensive delays before plan assets are actually distributed to plan participants.

Generally when defined benefit plans are terminated and assets are sufficient to fund at least those benefits guaranteed by the Pension Benefit Guaranty Corporation, benefits are provided in one of two ways:

A. Each participant receives an annuity contract issued by an insurance company pursuant to which the insurance company undertakes to pay the participant his or her accrued pension, or
B. Each participant receives a lump sum cash payment representing the value of his or her accrued benefit.

In some cases each participant receives an annuity contract. In others he or she is offered a choice between receiving an annuity contract or a lump sum cash payment. ERISA does not permit a terminating pension plan to distribute lump sums without offering the choice of an annuity contract but does permit the distribution of an annuity contract without offering the choice of lump sum.

Example 5. Assume the facts are as in Example 1. Robert Andrews, who is 45 years old, is entitled to an accrued benefit of $100 per month beginning at age 65. Andrews is offered the choice of an annuity contract for the sum of $3,000 in cash, the purchase price of that contract.

Date of Termination

It is often very difficult to fix the date on which a termination is considered to have occurred. The date which is chosen has important repercussions on the way participants' benefits are classified on termination. The reason for this is that ERISA requires that all participants' accrued benefits be fully vested at the time a plan is terminated. (At this point you should note that this Internal Revenue Service requirement of full vesting on plan termination does not affect the Pension Benefit Guaranty Corporation priorities described earlier, since the Pension Benefit Guaranty Corporation does not guarantee benefits which become vested by reason of plan termination. Those benefits are in the lowest Pension Benefit Guaranty Corporation priority category.)

If employees with nonvested benefits are laid off immediately prior to a plan termination their benefits will be forfeited. If the layoff takes place after the date of plan termination their benefits will be vested and must be paid if plan assets are sufficient for that purpose.

Example 6. Assume the same facts as in Example 1 except that the employees whose benefits are in the lowest priority are fired 30 days before Wondrous Gizmo formally terminates its pension plan and that plan assets are $2,500,000.

If the Internal Revenue Service accepts the termination date chosen by Wondrous Gizmo the former employees in the lowest priority will receive no benefits, since they forfeited their nonvested benefits when they were terminated. Instead Wondrous Gizmo will receive a refund of $1,000,000 because the plan is overfunded by that amount.

However, if the Service takes the position—as it often does—that the *plan* terminated when Wondrous Gizmo began firing its employees, they will all be fully vested and (in this example) all of the employees in the lowest priority will receive their full accrued benefits. Wondrous Gizmo will receive a refund of $500,000, as in Example 1.

Partial Terminations

Example 7. The Wondrous Gizmo pension plan covered 1,000 employees during 1980. In 1981 Wondrous Gizmo shut down its unprofitable Gadget division and fired 500 employees. The Internal Revenue Service will consider Wondrous Gizmo to have terminated the pension plan as to the employees in the Gadget division. These employees will become fully vested.

Often an employer will reduce its work force but not consider its pension plan as having been partially terminated. Sometimes the Internal Revenue Service disputes the employer's position and decrees a partial termination to have occurred. Usually these disputes are settled administratively but sometimes litigation is required to resolve it.

Even when a partial termination is conceded to have occurred, it is not always clear what follows. If plan assets are sufficient, all participants in the division or subsidiary that was terminated will get their full accrued pensions. If plan assets are not sufficient they will receive only a portion of their accrued benefits, but it is not always clear how assets are to be divided between the segment of the plan that is terminated and the ongoing portion.

The Pension Benefit Guaranty Corporation does not guaranty benefits in a partial termination. Therefore if plan assets are insufficient, it is possible for a participant to receive a smaller portion of his or her pension if he or she is involved in a partial termination than if the entire plan were terminated.

However, the Pension Benefit Guaranty Corporation has the power to completely terminate a partially terminated plan and guarantee benefits thereunder. It will do so if it believes that plan benefits will accrue at a greater rate than plan assets would accumulate if it allows the plan to continue to operate.

Defined Contribution Plans

Terminations of defined contribution plans are much simpler than terminations of defined benefit plans. In the case of a defined contribution plan, each participant's accrued benefit is the balance in his or her account. There is no possibility of a defined contribution plan's being overfunded or underfunded since the plan's assets will always equal the sum of all account balances.

The Pension Benefit Guaranty Corporation does not guarantee benefits accrued in defined contribution plans and is therefore not involved in the termination of such plans.

The Internal Revenue Service reviews the termination of defined contribution plans in much the same way as it does defined benefit plans. However, it is rare that the Service would object to the manner in which an employer proposes to distribute assets on termination of a defined contribution plan.

The questions of the date on which a defined contribution plan is considered to have terminated, and whether a partial termination has occurred arise in much the same way in the case of defined contribution plans as they do in defined benefit plans.

What Can You Do to Protect Your Interest If Your Employer Decides to Terminate Its Retirement Plan?

First, you will be notified when your employer files a Notice of Termination with the Pension Benefit Guaranty Corporation and a request for a determination with the Internal Revenue Service. You can keep track of the progress of the termination and you may intervene in these agency proceedings if you feel that the manner in which your employer proposes to allocate or distribute plan benefits in connection with the proposed termination is unfair or improper.

Even when there is no question as to the fairness or correctness of the proposed allocation of assets, you will often be presented with choices. For example, you may be offered the choice of a lump sum at the time of plan termination or a pension at some later time. The considerations are generally similar to those discussed in Chapters 13 and 14 on early and normal retirement.

MERGERS AND REORGANIZATIONS

In the first part of the chapter we considered a situation which involved only single company situations in which an employer was compelled to terminate a retirement plan because of financial necessity. While such plan terminations occur from time to time, they do not occur nearly as frequently as do changes in pension plans resulting from mergers of companies, acquisitions of one company (or a division of one company) by another, and reorganization within a single company where subsidiaries or divisions are merged or otherwise reshuffled.

The manner in which retirement plans are handled in these transactions follow established patterns. The following are examples of typical transactions and their effect on retirement plans.

Acquisition of One Company by Another

> *Example 8.* Acme Widget, a company which employs 5,000 people acquires Alliance Gadget, a smaller company which employs 1,000 people. Each of these companies, prior to the acquisition, maintained a pension plan covering substantially all of its employees. Acme decides that both plans shall continue to be maintained without change.

In most cases of the acquisition by one company of another the pension plans maintained by both the acquiring and the acquired corporation will remain unchanged. Therefore, most employees will not have their accrued pensions or their pension expectancies affected in any way as a result of the transaction.

However, even in situations where this is so, the key executives of the companies may be asked to transfer from one to the other in order to improve efficiency or for other business reasons. Where this occurs, special attention must be given to the pension rights of the transferred executives in order to make certain that their pension benefits are not inadvertently reduced. This problem has already been discussed in Chapter 12.

However, in some cases the acquiring company may decide either to terminate the retirement plans of the acquired company or to merge them into its own plan in order to have a uniform retirement benefit structure for all of its employees. This can be done in a number of ways.

> *Example 9.* Assume the same facts as in Example 8 except that Acme decides that it prefers to have all of its employees

covered by a single defined benefit pension plan. It therefore terminates the Alliance pension plan. Each participant is offered the choice of either receiving a lump sum distribution of the balance in his account under the pension plan or of leaving that balance in his account until he retires, at which time it would be distributed to him in accordance with the provisions of the plan.

The procedure on plan termination is the same as that discussed earlier in this chapter. The factors to be taken into consideration in deciding whether to take a lump sum immediately and roll it over into an individual retirement account, or to leave it in the pension plan have also been previously discussed.

Where an acquiring company terminates an acquired company's plan in this fashion, it generally provides benefits to the employees of the acquired company under its own plan only for the period of employment after the acquisition date. However, service with the acquired company is generally recognized for the purposes of eligibility and vesting in the acquiring company's retirement plan.

Example 10. Acme Widget acquired Alliance Gadget on January 1, 1981. Alliance did not maintain a pension plan for its employees. Acme amended its retirement plan to provide that all Alliance employees will begin to accrue benefits under the Acme pension plan effective January 1, 1981. However, for the purpose of eligibility and vesting under the Acme pension plan, service prior to January 1, 1981 with Alliance will also be recognized.

Joseph Smith began working for Alliance in 1965. Thus, on January 1, 1981 he had completed more than ten years of service, the period of time necessary to become vested under the Acme pension plan. Smith will immediately begin participating in the Acme pension plan (even though it has a one year waiting period for new employees) on January 1, 1981 and he will be immediately fully vested in all benefits which he accrues under the Acme plan after that date.

Acquisition of a Division or Subsidiary of One Company by Another

In the situation previously discussed, one company acquired all of the stock or assets of another company. In many cases, however, one company acquires only a division, subsidiary, plant or other facility of another company where employees of the acquired entity are covered by a pension plan which continues to cover other employees of the selling company.

Pension arrangements for the transferred employees are generally handled in one of two ways:

1. The selling company will continue to provide pensions to the transferred employees based upon their period of employment prior to the date of the sale, while the acquiring company will provide pension benefits for the transferred employees under its own pension plan for the period of service beginning after the date of the sale.

2. The selling company will, in effect split up its pension plan, and transfer an appropriate amount of plan assets to the pension plan of the acquiring company. In exchange, the acquiring company will provide pension benefits to all of the transferred employees as though they always worked for the acquiring company.

Under the first alternative, an employee could wind up receiving two pension checks, one from the selling company and the other from the acquiring company. Generally, both the selling company and the acquiring company will recognize the employee's period of employment with the other company under its pension plan for the purpose of vesting in benefits accrued under the other plan.

> *Example 11.* Reliable Furniture Company sells its mattress division to Famous Bedroom Corporation on January 1, 1981. Both Reliable and Famous maintain pension plans for their employees. They agree that Reliable will provide pensions to the mattress division employees equal to the benefits which they accrued prior to January 1, 1981, while Famous

will provide pensions to those employees equal to the benefits which accrue after December 31, 1980.

Reliable and Famous each recognize service with the other for the purpose of vesting in the benefits accrued under their respective plans.

Example 12. Assume the same facts as in Example 11 except that Famous provides benefits under its pension plan to all mattress division employees for both employment by Reliable prior to January 1, 1981 and for employment by Famous after December 31, 1980 and recognizes all service with Reliable for eligibility and vesting under the Famous pension plan. Reliable transfers assets from its pension plan to that of Famous in an amount sufficient to provide those benefits.

Mary Trimble joined Reliable at age 30 on January 1, 1976 and on January 1, 1981 had accumulated a benefit of $50.00 per month payable for life beginning at age 65. She remained employed by Famous until January 1, 2011 at which time she retired having accrued an additional $950 per month.

In Example 11, Trimble will receive two checks, one for $50.00 per month from the Reliable pension plan, and another for $950.00 per month from the Famous pension plan.

In Example 12, Trimble will receive one check, for $1,000 per month from the Famous pension plan.

Chapter 17

MARRIAGE AND DIVORCE

GETTING MARRIED

Although this chapter is called "Marriage and Divorce," the bulk of the discussion concerns divorce rather than marriage. This is not a social commentary, but simply a recognition of the fact that there is little pension planning customarily done at the time a marriage (or other live-in relationship) is entered into other than what common sense would dictate—that is, changing beneficiary designations to protect the new spouse and discussing investment decisions such as whether to make maximum voluntary contributions. There are, however, a few simple facts that bear emphasizing here:

1. Only a legally married spouse is entitled to the joint and survivor annuity. You must file *an express beneficiary designation* to insure that a death benefit is provided to a person to whom you are functionally but not legally married.

2. In community property states it seems clear that a nonemployed spouse is deemed to accrue half of the pension earned by an employed spouse during the period of marriage.

Finally, in cases where both spouses come into the marriage with substantial assets and vested pensions, they may agree to renounce interests in each other's pensions by means of an antenuptial agreement.

Apart from these problems, and estate planning (whose pension ramifications were discussed in Chapter 11), pension questions rarely arise prior to the time a marriage is being dissolved.

GETTING DIVORCED

Pensions as a Marital Asset

A participant's accrued vested benefit under a pension plan is as much an asset of the employee as is a house or car and is subject to division or transfer when his or her marriage ends. Courts have recently held that accrued pension benefits may be considered marital assets *even if* the employee-spouse does not yet have any vested rights under the plan. The fact that (qualified joint and survivor rights aside) the nonemployee-spouse has not earned the benefit and has no right under the plan to demand payment does not affect this conclusion because most states (whether common law or community property) provide for so-called "equitable distribution" of marital property. This means that there is an equitable (or "fair") division regardless of in which spouse's name the title to the property is held. New York adopted equitable distribution of marital property in 1980.

There are two ways to account for the value of a pension when negotiating a marital property settlement. The spouses either divide the pension in some agreed proportion or the employee-spouse receives the entire pension and the nonemployee-spouse receives other property equal in value to his or her agreed share of the pension.

Before the nonemployee-spouse can receive assets equivalent to the value of a portion of the pension, it is, of course, first necessary to value the pension.

> *Example 1.* H and W are both employed and have assets worth \$900,000 net of liabilities, plus their accrued pensions with present values of \$200,000 and \$100,000, respectively. Upon their divorce, H & W agree to divide their \$1,200,000 in assets equally. Each will keep his or her pension plus assets equal to the difference between that pension and \$600,000. Thus H will receive \$400,000 of other assets and W will get \$500,000.

It is possible to value pensions this easily only if the amounts represent vested account balances in defined contribution plans or in the case of defined benefit plans, if the employee is fully vested and relatively close to retirement. If either H or W in Example 1 does not become vested, that spouse will have been seriously shortchanged in the marital property settlement.

Benefits accrued under defined benefit plans, even if vested, raise unique and difficult valuation problems.

> *Example 2.* Assume H in Example 1 is entitled to receive a pension of $24,000 per year for life beginning at age 65 based upon compensation and service accrued to age 45. H is fully vested. H and W have decided upon divorce and are attempting to value at the date of the agreement this accrued pension which will not become payable for 20 years.

As you will recall from Chapter 13 the present value of a future pension must be discounted using an appropriate interest rate and mortality table. The higher the interest rate used, the greater will be the monthly value of most optional benefits. However, the higher the interest rate, the lower will be the lump sum value of the anticipated pension benefit. Similarly the mortality table utilized—whether it is sex linked or unisex—can substantially affect the actual dollar benefit payable.

Many plans have special subsidy or adjustment features which further complicate the valuation process. For instance, assume that in Example 2 the employee-husband could have retired at age 60 and received the same $24,000 because the plan contained a fully subsidized early retirement feature (note that this calculation ignores increased service and compensation between the date of the divorce and retirement, which is unrelated to the marriage). This pension is substantially more valuable than an identical one without this feature. However, the employee-spouse may contend that he or she has no intention of retiring early. Since he or she will therefore not benefit from this provision, it should not be considered when valuing the pension.

It is possible that in this same situation, the accrued pension will also be increased to take into account all or a portion of increases in the Consumer Price Index after retirement. This is obviously a valuable feature, but what inflation rate should be assumed to be applicable 20 or 30 years in the future?

When H & W cannot agree on the present value of the employee-spouses' pension, it is necessary to use the alternative method of sharing actual payments.

> *Example 3.* Assume that H and W in Example 1 each agree not to offset their respective pensions against other assets but to offset their pensions against one another with an offsetting adjustment in favor of W. H and W each receive $450,000 of the other assets, W receives her pension and 25 percent of H's pension.
>
> Presumably the parties will agree that H is not compelled to retire at any particular time in order that W may commence collecting her share of his pension.

However, there are still problem areas in valuation. These are discussed below:

1. Options

So far, we have assumed that the employee-spouse will receive a pension which is a life annuity. However, as discussed in Chapter 6, benefits are generally payable under any one of an array of elective options. Under most plans, the qualified joint and survivor annuity will not be available to a spouse since he or she will not be married to the participant on his or her retirement pension starting date. Unless the parties agree in advance as to the option which the employee-spouse must choose, the nonemployee-spouse may be disadvantaged. Even if the spouses do agree upon an option at the date of the settlement, there may be subsequent changes in the law or in their personal circumstances which make the choice unwise. They may have to renegotiate this provision to determine who bears the cost of the changed circumstances.

> *Example 4.* Assume that in Example 3 H and W do not agree on the option which husband must choose. H selects an annuity with a 20 year certain future on retirement at age 65, reducing his pension from $24,000 to $19,000 per year, and provides that in the event he dies before the end of the 20 year period unpaid installments shall be payable to their children. W's pension is thus reduced from $6,000 per year

to $4,750 with no offsetting benefits to her unless the agreement is renegotiated.

Example 5. Alternatively, assume H elected the lump sum option and received $240,000. H turned 25 percent, or $60,000, over to W. H can roll over his $180,000 into an IRA, thereby postponing taxation until he withdraws it from the IRA. While the law is not entirely clear, it appears that W will be subject to tax on the remaining $60,000 since she does not have the option to roll it over into an IRA, because she was not paid directly out of the pension plan but rather was paid by H.

2. *Subsequent Benefit Improvements*

Suppose, in Example 3, five years after the divorce becomes final, H's employer increases benefit levels under the plan, raising H's accrued pension at age 45 from $24,000 to $30,000 per year. Unless the parties have agreed otherwise, W will not share in this increase.

3. *Other Contingencies*

H's employer may terminate the plan, in which case a portion of the expected benefit may not be payable if it was not funded or guaranteed by the PBGC.

More important, pensions are generally contingent on the employee's survival. If H does not live to retirement (or if an early survivor annuity is not available, for example because H has not yet reached early retirement age) W may receive 25 percent of nothing.

4. *Remarriage*

If H in the above example marries X after having divorced W, X may automatically acquire certain rights in H's accrued pension which are inconsistent with W's rights under the settlement. For example, under current law, as discussed in Chapter 6, H's pension must be paid in the form of a qualified joint and survivor annuity unless he elects otherwise. There are a number of bills in Congress which would eliminate H's right to elect out of the joint and survivor annuity without the permission of his spouse (in this case, X) at the date he makes an election. Therefore if this option is elected W may have her pension benefits reduced without her consent by reason of H's subsequent marriage to X and X's understandable desire not to waive her own rights in favor of a former wife.

Moreover if H were to die prior to age 65, X–not W–would receive the preretirement death benefit.

If you are in the process of negotiating a marital property settlement, it is important to make provision for all these contingencies by making sure that your matrimonial lawyer focuses on these problems. If you become involved in matrimonial litigation where the value of a pension is at issue, it may also be important to seek expert actuarial advice on your behalf.

Attachments of Pension Plan Interests for Nonpayment of Alimony, Child Support, or Maintenance

There has been a great deal of litigation recently regarding the circumstances under which a nonemployee former spouse may attach the employee former spouse's accrued pension benefit to satisfy arrearages of alimony, child support, or maintenance.

ERISA, on its face, prohibits all attachments or garnishments of an employee's interest in a pension or profit sharing plan. However, while a few courts have read this provision literally and refused to allow pension benefits to be attached for such arrearages, most courts have read an implied exception into the antiattachment provisions to permit an employee's pension benefit to be used for this purpose on the theory that pension plans were designed to protect an employee's family as well as the employee himself or herself.

The Service and Department of Labor have gone along with this position, which now appears generally to be the law.

Benefits Provided by Employer Contributions

However the Internal Revenue Service takes a position which is substantially more stringent than that taken by some courts. The Service has ruled that a plan would lose its qualified status if its fiduciaries complied with a court order garnishing or attaching benefits of an employee whose benefits were not then in pay status, i.e., of an employee who had not separated from service with a right to an immediate benefit, or retired.

> *Example 5.* H agreed to pay W maintenance of $1,000 per month when they were divorced. H, without justification, stopped making these payments a few years ago and is now $12,000 in arrears. He has no assets except for an account balance in his employer's profit sharing plan of $100,000 in which he is fully vested.
>
> After W sues for back payments, the state court issues an attachment order in the amount of $12,000 against H's account in the plan, and, in addition, orders the trustees of the plan to pay W an additional $1,000 per month in the future unless H resumes making the monthly payments directly.
>
> Since H is not retired and receiving benefits, the trustees can either respond to the court order and risk jeopardizing the qualified status of the plan, or refuse to honor it and risk being held in contempt by the court which issued the order.

This obviously puts plan administrators in an impossible dilemma which must ultimately be resolved by the government and the courts. It is impossible to hazard even an educated guess at this time as to the direction in which the law will develop. A bill recently considered by Congress would allow only plan benefits in *pay status* to be attached. And ERISA preempts contrary state law so one would think if this bill is enacted that would be the end of the dispute.

At this point, however, its prospects for immediate enactment are not bright. In any event, the courts tend to sympathize with a financially-strapped former spouse left without income to which he or she is entitled and strain to find a way to see that plan moneys may be made available to him or her.

Benefits Provided by Employee Contributions

The law is especially unclear as to whether employee contributions under pension plans (which a participant may often withdraw at any time) may be attached, and whether a court needs personal jurisdiction over an employee former spouse to compel the withdrawal of amounts contributed voluntarily under a plan.

Example 6. H, $20,000 in arrears on his support payments, contributes that amount to his employer's profit sharing plan which permits the kind of "catch-up" voluntary contributions discussed in Chapter 3. H has no other assets. A state court, having personal jurisdiction over husband, orders him to withdraw the $20,000 and pay it to wife. Is this order enforceable?

The Service, at the time of this writing, has not indicated whether a forced withdrawal would adversely affect the plan's qualified status and whether such an order may be recognized. So long as there is a chance that such voluntary contributions may be sheltered in this way, participants in arrears on marital obligations will probably try to make maximum voluntary contributions under their qualified plans and ex-spouses will seek to apply these assets against obligations which are in arrears.

IRAs

Since IRAs are not qualified plans, the provisions forbidding assignment or alienation of pension benefits are not applicable to amounts accumulated in an IRA. An IRA may be divided between the employee and non-employee spouses incident to a divorce without incurring federal income tax liability provided neither spouse withdraws money from the IRA.

Chapter 18

THE FUTURE OF PRIVATE RETIREMENT PLANS

The rule and practices governing private pension plans are undergoing rapid change. Some of the developments are reflections of fundamental social change—the proliferation of laws reflecting the changing status of women in society, the growing incidence of divorce, the greater perception of a need to protect a population that grows increasingly older—while others are being brought about by the current high rate of inflation which shows no sign of abating.

The following is a forecast of new developments which you can expect to see materialize in the next few years:

1. Increases in Individual Retirement Account Dollar Limitations

The current high rate of inflation tends quickly to make obsolete the annual maximum dollar limitation on contributions to an individual retirement account which is currently fixed at $2,000 ($2,250 in the case of a spousal individual retirement account).

It is to be expected that these dollar limitations will be increased from time to time.

Ultimately the maximum dollar limitation may be indexed to inflation in the same way as are Social Security benefits and the maximum pension benefits that pension plans are permitted to pay.

2. Changes in Social Security Benefits

The Social Security system is in very serious financial difficulty. It is likely that benefits will be reduced in the future, either by raising the age at which a person may retire and receive full benefits (probably from age 65 to age 68, or even later) or reducing or even eliminating the automatic cost of living increases in pensions which are currently a very important feature of the program.

3. Greater Protection to Surviving Spouses and Other Dependents

Pension benefits must be paid in the form of a qualified joint and survivor annuity unless the participant elects otherwise. While a plan may provide that the spouse's consent is required in order to elect an option other than a qualified joint and survivor annuity, it is not required to do so.

There is considerable support, especially among feminist groups, for the principle that it is inequitable to permit a surviving spouse to be deprived of a survivorship annuity without her (or his) consent.

There is even support for the proposition that a plan should be required to honor an agreement entered into between a participant and a nonspouse dependent to elect a survivorship annuity. For example, a plan participant may be living with a person without having entered into a formal marriage ceremony. Arguably, that individual is also entitled (at least to some extent) to the protection afforded to a lawfully wedded spouse.

4. Greater Protection to Divorced Spouses

The courts have generally held that a divorced spouse has an interest in the pension earned by his or her spouse during the term of their marriage. The Internal Revenue Service and the Department of Labor have generally accepted this view.

However there is no uniformity among the states as to how such a spouse's interest is measured. The uncertainty is magnified in the case of multiple divorces or where an employer's pension plan is changed during or after the term of a marriage.

There is a great need for federal rules for calculating the portion of a pension which has accrued during the term of a marriage.

> *Example 1.* John and Mary were married on January 2, 1965 and were divorced on December 31, 1979. John was not covered under a pension plan until January 1, 1975, and

while he accrued a pension of $50.00 per month on December 31, 1979, he was not vested on that date. John and Alice were married on January 2, 1985 and divorced on December 31, 1990. John's accrued pension on January 2, 1985 was $150.00 per month and on December 31, 1990 was $330.00 per month. John will not be eligible to retire until January 1, 2000 when he will be age 60.

There is presently no rule for determining how much of John's pension is attributable to the period of his marriage to Mary and how much to his marriage to Alice. (Of course, at the time of the divorce proceeding with Mary the marriage to Alice still lay in the future.)

Similarly, there is no rule for determining how Mary and Alice's rights are affected if John marries for a third time and is survived by a widow.

The tangle of litigation which will develop in the case of some complicated series of marriages and divorces will ultimately persuade Congress to adopt rules apportioning pension accruals over a participant's career for the purpose of allowing local courts to make alimony, child support and property division awards.

5. Age Discrimination

Employees cannot ordinarily be required to retire before age 70. This protection is afforded by federal law. However pension plans are not currently required to recognize service rendered by employees after normal retirement date, generally age 65.

The EEOC is presently contemplating the issuance of a regulation requiring pension plans to recognize service rendered up to age 70. If these rules are adopted they will undoubtedly be challenged in the courts.

Ultimately it is to be expected that legislation requiring the accreditation of service rendered after normal retirement age will be enacted.

6. Faster Vesting

Although ERISA required pension plans to adopt relatively rapid vesting schedules there remains a substantial body of opinion that vesting should be accelerated still further. It is argued that the present vesting schedules are particularly unfavorable to women who tend to incur longer breaks in service than do men, in order to bear and raise children and to particular career groups, such as engineers, where "job hopping" is frequent.

Of course the further acceleration of vesting will raise the cost of pension plans to employers and if employers are compelled by law to accelerate the vesting of benefits they might not, because of budgetary restrictions, make other benefit improvements which they would have otherwise been inclined to adopt.

Nevertheless it is likely that the future will bring some form of accelerated vesting.

7. Revision of Plan Termination Provisions

The Pension Benefit Guaranty Corporation is sponsoring legislation to change the rules governing the termination of defined benefit plans to provide greater safeguards to plan participants and strengthen the insurance program which that agency administers.

A number of proposals have a chance of being enacted in the more distant future.

8. Compulsory Cost-of-Living Protection

There have been a great many complaints by retirees that their pensions, even if adequate at the time of retirement, are thereafter seriously eroded by inflation. Unless the rate of inflation is substantially reduced some means of protection must be devised for retirees.

A number of studies are now underway seeking to develop a means of protecting retirees without bankrupting their former employers. The federal government may ultimately have to sell to private pension plans indexed annuity contracts under which the monthly pensions of retirees are inflation adjusted in the same manner as are Social Security benefits.

9. Compulsory Minimum Pension Benefits

While ERISA requires plan sponsors to provide certain features in their plans, it does not require employers to establish plans in the first instance. Consequently, many employees, especially those working for small companies, have no pension protection at all.

There are a number of proposals to require such employers to adopt at least minimal benefit plans to give their employees some level of retirement protection over and above that provided by Social Security.

It must be remembered that such pension proposals constitute a kind of tax against employers. If adopted without regard to the ability of less successful employers to afford them, they may hasten the demise of marginal businesses, thereby making our economy increasingly vulnerable to the threat of imports and the accompanying loss of jobs.

10. Unisex Pension Benefits

Pension plans have traditionally calculated their benefit options using actuarial tables which incorporate the well-documented fact that women as a class live longer than men as a class. This means that a woman and a man with an identical service and earnings history who elected the same option under a pension plan would not receive the same dollar monthly benefit or the same lump sum equivalent of their pension benefit. Since the Supreme Court's decision in *Manhart*, great pressure has been placed upon pension plans to eliminate all differences in the treatment of similarly situated male and female participants, including those based on average life expectancies. The most practical solution for pension plans would be to pay benefits midway between the current levels for male and female participants, although it is not now clear that such a changeover in benefit practices would not violate Title VII of the Civil Rights Act of 1964 and certain provisions of the Internal Revenue Code. Ultimately, the law will probably permit such a changeover to unisex benefits and require plans to eliminate all gender distinctions.

The financial implications of mandated pension improvements must not be overlooked. It is therefore very hazardous to make long range predictions as to the future of private pension plans. Nevertheless, we feel that the future will bring at least some of the changes outlined in this chapter.

GLOSSARY OF PENSION TERMS

ACCRUAL OF BENEFITS—The accumulation of benefit credit. Benefits must be accrued, or accumulated, at no slower than a relatively even rate over the working lifetime of a participant. A participant may or may not be entitled to receive payment of his or her accrued benefit upon termination of employment, depending upon whether the participant is *vested.*

ACTIVE PARTICIPANT—A Defined Contribution Plan participant who has had contributions or forfeitures allocated to his or her account during a plan year, or a Defined Benefit Plan participant who has accrued a benefit during a plan year.

ACTUARIAL ASSUMPTIONS—The projections regarding long term interest rates, turnover, mortality, salary scales and retirement patterns which are used to calculate and fund benefits.

ACTUARIAL EQUIVALENCE—Actuarially equivalent benefits have the same value, calculated using the plan's Actuarial Assumptions.

ANNUAL REPORT—Form 5500, 5500-C, 5500-K, or 5500-R which must be filed by a plan sponsor for each year in which the plan is in operation. Annual reports contain participant counts and detailed plan financial information.

BACKLOADING—Accrual of benefits at a faster rate in the years immediately preceding retirement than in the earlier years of plan participation. Backloading is prohibited by ERISA except within certain narrow limitations.

BREAK IN SERVICE—Termination of plan participation. In an Hours of Service plan, a Break in Service occurs when fewer than 501 hours of Service are completed in a year. In an Elapsed Time Plan, a Break in Service is twelve months during which no services are performed.

BUYBACK RULE—An ERISA regulation affecting employees who receive benefit payments and then are reemployed prior to incurring a Break in Service. The rule provides that by repaying the benefits received, such employees may have any forfeitures of their accrued benefits restored. This means that they may not be penalized for short breaks in employment.

CAREER COMPENSATION PAY PLAN—A Defined Benefit Plan under which benefits are based on a participant's compensation over his or her period of plan participation.

CASH AND DEFERRED COMPENSATION PLAN—A form of Defined Contribution Plan under which participants may elect to receive a current cash distribution of a portion of their annual allocations.

CONSTRUCTIVE RECEIPT—A theory under which the Internal Revenue Service sought to tax amounts "made available" to plan participants prior to their actual distribution from the plan. Constructive receipt defeats the tax deferral purpose of Qualified Plans. Application of the Constructive Receipt doctrine was avoided if a plan contained withdrawal penalties or provides for prior irrevocable elections to receive deferred benefit payments. ERTA makes the constructive receipt doctrine inapplicable to qualified plans in and after 1982.

CONTINGENT ANNUITANT OPTION—A form of Joint and Survivor Annuity under which the "contingent annuity", or survivor benefit may be payable to anyone selected by the participant.

COST OF LIVING CLAUSE ("COLA")—The most common method by which plan benefits already in pay status are adjusted to compensate for inflation. Under a COLA clause, benefits are increased in proportion to increases in one of the consumer price indices. There is usually a cap, or ceiling, limiting the annual adjustment which may be made.

COVERED COMPENSATION—A term used in certain integrated Defined Benefit Plans to represent the average social security taxable wage base over a participant's career. All employees born in the same year have the same Covered Compensation amount. The Internal Revenue Service publishes official tables of Covered Compensation to be used in such plans.

DEFERRED RETIREMENT—Retirement on or after a Participant's Normal Retirement Date. Deferred Retirement benefits may reflect continued service and compensation credit, and may also be actuarially adjusted to reflect the shorter projected payout period or payment of interest if a participant retires after rather than at the Normal Retirement Date.

DEFERRED RETIREMENT CREDIT—A benefit increase under the Social Security system for employees who work beyond age 65.

DETERMINATION LETTER—A document issued, at the Plan sponsor's request, by the Internal Revenue Service to indicate that on the basis of its written terms and coverage, a plan is tax qualified.

DEFINED BENEFIT PLAN—A form of pension plan under which benefits are determined or "defined" under a formula related to compensation and length of service. In a Defined Benefit Plan the plan sponsor gets the benefit of good fund investment performance in the form of decreased future contributions. Benefits provided under Defined Benefit Plans are guaranteed by the insurance program administered by the Pension Benefit Guaranty Corporation.

DEFINED CONTRIBUTION PLAN—A form of Qualified Plan under which individual accounts are maintained for participants and contributions are calculated as a percentage of compensation. In a Defined Contribution Plan the participants benefit from investment gains and good investment return. Profit Sharing Plans and Money Purchase Pension Plans are two kinds of Defined Contribution Plans.

EARLY RETIREMENT AGE—See Early Retirement Date below.

EARLY RETIREMENT DATE—The earliest age prior to Normal Retirement Age at which a Participant may, under the terms of his or her plan, retire and be entitled to immediate pension benefits. Age 55 (often coupled with a ten year service requirement) is the most common Early Retirement Age.

EARLY SURVIVOR ANNUITY—A death benefit equal to at least 50 percent of a Participant's annuity (calculated on a Qualified Joint and Survivor Annuity basis) which ERISA requires to be paid by all plans which pay benefits in annuity form. The Early Survivor Annuity must be made available to spouses of all married employees who die while in active employment after the plan's Early Retirement Age. Participants may be made to bear the cost of the Early Survivor Annuity.

ELAPSED TIME PLAN—A plan under which employees are given service credit for all time during which they are employed, regardless of the number of Hours of Service worked.

ELIGIBLE INDIVIDUAL ACCOUNT PLAN—A Defined Contribution Plan whose provisions authorize investment of more than 10 percent of plan assets in stock of the employer. ESOPs and TRASOPs (Tax Credit ESOPs) are special kinds of Eligible Individual Account Plans.

EMPLOYEE STOCK OWNERSHIP PLAN (ESOP)—An Eligible Individual Account Plan which borrows to finance its purchases of employer stock. ESOPs must be designed to invest *primarily* in employer stock, although they may have other assets.

ERISA—An acronym for the Employee Retirement Income Security Act of 1974, the federal statute that governs the operation of retirement plans. Parts of ERISA are administered by the Internal Revenue Service, the Department of Labor and the Pension Benefit Guaranty Corporation.

FLAT BENEFIT PLAN—A Defined Benefit Plan which provides a benefit equal to a fixed number of dollars for each year of service.

FIDUCIARY—A plan or corporate official who has discretion and control over plan assets. Fiduciaries include trustees, investment managers and plan committee members. ERISA requires that fiduciaries operate their plans for the exclusive benefit of participants and their beneficiaries.

FINAL AVERAGE PAY PLAN—A type of Defined Benefit Plan under which benefits are based on the average compensation earned in a short period (typically five years) immediately preceding retirement rather than on compensation earned during an entire career.

FOUR-FORTY VESTING—A Vesting schedule under which Participation are 40 percent vested after completing four Years of Service and continue to vest at a graduated rate until they are fully vested after 11 Years of Service. The Internal Revenue Service often requires small plans to contain Four-Forty Vesting.

HOUR OF SERVICE—The basic unit used to count service under most pension plans. Each hour for which an employee is paid, or entitled to be paid, for services (including vacation, paid leaves of absence, jury duty and time covered by back pay awards) must be counted as an Hour of Service.

HOUR OF SERVICE PLAN—Any Qualified Plan under which service is measured by the number of Hours and Years of Service completed.

INDIVIDUAL RETIREMENT ACCOUNTS (IRAS)—Plans under which individuals who receive earned income may make deductible contributions to fund their own retirement benefits (Deductible IRA's) or under which any employee may defer taxation of plan distributions which he or she has received (Rollover IRA's). The maximum deductible IRA contribution which may be made by an unmarried employee or a married employee who does not have a nonworking spouse is $2,000. This limitation does not apply to nondeductible rollover contributions.

INTEGRATION—A method used to skew plan benefits in favor of the highly paid by making greater contributions based on compensation in excess of the Taxable Wage Base than those made based on compensation not subject to Social Security Tax withholding. Integrated plans are either of the excess or offset type.

JOINT AND SURVIVOR ANNUITY—A payment option similar to the Qualified Joint and Survivor Annuity except that the survivor benefit may be payable to an individual other than the participant's spouse. Joint and survivor annuities may be combined with period certain options to add a minimum guaranteed payout period.

KEOGH PLAN—The type of Qualified Plan adopted by partnerships and self-employed individuals. Keogh plans may be of either the Defined Contribution or Defined Benefit type, although Defined Contribution Keogh plans are more common. The maximum annual deductible contribution which may be made to a defined contribution Keogh plan is the lesser of 15 percent of earned income or $15,000. Only the first $200,000 of compensation may be recognized under a Keogh plan. Keogh plans are also called H.R. (10) plans after the number of the bill in the House of Representatives, sponsored by Rep. Keogh, which authorized noncorporate pension plans for the first time.

LIFE ANNUITY—Any form of benefit which is calculated based on projected life expectancies. Payments under a life annuity option which has not been combined with any death benefit feature cease at the former Participant's death.

LUMP SUM—Payment of the entire amount to a Participant's credit under a plan in one tax year of the Participant (usually, in one calendar year). Lump sums are not eligible for special favorable income tax treatment. However, a lump sum payable on account of a Participant's death and for which favorable income tax treatment has been elected will be included in the Participant's gross estate.

MONEY PURCHASE PENSION PLAN—A Defined Contribution Plan under which mandatory employer contributions equal to a fixed percentage of participants' compensation must be made each year.

NORMAL RETIREMENT AGE—See Normal Retirement Date below.

NORMAL RETIREMENT DATE—The earliest age under a plan at which a participant may retire entitled to an immediate unreduced benefit. Although age 65 is the most common Normal Retirement Date, it is possible to delay Normal Retirement Date until the 10th anniversary of plan participation. All Qualified Plans must provide for immediate full vesting at Normal Retirement Date.

PARTIAL TERMINATION—The discharge of a significant percentage of plan Participants, often resulting from the closing of a significant business operation. All affected participants must be fully vested upon a Partial Termination.

PARTICIPANT—An Employee who is or formerly was an Active Participant.

PARTIES-IN-INTEREST—Certain related entities and individuals enumerated in ERISA who may not enter into sales, extensions of credit or other transactions with their plan.

PASS THROUGH OF VOTING RIGHTS—The right of Participants in Eligible Individual Account Plans to direct how the shares in their accounts are to be voted.

PAST SERVICE BENEFIT—A benefit based upon service completed prior to the adoption of the plan or of a plan amendment.

PENSION BENEFIT GUARANTY CORPORATION—("PBGC") The government agency which insures benefits provided under Defined Benefit Plans. The PBGC must be notified before a Defined Benefit Plan is terminated.

PERIOD CERTAIN OPTION–A payment method under which annual benefit payments are made over a fixed period of years.

PRIMARY INSURANCE AMOUNT ("PIA")–The basic amount payable under the Social Security System. The PIA is based on an employee's average indexed monthly earnings.

PRIMARY SOCIAL SECURITY BENEFIT–The portion of the PIA which is subtracted from the base benefit in a Defined Benefit Plan which is integrated using the Social Security offset method. The Primary Social Security Benefit is calculated without regard to any survivor, disability, or other benefits which may be paid out by the Social Security System. The Social Security offset is usually proportional to Years of Service. This insures that shorter service employees do not have a full offset applied against their benefits.

PROFIT SHARING PLAN–A Defined Contribution Plan which provides that employer contributions may be made only out of profits or retained earnings. Annual contributions are further limited to 15 percent of the aggregate compensation of participants. Employer contributions under a Profit Sharing Plan may be either mandatory or discretionary.

PROHIBITED GROUP–Officers, shareholders and highly compensated employees.

PROHIBITED TRANSACTION–Any transaction between a Qualified Plan and one of its Parties In Interest which has not been exempted under ERISA. The Internal Revenue Code imposes penalty taxes on Prohibited Transactions.

QUALIFIED JOINT AND SURVIVOR ANNUITY–A benefit payable over the joint lives of a participant and his or her spouse which provides a spouse's death benefit equal to at least 50 percent of the benefit payable during the participant's lifetime. ERISA requires that the Qualified Joint and Survivor Annuity be paid to all married participants who retire after the plan's earliest retirement age unless they have declined in writing during a special election period to receive benefits in Qualified Joint and Survivor Annuity form.

QUALIFIED PLAN—Any pension or profit-sharing plan which, because it satisfies the requirements spelled out in the Internal Revenue Code, entitles the employer sponsoring the plan and the Participants to valuable tax benefits. Qualified Plans may not discriminate in favor of the Prohibited Group.

REPLACEMENT RATIO—The ratio of a Participant's pension to his or her salary in the period immediately preceding retirement. The Replacement Ratio is a common measure of the adequacy of a pension plan.

RETIREMENT EARNINGS TEST—The test applied under the Social Security system to determine whether retirees' benefits should be reduced if they work while collecting benefits. If earnings are too high, benefits will be reduced $1 for every $2 earned.

ROLLOVER—Tax free transfer of a portion of a Lump Sum plan distribution to an Individual Retirement Account. To qualify as a Rollover, the transfer must be made within 60 days of the distribution.

RULE OF 45—One of the three statutory minimum vesting schedules under ERISA. Under the Rule of 45, a participant becomes 50 percent vested when the sum of his or her age and Years of Service equals 45, but not before completing 5 Years of Service or after completing 10 Years of Service. Participants then continue to vest at a rate of 10 percent per Year of Service.

RULE OF PARITY—The rule which permits a plan to disregard service prior to a Break in Service if the length of the Break in Service exceeds the period of Service prior to the Break in Service.

SEGREGATED ACCOUNT—An account under a Qualified Plan which is separately invested in accordance with the Participant's instructions. Segregated accounts do not share in trust fund gains and income or losses, but are credited with gains and debited with losses and expenses resulting from their separate investment.

SERVICE SPANNING—A rule which must be used in Elapsed Time Plans under which breaks in employment shorter than 12 consecutive months are ignored for purposes of eligibility and vesting.

SIMPLIFIED EMPLOYEE PENSION PLAN—A relatively new arrangement under which employers may contribute up to $15,000 per employee to employee Individual Retirement Accounts. Employees are always vested in these contributions.

SPINOFF—The splitting up of a retirement plan, usually when a division or subsidiary is sold.

SUMMARY ANNUAL REPORT—A summary of the financial information in the plan's Annual Report, which is required to be distributed to participants prior to the end of the 9th month following the close of the plan year.

SUMMARY PLAN DESCRIPTION ("SPD")—A summary of the plan's rules regarding eligibility, vesting and benefit accrual which must be written in language understandable by the average plan participant. Participants must be given SPD's within 90 days of their entry into a plan.

TARGET BENEFIT PLAN—A plan which is a hybrid combining the certain features of Defined Contribution Plans and Defined Benefit Plans. Although individual accounts are maintained for participants in a Target Benefit Plan, there is a benefit goal towards which the plan sponsor funds.

TAXABLE WAGE BASE—That portion of an Employee's compensation which is subject to Social Security Tax withholding. In 1982, the first $32,400 of an employee's compensation is in the Taxable Wage Base. In subsequent years, it will be raised in accordance with increases in the Consumer Price Index.

TEN YEAR CLIFF VESTING—One of the three statutory minimum vesting schedules under which a participant is fully vested after the completion of ten years of service but is not vested at all prior to that time. Most large retirement plans use Ten Year Cliff Vesting.

TEN YEAR FORWARD AVERAGING—The favorable tax treatment available for Lump Sum Distributions. Under Ten Year Forward Averaging the lump sum is taxed (sometimes after an exempt amount is subtracted) without regard to other income earned at

10 times the tax imposed on 1/10 of the Lump Sum Distribution under the tax tables applicable to unmarried taxpayers.

THRIFT PLAN (sometimes called a "Savings Plan")—A Defined Contribution Plan under which the employer matches employee contributions by contributing a percentage of employee contributions made.

TRASOP—(Tax Credit ESOP) An Eligible Individual Account Plan which distributes employer securities to participants. The employer claims a tax credit for the value of the employer securities contributed to the plan.

UNIT BENEFIT PLAN—A Defined Benefit Plan under which a "piece" of the retirement benefit is earned in each Year of Service. A plan which provides a benefit equal to 1 percent of compensation for each Year of Service is a Unit Benefit Plan.

VESTED SEPARATED (or "Terminated") PARTICIPANT—A Participant who terminated employment with a vested right to a benefit which will not become payable until some time in the future.

VESTING—The earning of non-forfeitable rights to benefits. A benefit which is vested will not be lost even if the employee quits or is discharged. ERISA requires that vesting be no slower than statutory minimum vesting schedules and that participants become fully vested at Normal Retirement Date.

VOLUNTARY CONTRIBUTION—A nondeductible employee contribution to a plan which may not exceed 10 percent of compensation during the period of plan participation. Taxation of income earned by Voluntary Contributions is deferred until the earnings are distributed to the participant. Beginning in 1982, plans may permit employees to make *deductible* voluntary contributions of up to $2,000 per year subject to rules similar to those governing deductible contributions to IRAs.

YEAR OF SERVICE—The unit used to determine eligibility vesting, and benefit credit under ERISA. In an Hours of Service Plan, each year in which at least 1,000 Hours of Service are completed counts as a Year of Service. In an Elapsed Time Plan, 12 months of service equal a Year of Service regardless of the number of Hours of Service completed.

INDEX